'Mr. Cecil Gray, who writes primarily as a friend concerned to present Philip Heseltine in a true light and to dispel certain current falsities, has produced a book which, even on those who neither knew Heseltine nor know Warlock's music, may well exercise the fascination of a novel without losing the direct appeal of a true story. It is a story of a dual personality, or, strictly speaking, of a fictitious personality called into being to represent the "self" of a man's frustrated desires and so successfully acting that, in time, as with Frankenstein destroyed its own creator.'

THE LIFE & LETTERS
SERIES.   VOLUME 84
PETER WARLOCK

❡ The *Life and Letters Series* is a selection of non-fiction books previously published at a higher price and now re-issued in a uniform format and at a uniform price

❡ A list of other titles in the series can be obtained on application to the publishers

PETER WARLOCK (*circa* 1924)

THE LIFE AND LETTERS SERIES NO. 84

CECIL GRAY

PETER WARLOCK

A Memoir of Philip Heseltine

With Contributions by
Sir RICHARD TERRY
and
ROBERT NICHOLS

Foreword by
AUGUSTUS JOHN

With four illustrations

London - JONATHAN CAPE - Toronto

FIRST PUBLISHED OCTOBER 1934
SECOND IMPRESSION JULY 1935
RE-ISSUED IN
THE LIFE AND LETTERS SERIES
1938

JONATHAN CAPE LTD.   30 BEDFORD SQUARE, LONDON
AND 91 WELLINGTON STREET WEST, TORONTO

PRINTED IN GREAT BRITAIN IN
THE CITY OF OXFORD AT THE ALDEN PRESS
AND BOUND BY A. W. BAIN & CO. LTD.
PAPER MADE BY JOHN DICKINSON & CO. LTD.

CONTENTS

FOREWORD, BY AUGUSTUS JOHN 11

PREFACE 17

INTRODUCTORY 21

PART ONE

PHILIP HESELTINE

I EARLY YEARS: DELIUS 33

II AT OXFORD: A MEMOIR BY ROBERT NICHOLS 61

III THE WAR AND D. H. LAWRENCE 93

PART TWO

BOUVARD AND PÉCUCHET

I CHELSEA DAYS 125

II IRISH YEAR 158

III *THE SACKBUT* 200

PART THREE

PETER WARLOCK

I EYNSFORD 241

II RECAPITULATION: CODA 278

LIST OF WORKS 307

INDEX 315

ILLUSTRATIONS

PETER WARLOCK (*circa* 1924)   *frontispiece*

PHILIP HESELTINE (*circa* 1915), WITH
   JACOB EPSTEIN AND LORD TREDEGAR   *facing page* 94

PETER WARLOCK (*circa* 1927)   200

PHILIP HESELTINE (*circa* 1929)   278

FOREWORD

WITH the renovation of the Café Royal, disappeared the one and only example in London, or indeed in England, of the Continental style of public-house (with the sole exception of the small but charming Café Verrey, which now too has undergone a bewildering transformation). Successor to the tavern of the preceding century, it fulfilled the same function as a meeting place of Character, Wit and Fashion, and its history is largely that of the figures, eminent, eccentric or infamous, who sat at its marble tables. Now that the famous haunt has been overshadowed by the added eating accommodation, the uneasy ghost of pre-war days that ventures within its doors must turn away, affrighted, before an endless vista of glittering napery, and resort in despair to the doubtful consolations of club or pub, or merely retreat to bed – a beaten ghost. Survivors of the pre-war period will remember the various well-differentiated groups who habitually assembled under the fly-blown rococo of the famous saloon. In one section, under the bar whose façade glittered with the almost Byzantine splendour of a steam roundabout, were established members of the sporting fraternity, loud raucous-voiced men seeking to intimidate each other into bets. Near these the pleasant clatter of dominoes proclaimed a colony of our future allies *d'outre-manche*. Farther off again a gathering of unusually bulky and grave persons, collected from the vicinity of the British Museum, conversed in voices pitched like the squeaking of bats so high as to be inaudible except to the trained ear (if I am not mistaken the females of this group alone *portaient barbe*). Next could be observed what may be described as a *schlemozzle* of Cubist painters, presumably endeavouring to solve the problem of fitting a square peg into a round hole; while not far off the leader of the Avorticist movement with his lieutenants kept a vigilant eye on the balance of power as indicated by the number and consuming capacity of the different parties. From a carefully chosen point of vantage a well-dressed gang of blackmailers, pimps, con-men, *agents-provocateurs* and bullies, secure in the well-tried loyalty of the staff, laid their plans for the next operation. Here in the dangerous neighbourhood of a whooping Anglo-Irish practical-joker and a cluster of intoxicated social reformers, a body of exquisite Old Boys of the 'nineties, recognizable by their bright chestnut wigs and raddled faces, exchanged unctuous *facetiae* in the sub-dialect of the period. Within easy reach of the exit a mixed company of poets, prostitutes and portrait painters drank shoulder to shoulder under the unceasing observation of a hawk-eyed private detective, and usually the presence of a sprinkling of the less reputable nobility added a note of ambiguous distinction to the *ensemble*. Needless to say, the clientèle included others of less interest, however, to the historian than to the management.

The entrance of Philip Heseltine into The Café, long before I made his acquaintance, always excited my curiosity. This tall blond young man, with a strange derisive smile for ever about his pale handsome features, who and what might he be? I decided he was a writer, perhaps a poet; for, always accompanied by three or four young females carrying portfolios and scrolls of paper, he appeared to me to be engaged, with his *amanuenses*, on some urgent and evidently important literary work. I had guessed partly right, for at that time he was busy editing *The Sackbut*, a musical journal (to which later I myself contributed at his request a drawing which unfortunately I have never been able to recover). When eventually I met Heseltine, I was at once impressed and charmed with his admirable conversational powers, his wide and curious scholarship, and his gargantuan brand of humour; while the sardonic smile which previously had aroused in me a feeling of vague discomfort, as if I myself might in some way be the innocent cause of it, I learned to attribute to the contemptuous amusement which the endless spectacle of human imbecility excited in a nature at once supersensitive and bellicose.

It may be worth while recounting a motoring trip I once shared with Philip, E. J. Moeran, John Goss and a lady. Setting out from Eynsford in Kent our goal was the Windmill Inn at Stalham in Norfolk where of a Saturday evening several local folk-singers were known to gather, chief among whom was one Harry Cox, a first-rate singer with a large *repertoire* of traditional songs. Philip on this occasion wore a *beret basque* which was probably the first example of this now common form of head-gear to be exhibited in East Anglia, and I could see that the resentment and suspicion the sight of it aroused in the natives was only with difficulty overcome by Philip's charm of manner and their own natural politeness. Arriving without mishap at the Windmill, Philip at once hired a somewhat defective motor-cycle with which to proceed to a neighbouring village where lived a lady of musical tastes whose presence was desired. She duly came along, to be secretly accommodated with a seat in the next room to the public bar where our folk-singers were to perform, the door being left discreetly ajar, for as is well known, countrymen are apt to lose voice, memory and nerve in the presence of the more refined sex.

The evening's entertainment passed off with the greatest success until it was brought to an abrupt conclusion by the following occurrence. While in the midst of a brilliant discussion which, though a little over the heads of the audience, was listened to with fascinated attention, Philip suddenly collapsed on the floor as if struck down by some mysterious seizure. All our efforts to arouse him proved unavailing, so, reverently covering what appeared to be a corpse, we left it where it lay till the next morning when to our great relief our friend reappeared completely restored to life and indeed by far the freshest and liveliest of the party.

I found that this behaviour was characteristic of Philip, whose intellectual activity never languished or slowed down, but at a given moment would just stop dead, blown out, as it were, like a candle. As in the tropics, there was with him no intermediate period of twilight between light and darkness. On the same motor journey Philip displayed his well-known, quite Baudelairian devotion to cats by insisting on repeated stops when he descended from the car to caress with loving words some handsome tabby by the roadside, but Moeran, who was in command, definitely refused to make a détour in order that Philip might inspect a fine rood-screen which he believed to exist in a church near by, for our objective was a certain inn where the beer was good, and where we were timed to arrive precisely at opening-time, so we were not to be further delayed by any less pressing matter. It was that evening after our punctual arrival at this inn that a thoroughly nerve-shaking event took place. Philip, his girl friend, John Goss and I were visiting the parish church – a fine example of Perpendicular. Philip had just given a rendering of Harry Cox's beautiful but profane song 'Down by the Riverside' upon the organ, and we were about to leave the building, when, moved by a perverse whim, I proposed to revive the rites of a more ancient cult by there and then offering up Miss —— on the altar. My ill-timed pleasantry had hardly been uttered when, with a deafening crash, a thunderbolt struck the building, instantly filling the interior of the church with smoke and dust, and with electric cracklings on every metal surface and the screeches of a distraught charwoman adding to the general confusion, one received a vivid impression of Hell being opened and all its devils loose! Philip with his peculiar beliefs in 'Principalities and Powers' was the most shaken, especially as he was about to mount the tower of which a pinnacle now lay shattered on the ground outside. I believe he composed, at the vicar's request, a hymn tune for the church 'as a thanks-offering for our providential escape'. At another time I accompanied Philip and Cecil Gray to Oxford on the rare occasion of the performance of an opera by Monteverde. Having an hour or two to dispose of we naturally visited an inn renowned for its excellent but extra-potent ale. In due course we reached the concert-hall and without much difficulty found our seats; but it remained for the non-musician to appreciate as best he could the, to him, unfamiliar beauties of Monteverde, for his two more learned friends passed at once into a state which might have been ecstasy but to which I am convinced no material sounds contributed.

If Philip's ribaldry and violence of language could be at times disconcerting – Socialism and the problems of over-population particularly inciting him to the most lurid invective – this and his sense of the comic which was both colossal and elaborate could not by any means conceal the fundamentally romantic nature which was his. I was often struck during his visits to Dorset, where I then lived, by his emotional response to the changing beauties of the landscape; and, indeed, whatever mood might at the moment possess him, his unceasing intellectual alertness was to me a source of continual admiration. Fantastic and visionary as might appear to a man of business some of his more eccentric views and predilections, at least his unfulfilled intention to acquire an ancient penny-farthing bicycle with which to perambulate the country was eminently practical, in that by such means he would be enabled to see over the hedges which too generally screen the view from pedestrian and motorist. My memories of this extraordinary being will always be charged with the bitter and futile reflection that, had we but set out in time on a tour into Wales we had projected, that fatal hour might have been perhaps averted when he put the cat out, locked the door, and turned on the gas.

AUGUSTUS JOHN

Road to Freedom

Black Boy / R. Wright

Native Son

leaves of Grass

PREFACE

EVERY attempt at a biography such as this must inevitably owe a large measure of whatever merit it possesses to the collaboration of others besides the author; in the present instance the latter's debt is more than usually heavy, and demands more than the customary conventional acknowledgment.

My thanks are due, firstly, to Mr. Augustus John, Mr. Robert Nichols, and Sir Richard Terry, for contributing a foreword, an entire chapter, and a short essay respectively; secondly, to Mr. Frederick Delius, for placing at my disposal the immense collection of letters he received from his friend, without the aid of which, indeed, a study of the years of growth and adolescence would have been impossible, and for allowing me in addition to quote extensively from his own letters in reply; thirdly, to all those other correspondents who have similarly provided me with much valuable material; also, not least, to Mrs. Edith Buckley Jones for much interesting and vital information, particularly relating to her son's early years.

But my deepest debt of gratitude, which I reserve to the end, is that which I owe to Mr. Bernard van Dieren; not only in his capacity of literary and musical executor, by allowing me free access to all papers and documents in his possession but also for his constant encouragement, without which the book would never have been written, and for his many valuable constructive suggestions and criticisms without which it would have been even more imperfect than it is.

C. G.

S.S. *Almeda Star*,
   SOUTH ATLANTIC,
     NEAR RIO DE JANEIRO,
March 27th, 1934.

N.B.—Since writing the above Frederick Delius has passed away. I leave unaltered what I have written, for my debt of gratitude remains, although alas! it can never now be repaid.

Si on me presse de dire pourquoy
je l'aymois, je sens que cela ne se
peult exprimer qu'en respondant
'Parce que c'estoit luy; parce que
c'estoit moy'

MONTAIGNE

INTRODUCTORY

FROM the time when the first songs bearing the signature of 'Peter Warlock' were published, in 1919, up to the present day, there has been a remarkable unanimity of opinion among musical critics in recognizing and paying tribute to the fine talent of the musician who chose to conceal his identity under this pseudonym: always subject to the qualification that, since he wrote no works on a heroic scale, and very little music for the larger instrumental or vocal combinations, he cannot be conceded to be a figure of the first importance, or even one of any real importance at all. Peter Warlock, in short, is admitted to have been a charming miniaturist, but nothing more, and is therefore dismissed as virtually negligible in comparison with many of his contemporaries who have achieved operas, symphonies, symphonic poems, oratorios, cantatas, and so forth.

This naive and touching faith in the positive merit of physical bulk and weight is, so far as I know, confined to musical criticism and to the aesthetic standards of female beauty which obtain among the Hottentots and Bushmen; in no other art, in no other walk of life or manifestation of nature even, does this steatopygous code of values prevail. Is Betelgeuse, a star no less than three hundred times the size of the sun, of more importance in the scheme of things than our modest little earth? Is the *Diplodocus Carnegii* in the Natural History Museum at South Kensington a more consummate achievement on the part of nature than, say, the lion or the tiger? In the aesthetic sphere, is an easel picture, as such, necessarily inferior in merit to a gigantic fresco or ceiling painting, or an ode or sonnet to an epic? Is not rather the contrary nearer the truth, namely, that sheer size in itself is generally found in inverse proportion to aesthetic or any other kind of significance? In nature the smaller organisms are almost invariably the most efficient and highly developed, and it would be easy to make out a

21

very plausible case for the same contention in the field of art. Edgar Allan Poe, indeed, has actually done so as regards poetry, in his essay on *The Poetic Principle*, where he argues convincingly that the epic intention is based upon a primitive and imperfect sense of art, that the day of such ungainly artistic anomalies is as surely over as that of pre-historic monsters, and that only poems of comparatively modest dimensions can be considered to be the highest manifestations of poetic art. In this he was followed by Baudelaire, in whose opinion (see his letter to Armand Fraisse, February 2nd, 1860) long poems are written only by those who have not sufficient talent or concentration to compose short ones.

It is certainly true that an obsession with the colossal is generally symptomatic of immaturity or arrested mental development in an artist. Practically everyone starts off by trying to outdo the monumental creations of a Michelangelo, a Beethoven, a Goethe; those who so continue in later life – and how well we know them! – have invariably second-rate minds. Even in the humbler activities of criticism and appreciation we know from personal experience that we are nearly always attracted at first to the vast, the gigantic, the grandiose, and only learn to appreciate the subtler and discreeter qualities as our taste matures. As Mr. E. M. Forster says, 'It is the vice of a vulgar mind to be thrilled by bigness', and this is as true in music as in anything else. It could reasonably be contended, therefore, that Peter Warlock's deliberate avoidance of the larger forms, so far from being regarded as a fault, ought rather to be accounted to him as a positive virtue; that large girth and proportions, so far from being the concomitant of the highest achievements, are rather antagonistic to them. If I do not propose to do so, however, the reason is simply because I am unable to see that the material dimensions of a work of art have any relation whatsoever to its merit. Excellence is absolute, and cannot be compared to its disadvantage with another example of excellence in a different category.

Even if one were to concede, in theory, that, everything else being equal, as it were, a talent for large-scale works is superior to a talent for small-scale works, in practice this belief is definitely pernicious, and has only too often led admirable artists to attempt tasks of which they were by nature incapable, and to disdain or neglect the powers which they genuinely possessed. Granted, if one happens to be a Bach or a Beethoven, one may freely indulge in a taste for the colossal; but unfortunately such figures, it may have been noticed, are of somewhat rare incidence. With artists of a different order of talent – lesser if you will – the outcome is generally fatal. No better warning example of this could possibly be found than that exquisite and charming miniaturist, Gustav Mahler, who chose to squander his natural gifts in a vain attempt to achieve the monumental and the colossal. His huge symphonies struggle hard for survival because we must search them for the qualities that easily keep alive his *Des Knaben Wunderhorn* songs, the *Kindertotenlieder* and other settings of poems by Rückert, in which he achieves all that provides the greatest attraction of his gigantic symphonies.

Even if it were true that Peter Warlock's talent was exclusively miniaturist and lyrical, so for that matter has been that of many of the greatest in the history of every other art. The achievement of a Catullus or a Propertius, a Baudelaire or a Verlaine, is no longer – if indeed it ever was – considered to be in any way inferior to that of a Virgil or a Lucretius, a Hugo or a Lamartine (rather the opposite, indeed), in spite of the fact that none of the first-named ever wrote a long poem in his life; and so it is, or rather should be, in music. And if Warlock confined himself almost exclusively to works in the smaller forms the reason was not so much that he was any more incapable of writing large works than many composers who have done so, as that he deliberately chose to concentrate his powers rather than to disperse and dissipate them, believing, rightly, that a first-rate small work is of infinitely greater value and significance than a second-rate large one. The consequence may well be that the best of his music will be remembered and performed long after many more pretentious and grandiose efforts of his contemporaries have been deservedly forgotten. For whatever may be the relative merits of large and small works it is at least indisputable that the latter enjoy a very much higher chance of survival. He travels furthest who travels lightest, in time as in space, and the lyricist or miniaturist penetrates more often to a later age than the epic poet, or the composer weighed down by bulky symphonic baggage. The number of large works of a generation which take a permanent place in the repertory is small indeed, only the minutest proportion of the output, but many an artist is assured of immortality by virtue of merely one or two perfect small things. The name of William Cory, for example, will live as long as the English language itself, solely on account of one exquisite lyric, which itself is only a translation from the Greek – 'They told me, Heraclitus' – while the innumerable vast epics of his more ambitious colleagues are already forgotten; and so it may well be with Peter Warlock. As he himself wrote to his friend and master, Bernard van Dieren, in a letter which is highly revealing in that combination of humility and pride which is the sign of the true artist – humility in comparing himself with the great masters, and pride in contemplating contemporaries: 'Sometimes I feel that this exiguous output of tiny works is too futile to be continued – though I have neither the impulse nor the ability to erect monuments before which a new generation will bow down. And then when I think of some of the "monumental" composers in present-day England alone, I feel that I would rather spend my life trying to achieve one book of little songs that shall have a lasting fragrance, than pile up tome upon tome on the dusty shelves of the British Museum. I should be more than happy if at the end of my days I could look back upon an achievement comparable to that of Philip Rosseter, who left behind him but one small book of twenty-one immortal lyrics' (Jan. 24th, 1920).

He certainly achieved this ambition, and more than achieved it. Philip Rosseter admittedly wrote some beautiful songs, but I do not hesitate to say that in my opinion there are very many more than twenty-one out of Warlock's hundred-odd which are

24

not merely as fine as, but finer than, any of Rosseter's, and some that are equal to the finest in the whole literature of English song. If we provisionally exclude Henry Purcell, whose solo songs as a whole are still unfortunately inaccessible and cannot therefore be taken into account in this connection, Peter Warlock seems to me, both by virtue of the number and excellence of his best examples, to be, quite simply, the best song-writer this country has produced since the death of John Dowland some three centuries ago, and there is no other than this one single name that I would place above his in any period. And this is not all, for he wrote admirable works in other categories as well. Even Mr. Ernest Newman who, I gather, does not altogether share my high estimate of the songs, wrote as follows concerning the choral works *Corpus Christi*, *As Dewe in Aprylle*, and *Balulalow*, on the occasion of their performance at the memorial concert of his works which took place in the Wigmore Hall in February, 1931: 'The young man who could conceive these exquisite things, and realize them so perfectly in music, must have had the root of the matter in him; they are three gems that will of themselves keep his name alive as a composer.' And, lest it be thought that my high estimate is attributable to personal friendship, that of Mr. Newman to the obituary circumstances of the performance, and both to some extent to a tendency to appraise unduly the art of a fellow countryman, I quote here the striking tribute paid to Peter Warlock by the eminent French composer and critic M. Paul Ladmirault in an article published in the weekly journal *Chantecler* during his lifetime, in which he says of him that he was not merely *un des plus grands compositeurs anglais de notre époque*, but also *le musicien peut-être le plus remarquable d'après guerre*. This tribute, coming as it does from a representative of musically the most insular country in Europe, the least given to the admiration or acceptance of the music of other races, suggests that Peter Warlock is a much more, and not a less, important figure in contemporary music than his compatriots suppose, and also the possibility that his work may penetrate more successfully into other countries than that of many English composers whom we ourselves consider more highly. Such a development would not, in fact, be at all surprising in view of the Elizabethan element in his work which links him up with the sixteenth-century tradition which was common to all countries, whereas the art of most modern English composers, whatever its merit, speaks in a language that can only be apprehended fully by listeners acquainted or in sympathy with the more specifically national aspects of the English spirit.

In addition to his achievement as a composer, the debt we owe him for his work as a transcriber and editor of old, and principally Elizabethan, music, cannot be exaggerated; I leave the estimation of it in the far more capable hands than mine of Sir Richard Terry, himself a pioneer and master of all subsequent workers in this field, and the greatest living authority on the subject. (See p. 267). Furthermore there is his considerable activity as a critic and musicologist. His studies of *Frederick Delius*, *The English Ayre*, and the music of Carlo Gesualdo, Prince of Venosa, are among the most valuable contributions that have been made in modern times to the literature of music in this country.

All this is enough, I think, and more than enough, to justify the existence of the present memoir. Over and above this tangible achievement as creative artist, scholar, and critic, however, there is the man himself, as revealed in the comedy and tragedy of his life and death – one of the most vivid, picturesque, fascinating, and enigmatic personalities of our time and, to those who knew him, at least, one of the most lovable. It is often said that the greater an artist is, the less important are the details of his personality and private life. No doubt this is true enough of the greatest; concerning Homer, Bach, Shakespeare, we know next to nothing, and we are not conscious of any real loss occasioned thereby. Their lives could tell us nothing that is not to be found in their works, because everything is contained there. Other artists there are, however, whose personalities are bigger than their works. No one to-day, for example, ever thinks of reading the poetry of Lord Byron, and in truth it is for the most part sorry stuff. But Byron the man, the legend, is even more alive now than he ever was in his lifetime. The same is true of Dr. Johnson.

Similarly Peter Warlock, in his different way, may have been, and probably was on the whole, a bigger man than he was an artist, but the peculiar gift of personality which he possessed is, I think, just as rare a quality as creative genius itself, just as valuable, and just as enduring, as we see from the examples mentioned. Hence it is that the following pages are primarily concerned with his life rather than his work; the latter can safely be left to speak for itself.

No one could be more conscious than I of the manifold faults and deficiencies of the following attempt. I would only plead in self-defence that some at least of them were unavoidable, and inherent in the nature of the undertaking. For example, in writing about one so recently dead, and especially one who led such a stormy and controversial existence as Peter Warlock did, it is obvious that much, if only for purely practical legal reasons, must necessarily be omitted which might conceivably reflect hatred, ridicule or contempt, as the phrase goes, upon living persons. On the other hand, if I were to propose to wait patiently until everyone who had been intimately connected with him were dead, the odds are that I should be dead myself as well, and I must confess that the notion of writing the book now and putting it away in a drawer indefinitely, for the benefit of a posterity which might perhaps never read it, would have been too austere a solution of the problem to provide an incentive to the undertaking. Apart from all this, however, the chief object in writing the book at all was to show him as he was to the generation which had so misunderstood him, and to give the lie to many grotesque perversions of the truth concerning him which are now current. The book, I felt, if it was to be written at all, had to be written now and published now, in spite of the inevitable defects that this decision must entail. In consequence, while I can promise that what follows is the truth and nothing but the truth, it is certainly not the whole truth, which cannot yet for obvious reasons be told.

Some readers, on the other hand, will no doubt think that, so far from having left out too much, I have put too much in: that my errors have been of commission rather than of omission and that I have, in fact, been inexcusably candid, and even indiscreet. To this accusation I shall only enter the plea of another biographer placed in similar circumstances: 'Any chronicle of his doings must record both folly and extravagance, and I should think it very foolish to disguise the characteristics which during his life were so apparent to his friends. I know that it will appear to some that the portrait might have been as well done without so many realistic touches, and that the phenomenal aspects are illustrated at the expense of his inner life of high purpose and devotion: but . . . it is only the existence of truthful detail that can refute the irresponsible hearsay, which by natural selection of its spontaneous variations grows up at last to a coherent falsehood – like a portrait of Macaulay. His imprudent behaviour, too, which invited such lamentable gossip as I have heard, was merely the consequence of his indulging his actual feelings and conscientious beliefs in contempt of convention, and in spite of circumstances – as is often the way with a genius.'

These are the words of none other than the late Poet Laureate, Robert Bridges, in his memoir of the poet Digby Mackworth Dolben in *Three Friends*; what he so amply and convincingly justifies needs no apology from me – I am content to invoke this illustrious precedent. Apart from that, if ever I was sure of anything it is of this, that to write a timid, bowdlerized version of the life of Peter Warlock, of all people, would have constituted a gross and unforgivable betrayal of all that he was and all that he stood for. I have sought to show him to the best of my ability as he was and as I knew him, with all his faults, in the firm belief that the shadows which appear in the picture will only serve to enhance the brightness of the whole. If I have failed, the fault is that of the painter, not of the model, and I am well aware of my shortcomings in attempting a task and subject better fitted to the pen of an accomplished literary craftsman than to that of a mere musician.

In conclusion, however, I should like to say that I shall definitely consider myself to have failed if the book is favourably received in certain quarters, and if it is not as bitterly resented by those who were his enemies as much as it is appreciated by his friends. It is intended as a kind of prolongation of his life, his activities, and his ideals: as a kind of artificial limb to replace, however clumsily and inadequately, the arm which fought so valiantly and struck so hard in the eternal battle against everything small, petty, mediocre, philistine, pharisaical, puritanical, both in art and in life.

The letter from D. H. Lawrence to Middleton Murry and Katherine Mansfield which appears on page 113 is reprinted from *The Letters of D. H. Lawrence* by kind permission of Mrs. Frieda Lawrence and Messrs. William Heinemann Ltd.

PART ONE

Life put a hair brush in my bed,
A water jug upon my door,
A lizard down my back, and said
'What are you wanting more,
Now that your flesh is sore?'

R. MIDDLETON

CHAPTER I

EARLY YEARS: DELIUS

WHEN asked once for biographical information, Peter Warlock indulged his characteristically impish love of mystification by gravely replying that he was born on the Embankment. As so often in even his most fantastic statements there was an element of truth in the remark, for Philip Heseltine enjoyed the rare, and possibly unique, distinction of having come into the world by way of the Savoy Hotel, on October 30th, 1894.

His parents, however, were not as opulent as such an imposing natal address might lead one to expect. His grandfather, certainly, was a successful stockbroker, and two of his uncles who entered the family profession were exceedingly wealthy men; but his father, Arnold Heseltine, a younger son of a family of eleven, was merely a partner in a firm of solicitors, enjoying a comfortable but in no way exceptional practice.

There is considerable evidence of artistic and cultural interests in the family history. One of these stockbroking uncles, John Postle Heseltine, was a man of exceptional culture and artistic leanings; his large collection of bronzes, etchings, and drawings is well known to all connoisseurs, and in addition he was a member of the Committee of the National Gallery. Another uncle, Joseph, was by profession a painter – though not a very good one – and we shall come across him later in connection with an event of decisive importance in his nephew's life. His grandmother was a Greek and Latin scholar of brilliant attainments, and a cousin, Michael Heseltine, is responsible for the best modern edition and translation of the works of Petronius (in the Loeb Library). Of specifically musical talent, on the other hand, whether creative, executive, or even merely appreciative, there

C   33

is little trace, either amongst ancestors or collaterals. Believers
in heredity, however, may find partial consolation for this
anomaly in a lifelong passion for litigation, which might plausibly
be accounted for by the paternal calling.

His father died suddenly when he was only two years of age.
His early childhood was passed in Hans Road, near Sloane
Street, and about the age of nine he was sent to a private boarding-
school at Broadstairs. He had already had a few piano lessons
at the age of six, and disliked them intensely, but at Broadstairs
his interest in music was aroused by the son of the proprietor of
the school, who had a pianola, on which he played chiefly Chopin
and Liszt. As a scholar Philip was brilliant, and no term passed
without his winning a prize in one subject or another. He soon
reached the Upper Sixth, and became head of the school when
he was twelve years old. On leaving Broadstairs he won, but
did not take up, a scholarship at Eton, where he went in 1908;
but although he had thoroughly enjoyed his private school, he
detested Eton. His capabilities were far above the average for
his age, and the authorities, with the intention, no doubt, of
rectifying what to them must have seemed a most regrettable
abnormality in a public-schoolboy, placed him in a lower class
than that for which he was qualified, with the result that, as
Philip once remarked to an interviewer, 'I became a moody,
vindictive youth, and absolutely lost a real power of concentration
that I had.'

This statement must not be taken strictly literally. The report
for his last term at Eton – summer 1911 – has been preserved,
and reads as follows: – 'I have no words of praise too high for his
work and conduct all through the Half. I understand he is leaving
Eton, and he could not have ended his school-life with a better
record. He evidently has a good memory, and his English papers
have shown a command of style, as well as an intelligence of
thought, that is quite remarkable. His weakest point is Greek
prose, but even this is not at all bad. I think he takes a greater
interest in English subjects than in Classical, and I am of the

opinion that he will always be more successful in them. It has been a great pleasure to me to teach him.'

This presents a somewhat different picture from his own, so far as his scholastic capacities were concerned. That he was unhappy at Eton, however, is unquestionable. From remarks made at various times, I gathered that he had been subjected to the systematic bullying which is the melancholy distinction conferred upon practically every unusually gifted boy who has the misfortune to spend the most impressionable years of his life in the hell on earth which is called an English public school. The instinctive recognition of something different from, and superior to, themselves, invariably brings out all that is worst in a community of boys who, individually, may often be harmless and good-natured. No one who has not been through such an experience himself can ever realize how much a sensitive boy can suffer; he is marked by it for life, and personally I have no doubt whatever that the explanation of many aspects of his life and character that are difficult to understand is to be sought in the miseries and humiliations endured in those early years at Eton. He confessed to me once that the worst and perpetually recurring nightmare of his life was to dream that he was back at school again.[1]

In spite of the exceptional brilliance of his school record Philip

[1] At Eton, that is to say. Mr. Robert Nichols, it will be seen, formed quite a different impression which, although I disagree with it, I naturally allow to stand. (See page 72.) It is more than probable, however, that the solution of the question – the point of reconciliation between the two seemingly discrepant impressions of Mr. Nichols and myself – is to be found in a passage from Francis Thompson's essay on Shelley, significantly marked with pencil in the margin of Philip's own copy: 'That he escaped for the most part bodily violence is nothing to the purpose. It is the petty malignant annoyance recurring hour by hour, day by day, month by month, until its accumulation becomes an agony; it is this which is the most terrible weapon that boys have against their fellow boy, who is powerless to shun it because, unlike the man, he has virtually no privacy. His is the torture which the ancients used, when they anointed their victim with honey and exposed him naked to the restless fever of the flies. He is a little St. Sebastian, sinking under the incessant flight of shafts which skilfully avoid the vital parts.' The reader must form his own opinion on the point. It is quite possible, of course, that being a creature of violently alternating moods, he unconsciously exaggerated his sufferings to me and others, and minimized them to Mr. Nichols.

actually developed surprisingly late in some respects. His purely
intellectual capacity was, as we have seen, decidedly precocious,
his sensibilities were abnormally alert and acute, but in his
psychological development he was singularly backward. A letter
of his written to his mother in 1910 is very revealing in this respect.
The diction and composition show a high level of intelligence in
a boy of his age, the exquisite handwriting is indicative of an
unusual sensitiveness and delicacy of perception, but the order of
sentiments expressed, concerning the death of King Edward and
the accession to the throne of King George, for example, are
surprisingly childish and conventional. It is with something of a
shock that one realizes that the writer was, after all, sixteen years
of age. At a time when most boys of such outstanding intelligence
are red-hot revolutionaries and atheists, Philip's views on politics,
religion, and so forth, were of the copy-book order – the kind of
thing one would expect from a boy of ten, not more. Incredible
though it may seem, the young Peter Warlock was more than a
little of a prig. He had evidently not as yet begun to think for
himself, but merely accepted unquestioningly and gave forth
again the conventional standards of judgment inculcated at school
and in the family circle.

The explanation is, I think, to some extent at least,
physiological; everything points to an unusually late puberty.
But there is also a psychological explanation to be found in the
premature death of his father which inevitably resulted in an
undue strength and prolongation of maternal influence which, it
is well known, generally makes for backwardness in psychic
growth and independence of character and judgment. His mother,
it is true, married a second time during his childhood, but although
Philip and his stepfather were always the best of friends and
companions, such a relationship can never be an entirely satisfactory substitute for that which subsists, or should subsist, between
father and son.

Again, even where music was concerned, Philip was the very
reverse of an infant prodigy. Indeed, up to his fifteenth year or so

his pronounced liking for music does not seem to have been appreciably greater than that shown by many other quite intelligent and imaginative children who subsequently develop no positive talent for it. At Eton, however, he was fortunate in finding a sympathetic and stimulating influence in the person of the assistant music-master, Mr. Colin Taylor, from whom he received piano lessons which he now actually enjoyed, though he was never to attain to any great proficiency on the instrument. In addition he played percussion in the orchestra of the Eton College Music Society, and began to compose small pieces, mostly songs. It was not until the latter part of 1910, however, that he first became acquainted with the music of Frederick Delius – the particular occasion was the performance of the unaccompanied part-song *On Craig Dhu*, to words of Arthur Symons – which came as a veritable revelation to him. He did not rest until he had procured every work of Delius which was then accessible, and from that moment onward music possessed his thoughts to the exclusion of all else.

The influence of Delius was destined to become a more than purely musical one. By one of these mysterious coincidences which almost seem to suggest at times the illusion that there is a meaning and a logic in life, Philip, shortly after thus becoming acquainted with the music of Delius, was spending a short holiday in France with his uncle Joseph, the above-mentioned painter, at his home in Marlotte, a little village on the outskirts of the forest of Fontainebleau. To his astonishment and joy he discovered, quite by accident, that not only did Delius live within a few miles from where he was, at Grez-sur-Loing, but also that his uncle knew him well personally. During his stay at Marlotte he duly became acquainted with the composer, and thus began the close friendship between the two which lasted uninterruptedly for twenty years, and was only terminated by death.

That such a close and enduring friendship should exist between two people of such disparate ages may perhaps seem surprising, or at least unusual – Delius was a man of close on fifty when they

37

met for the first time – but all his life Philip possessed the rare gift of being able to surmount the invisible barriers which ordinarily cut off one generation from complete intimacy with another; he was always able to establish as close a contact and as real an equality with persons much older and much younger than himself as with those of his own age. The relationship with Delius, however, was of a deeper and more comprehensive order than that of ordinary friendship; it comprised also that of master and disciple, and almost of father and son. In the years of Philip's adolescence, indeed, from sixteen onwards till about twenty-three, Delius was not merely his guide and mentor in questions of music and art generally, but also in the affairs of ordinary life, and it is admirable and touching to see from their correspondence how often Delius would lay aside his work in order to write long letters of help and advice to his young friend concerning religion, sex, the choice of a career, and all the other hundred and one problems which beset adolescence. In return Delius found in Philip not only an indefatigable propagandist for his art, but also an invaluable assistant in such matters as the making of transcriptions of orchestral scores, correcting proofs, and in innumerable other services of a similar nature.

Delius, it is interesting to note, seems to have carefully preserved all the letters written to him by Philip, and these provide the chief material for following his course of development in these early years. In reading the extracts from them which follow – and, for that matter, from letters written to other correspondents – it must always be borne in mind that the perpetually recurring mood of acute melancholy and self-distrust, while certainly genuine enough, represents only one side of the picture. It is absolutely essential that this side should not be concealed or minimized but rather, on the contrary, stressed, if only as a salutary and necessary corrective to the popular conception of the boisterous and ribald Peter Warlock, but it would be a great mistake to suppose that he was continually wrapped in sable gloom. In common with most people who are passing through the uneasy stage of development called youth, Philip perpetually oscillated between the highest exaltation and the deepest depression; and if the latter mood predominates in the letters the reason is that one does not ordinarily, at that time of life, sit down solemnly to write letters when things are going well – one is much too busy enjoying oneself – but only when one is in need of advice in some difficulty, of consolation in some sorrow, or catharsis in some black and despondent state of mind.

The first letter from Philip to Delius – or at any rate the first that has been preserved – was written at the age of sixteen, while he was still at Eton, but after he had become acquainted with the composer during his visit to France two or three months previously. The concert to which reference is made was the Delius Concert given by Sir (then Mr.) Thomas Beecham at the Queen's Hall in June, 1911, when the first performance of the *Songs of Sunset* took place.

PHILIP TO DELIUS

Eton College
June 17th, 1911

Dear Mr. Delius,

I feel I must write and tell you how very much I enjoyed your concert last night, though I cannot adequately express in words what intense pleasure it was to me to hear such perfect performances of such perfect music. I hope you will not mind my writing to you like this, but I write in all sincerity, and your works appeal to me so strongly – so much more than any other music I have ever heard – that I feel I cannot but tell you what joy they afford me, not only in the hearing of them, and in studying vocal scores at the piano (which until last night was my only means of getting to know your music), but also in the impression they leave, for I am sure that to hear and be moved by beautiful music is to be influenced for good – far more than any number of sermons and discourses can influence.

It was extremely kind of you to see me in the interval, especially as you had so many friends to talk to. I am most grateful to you for allowing me to make your acquaintance, and I shall value it very highly.

If you would be so kind as to do me the honour of a visit in Mr. Beecham's motor, as you suggested, I should be overjoyed to see you and Mr. Beecham any Tuesday, Thursday or Saturday afternoon, this or next month, and I will show you everything you may wish to see in Eton and Windsor.

I was immensely struck by Mr. Beecham's magnificent conducting: I have never seen him conduct in a concert hall before, though I was lucky enough to hear him do all three Strauss operas. I am so glad the concert was such a success.

I cannot thank you enough for allowing me to meet you and for the most glorious evening I have ever spent.

Believe me,
Your very sincere admirer . . .

On leaving Eton at the end of the summer term (1911) the problem of choosing a profession presented itself. It was intended first that he should go on the Stock Exchange, then that he should enter the Civil Service, but pending a definite decision it was arranged that he should spend some months in Germany, learning the language, which might be of use to him in any career ultimately chosen, and also studying music for his own pleasure at the same time. Consequently in the autumn of the same year we find him writing to Delius from Cologne.

PHILIP TO DELIUS

Brusselerstr. 98 III
Cöln a-Rh.
Nov. 25th, 1911

Dear Mr. Delius,

To my intense joy I managed to hear a performance of *Brigg Fair* yesterday in Coblenz! I know whenever one of your works is going to be performed within reasonable distance of Cöln, so yesterday I took the first opportunity of hearing *Brigg Fair*, which I understand is given the most often in Germany.

By way of contrast to the music I was going to hear, my only

40

fellow passenger between Bonn and Coblenz in the train was an opera singer, who rehearsed the part of Mephistopheles from Gounod's *Faust* in loud tones all the way! I cannot possibly tell you how much I enjoyed hearing *Brigg Fair*; it is absolutely marvellous! – and it was a very great additional pleasure to me that I knew the score, although the actual performance entirely shattered my preconceived notion of the tempi. I am probably wrong, I expect, but I should be very interested to know whether your direction 'With easy movement' (dotted crochet $= 66$) is best carried out by beating a rhythmical one in a bar, or by three beats in a bar: the conductor at Coblenz adopted the latter method, and I am quite sure certain his tempo was considerably slower than 66; anyway, it seemed to me that by beating three the 'easy-going' of the movement was seriously impaired. But of course I do not know, since I have never heard the work before. The second 'easy movement' (section 22) seemed much nearer the proper time, but the next movement suffered, I thought, from a fault in the other direction; the conductor just doubled the time, making a crochet of $\frac{3}{4}$ equal a quaver of $\frac{4}{4}$, which, since the preceding movement was taken fairly fast, did not seem to carry out your direction 'Slow – with solemnity', and the 'Maestoso' sounded positively hurried! The return to $\frac{3}{8}$ was treated in much the same way as the first $\frac{3}{8}$ movement. The orchestra, however, was good, except for some very shaky playing of the wind in the introduction. Of course, I ought not to criticize the conductor, being no musician myself, but I hope you will forgive my doing so, since I am so very anxious to know all that I possibly can about your music, down to the correct interpretations of the scores. I would give anything to hear the work under Mr. Beecham's direction: I could then be quite certain as to the right reading of it.

Life here continues to be quite heavenly for me, the more so by contrast to the dull monotony of Eton and the depressing effect of being surrounded there by people whose chief ideal in life is to excel at football or some such thing!

I am hearing a perfect deluge of music: the opera performances are very good indeed. *Der Rosenkavalier* is played regularly once or twice a week to crowded houses. I have heard it twice:

it is very amusing and interesting musically in parts, but I must confess that three hours and a quarter of Strauss (exclusive of intervals between the acts) is rather more than I altogether care for! Hearing *Heldenleben* last night after *Brigg Fair* filled me with disgust: the only part I liked at all was the 'Adversaries' section which is distinctly amusing.

The last Gurzenich concert, consisting of French music, was exceedingly interesting. The programme contained Berlioz's *Queen Mab*, which I love, and a quite wonderful *Image* of Debussy – *Ibéria*, which I thought magnificently impressionistic and 'stimmungsvoll'. The audience hissed at the end of it!

I have just lately finished scoring a suite of six numbers from Ingelbrecht's *Nursery*, and so I have at present no interesting musical work, for I do not count piano finger exercises as music! I should very much like to make another piano arrangement of one of your works, since I found copying *Brigg Fair* so very interesting and instructive. I am thinking of getting the score of *In a Summer Garden* to do, as I do not know the work at all, but since you were kind enough to say that you thought my transcription of *Brigg Fair* was not altogether bad, I venture to ask you first whether there is any other work I could do, either copying or arranging, that could be of use to you also, for I should consider it a very great honour to do the smallest service to you. If not, I shall get a copy of *In a Summer Garden* and make a two-piano arrangement. We have two pianos in one room here, and it is much better than four hands on a single instrument. I found orchestration a very interesting study, especially after the very valuable advice you gave me at Grez. I cannot tell you what a difference that made to me: I felt that the work was quite different after you had corrected the number I brought to you, and I re-scored all the numbers I had done previously. I am afraid, however, they are still very bad, as a beginner's work must inevitably be, but it gives me such pleasure to do – it is, I suppose, the next best thing to composing, which I cannot do, except by finding every chord at the piano, which is far from satisfactory!

I hardly like to take advantage of your exceedingly kind offer to look over some of my work, when I have only such poor stuff to shew for it, but since you were good enough to say you would look over some, I should be overjoyed if you would allow me to send you perhaps one or two numbers of the *Nursery* suite and a song or two – they are all very short, and you can burn them as soon as they arrive, if you like – I shall be quite content with the privilege of being allowed to send such nonsense to you.

I am having piano lessons, but for five weeks now I have been given nothing but finger exercises to practise which, I am sorry to say, bore me horribly, since I have not the slightest wish to become proficient on the piano.

I am looking forward immensely to the coming production of *A Village Romeo and Juliet* at Elberfeld. I shall attend every performance if I possibly can, as I have long known and loved the piano score of it.

I quote this letter at length primarily for its interest in showing what a clear and precise intuition the young writer had already of the *minutiae* of a score such as that of *Brigg Fair*, the rhythmical organization of which is so subtle and wayward that its correct interpretation even to-day is a rare occurrence. As will be seen in the following reply from Delius, his criticisms of the performance are confirmed on all points.

DELIUS TO PHILIP

I am so glad you like the sound of *Brigg Fair*, and am sorry you did not hear it conducted in a better way, What you say is perfectly correct – one must beat one in a bar; three makes me shudder. Then again the slow section cannot be taken slow enough; the maestoso section must be taken solemnly and not hurried – in other words it seems to have been a miserable performance!

There is no piano score of *The Summer Garden* as yet, or of the *Dance Rhapsody*. Do one of them for two pianos and I will hear it when I next come to Germany – perhaps in March. Send me the pieces you have orchestrated and I will be very glad to help you. You have a great talent for orchestration – that I could see from the two pieces you showed me.

I think it is absurd that your teacher only gives you finger exercises. I would simply tell him that you did not come to Cologne for that purpose. If I were you I would go to the best theorist in Cologne and learn what you can from him; as a critic and writer it may be of some service to you – as a composer none whatever. I do not believe in any music constructed knowingly on any harmonic scheme whatsoever. All the people who write about the harmonic system or try to invent other systems – quarter tones etc. – don't seem to have anything to say in music. Systems are put together from the compositions of inspired musicians. I don't believe in learning harmony or counterpoint. Never lose your own sense of criticism, and don't be 'imponirt'. Write as much as possible.

I am writing a new choral work. You must have thought very much about *Brigg Fair* on the 25th, for I was quietly reading in my room, when suddenly I could only think of *Brigg Fair*, and I was obliged to get up and play it through, and the rest of the evening it quite haunted me. Telepathy! Write again soon.

PHILIP TO DELIUS

Cöln

Dec. 10th, 1911

Dear Mr. Delius,

I am so glad to know for certain about the tempi in *Brigg Fair*. I felt sure that the old man at Coblenz (who by the way looks a little like Hubert Parry!) knew nothing at all about it. Perhaps he did not understand the English directions on the score.

. . . I am exceedingly interested in the incident of November 25th. I fear you would not have very much peace if the same thing occurred every time I thought of or played one of your works! As a matter of fact, I spent the whole evening of the 25th writing my first letter to you which, although not finished until two days later, contained my description of the Coblenz concert in the first part, which I wrote on the 25th! I think it was undoubtedly telepathy, in which I believe very strongly, as also in many other occult and, at present, undeveloped sciences, though many people laugh at them, because they themselves cannot understand them, owing to the fact that the necessary discoveries leading up to the development of the science have not yet been made. . . .

. . . I look forward with immense pleasure to your visit to us in Wales. My uncle told me you were very fond of Borrow's glorious book *Wild Wales*: it is one of my most treasured possessions, which I have always by me, and read constantly, over and over again, it is wonderful how Borrow caught the spirit of that heavenly country, and described it in such delightful style! I adore Wales, and never tire of such a delicious picture of it! When you come to Cefn Bryntalch you can visit Bala, Mallwyd, Machynlleth, Devil's Bridge, Plynlimmon and the three sources thereon, and many other places described by the inimitable Borrow, and you will, I am sure, enjoy them all the more by having read such living descriptions of them!

I was highly delighted at what you said about my piano teacher. I am sure it is useless for anyone who is not going to study seriously for three years at least, to learn, from the foundations, any of these complicated 'methods', good as they may be for professional pianists. I have very little enthusiasm for playing the piano, except for the purpose of studying piano scores of operas and orchestral works.

You tell me to write as much as possible. There is nothing in the world I should like better, but how am I to do it? If I had ideas, I could not write them down without a piano, and it is such an unsatisfactory feeling that one must seek ideas at the piano.

If I am to make music my profession, which is of course my great wish, I do not see what I can do except become a critic – a writer on but not of music.

DELIUS TO PHILIP

Forgive me for keeping you waiting so long; I have been very busy with a new work. The arrangement of my *Summer Garden* I think is excellently done and I hope you will play it to me on my way through Cologne. I shall be in Germany in a fortnight – first Berlin and on my way back I hope to see you in Cologne.

The only fault I find with the orchestration of the *Nursery* is that you employ far too big an orchestra. The matter is too slight for such an enormous apparatus. Otherwise it is orchestrated with great taste.

Your songs are beautiful. In one or two I have made slight alterations – only a suggestion, mind – you come back so persistently to E flat in one of them. It is of no importance whether you write at the piano or not as long as you feel you want to express some emotion. Music is nothing else. Excuse this hasty scribble.

PHILIP TO DELIUS

Cöln
Feb. 28th, 1912

Alas! I shall not be in Germany in a fortnight's time – in fact I shall not be here next week! Since my love of music is so *unpractical* I must take the next best work that comes along, and this being the English Civil Service, I shall have to sacrifice a good deal of what I should like to do, to what is necessary. I discovered last month that, to comply with the age-limit regulations, I shall have to enter for my first Oxford exam. very much earlier than I had previously supposed – in fact at the end of the present year and, to prepare for it, I have quite as much if not more, classical work before me than I can possibly cram into the succeeding nine months. On that account therefore, most unwillingly, I must return to England and recommence study of the classics at the beginning of next month. I leave here on Friday next. I shall, of course, return to Germany after this exam. is over, and also during the vacations when I am at Oxford, but for the English Civil Service exam, for which I enter in five years' time, classics and English are, of necessity, my chief subjects, German only counting one-tenth part of the total marks!

I am extremely sorry to miss seeing you here, as I had long been looking forward to your visit to Germany. But I continue to hope most ardently that you will come over and see us in Wales next August or September. I long to roam the wild hills with you, who understand them, who are in sympathy with them, and to whom they are not merely 'sights pleasing to the eye!'

I have crowded much music into this last month, chiefly opera – *The Ring*, complete, *Die Meistersinger*, *Figaros Hochzeit* and other works I have heard with great pleasure: also some pure 'hogwash' by Meyerbeer, which is attracting enormous audiences because of its elaborate staging . . . The opera here is splendidly done – acting, singing, and staging being alike excellent; but good novelties are very scarce. Dr. Fischer published last week an open letter to the 'Festspiel' committee, in which he urged them to put on *A Village Romeo and Juliet* on the stage here.

I hope Mr. Beecham will give another concert of your works this year. I suppose the new choral work will be ready soon. I am longing to hear more of your music after all the Strauss etc. that I have heard here with interest, but not much real enjoyment.

DELIUS TO PHILIP

March 11th, 1912

Thanks so much for your nice letter. Do not be afraid to write to me when you feel like it. I love to receive your letters and assure you that they are never a bore to me. If you don't always get a quick and lengthy reply please do not attribute it to lack of interest; it will be because I am occupied with something very absorbing. If you want some advice from someone who really likes you and feels real interest in your welfare you can come to me without the slightest restraint. On any subject or question whatever I will tell you what I really think, and I can assure you that very few people can tell one what they really think. When they do they are always invaluable.

We leave for Berlin to-morrow, and shall be away about eighteen days. It is so lovely here that I hate to go. The garden is full of daffodils, primroses, scyllas; and flowering fruit-trees. I should love to wander about the Welsh hills with you and hope to come to see you next September.

Philip thoroughly enjoyed his stay in Germany. The different conditions of life in a foreign country, the freedom from restraint and supervision after the irksome years at Eton, and, above all, the opportunities for hearing the best and the latest in music – all these factors combined to make this one of the happiest periods of his life.

I add here extracts from letters written to Colin Taylor about this time, which are of interest in showing what decided – and, it seems to-day, extraordinarily sound – views this youth of seventeen held concerning music.

PHILIP TO COLIN TAYLOR

Cologne
Dec. 6th, 1911

. . . At the end of the concert came Strauss's *Heldenleben* – a sad come-down, to my mind, after Delius. I think it is the worst piece of Strauss I have ever heard, though I liked *Salome* and *Elektra*. Last month a new orchestral work by Debussy was played here – *Ibéria* (*Images* No. 2). I will not weary you with any more of my enthusiastic superlatives, but I must say that, next to Delius, this is the finest orchestral work I have ever heard. I heard it twice, rehearsal and performance; it is perfectly marvellous in its subtle impressionism, and absolutely original. Who ever before has undertaken (and really achieved) a musical portrayal of *Les parfums de la nuit*, as Debussy has in this work? It is quite wonderful.

. . . At the same concert, Berlioz's delicious *Queen Mab* was played. I have become very enthusiastic over poor, neglected Berlioz since reading the splendid autobiography, which is one of the most wholly delightful books I have ever come across. I went to Aachen a fortnight ago to hear his *Requiem*, which is absolutely thrilling! The passage from the *Dies Irae*, quoted in his book on orchestration, where the four brass bands and the army of drums sound the last trump is immensely effective, and worth going any distance to hear. I liked the whole work very much indeed – far far better than the heavy, gloomy

Requiem of Brahms, which was the last work of this kind I heard. I suppose that would be called 'bad taste'! Have you any idea why Berlioz is so neglected? I should like to know, since all that I have heard of him has struck me as being particularly fine, interesting and modern.

. . . Sibelius's new symphony (No. 4 in A minor) is absolutely original, quite in a class by itself, and uninfluenced by anything, save Nature. It struck me as being genuine 'Nature music'. It is very strange and mysterious, but at the same time a work of great beauty which one could appreciate more and more on repeated hearings.

. . . Schönberg's *Five Orchestral Pieces* sounded not nearly as bad as one would expect from all accounts of it; sometimes it was quite fascinating – one gets now and then just a glimpse, as it were, of some weird, new country, and although one can only see it from a distance, there is a strange fascination in the idea of its further possibilities.

All this, observe, from a boy of seventeen, written more than twenty years ago.

On his return from Germany Philip settled down to study in earnest, with a series of parson-tutors, for his Oxford entrance examination, but a steady crescendo of dissatisfaction with the prospect reached a head early in 1913. As always in such moments he turned to Delius for help and advice.

PHILIP TO DELIUS

Cefn Bryntalch
Jan. 8th, 1913

I don't know what you will think of me for plaguing you with so many letters full of trivialities when you are busy with the greatest matters in the world, but you have been so good to me that I think perhaps you will forgive me if I ask your advice before taking or not taking a step which will be of the greatest importance to me; for there is no one to whom I feel I can turn at the present moment, sooner than to you, though I do hope that I am not making a nuisance of myself, with my petty affairs. It is this: I simply cannot go on with my present humdrum slavery to Greek and Latin for the next five years, for the sake of a possible post in the Civil Service, where I could vegetate complacently for the rest of my life on a large salary and pension thrown in. To begin with, I have the greatest possible aversion to the work which I should have to do for the next five years – and it involves incessant drudgery, even in vacations; also I believe (though of course I may be quite wrong) that such wholesale immersion in the 'classics' constitutes a real bar to one's development in other ways. I have the greatest respect for many of the great classical writers, but to study these exclusively is another matter. In addition, I have not the slightest enthusiasm for a post in the Civil Service, and without enthusiasm no one, I am sure, ever succeeded in a competitive examination. Enthusiasm seems to me to be a factor of the highest importance for success in any work. There is a passage in Arthur Symons's introduction to Dowson's poems which haunts me though I am at times a little sceptical as to its truth . . . 'For, there is not a dream which may not come true, if we have the energy which makes or chooses our own fate. We can always, in this world, get what we want, if we will it intensely and persistently enough.' Yet of course the mere Will to Power is a very different thing from having the ability and energy to attain it; even slaves have a Will to Power . . . There is only one thing I have a burning enthusisam for, only one thing I feel I could work for, come what may of adverse conditions, and that is, vaguely – Music. I say vaguely because I have absolutely no confidence in myself, or that I have the smallest ability to do anything in any specific branch of Music. At the same time, if I could but attain the meanest position in the world of music, I would sooner die like a dog there (if need be) than attain to a comfortable and conventional position in the Civil Service, or on the Stock Exchange. That is exactly how I feel about the matter.

When I was with you in Grez, nearly a year and a half ago, you advised me to abandon all other pursuits, and to devote myself to music. I was a fool not to do so at once, I suppose, but

at that time my ideas of what I was going to do were so utterly
confused that I had not the courage to take any decisive step.
Do you still advise me to do so? Can I rely on my enthusiasm,
the greatest I have for anything in the world, for the necessary
energy to make something of my project? Having no definite
talent in any particular branch of Music, I am not particularly
hopeful; my chief hope is that if I devote the next five years
seriously to the study of music, instead of wasting my time
at Oxford, I may be able to develop whatever slender ability
I may have to some degree of proficiency. This is but a vague
and general outline; details are hard to fix upon, and perhaps
unnecessary just at present. If I felt I could ever do anything
worthy of the name of composition I should have no hesitation
whatsoever. Of course, it is my greatest hope that by concentra-
ting all my attention and energy on music, I might, in time,
possibly attain even that but, frankly, I admit I am rather
taken aback by my present lack of ability to do anything whatsoever, and by the consequent lack of confidence in myself . . .
Perhaps after all I shall have to resign myself to the office stool
. . . But apart from composition, I would rather do anything
in the way of musical work than submit to the life I seem about to
enter upon . . . Perhaps I demand too much from life,
perhaps my castles in the air will fall with a sudden crash;
still, I simply cannot help building them up, even if they are
built in vain . . . At the present moment, what I really have
my eyes upon is – do not laugh at me too much! – musical
criticism! With five years' general study of music, I think I
could do that as well as some of the men whose columns one
reads in the Press. With this, I also include the writing of books
on musical subjects, and as many other musical tasks as I can
combine with it . . . Failing that, I might be able to scrape
along by copying orchestral parts, or even make piano transcriptions of orchestral works. I might learn some orchestral
instrument and so get to know the orchestra from the inside –
that is, if I could get into an orchestra at all; at least, I could
thrash the big drum! Or perhaps, after years of patient study
I might attain to the position of pianist to a cinematograph
theatre – I happened to see an advertisement for one yesterday

10492

in our little town. However, I do not want to study the piano unless it is absolutely necessary, but I should like to play in an orchestra . . . That is the rough outline of what I might possibly do if I devoted myself entirely to music for the next five years. Any of the courses I have mentioned above I should love to adopt – except perhaps the cinema pianist's job. However, my chief attention must, I think, be directed to the requirements of musical criticism . . . To descend to more sordid details – I have got to make a living out of it somehow. In three years' time, when I am 21, I shall have an income of £80 a year of my own; all my father's money was left to my mother for her life, so that anything over and above that £80 will have to come from her. But I do not for a moment anticipate any serious opposition . . . I have not come to this decision rashly, hurriedly or without very serious consideration; to begin a musical career would be the first step towards my highest ambitions; to renounce it for ever would be to bid farewell to the aspirations I have cherished for years – though perhaps I am a fool, and my ambitions but folly.

Please forgive me for inflicting all this on you, but I cannot help asking your guidance at the present time. I am, so to speak, at a crossroads; I must make a decision, one way or the other, within the next few days. At the end of next week or the beginning of the week after that, I am supposed to be going to live with *another parson* (!) and read Latin and Greek, Greek and Latin (world without end, Amen!) until I go up to Oxford in October. The whole prospect revolts me; I must get out of it somehow, if it is possible.

. . . I do hope you do not mind me writing to you like this. I cannot tell you what a help, what a relief it is to be able to turn to you and ask your advice at a time like this. If you still advise me to devote myself to music, I can assure you that nothing on this earth shall prevent my doing so.

Affectionately yours . . .

DELIUS TO PHILIP

Jan. 11th, 1913

Your letter interested me very much indeed, and I may tell you once and for all that I take the greatest interest in you and your career, and shall always be only too happy to help you in whatever way I can.

You ask me for advice in choosing between the civil service, in which you seem to have no interest whatever, and music, which you love. I will give it to you. I think that the most stupid thing one can do is to spend one's life doing something one hates, or in which one has no interest; in other words it is a wasted life. I do not believe in sacrificing the big things of life to any one or anything. In your case I do not see why you should sacrifice the most important thing in your life to your mother. You will certainly regret it if you do, later on. Children always exaggerate the duty they have to their parents. Parents very seldom sacrifice anything at all for their children. In your case your mother has certainly not, since she married again; in other words she followed her own feelings – and of course, did entirely right in so doing, and I should advise you to do the same. I was in exactly the same position when I was your age and had a considerably harder fight to get what I wanted. I chucked up everything and went to America. One has every chance of succeeding when one does what one loves and I can tell you personally that I have never once regretted the step I took. The greatest pleasure and satisfaction I have experienced in life has been through music, in making it and in hearing it, and in living with it. I should advise you to study music, so that you will be able to give lessons in harmony, counterpoint, and orchestration. You can always become a critic. I think that you are sufficiently gifted to become a composer. Everything depends on your perseverance. One never knows how far one can go. I will find out where you can receive the most modern and the best musical instruction – perhaps in Paris, perhaps in Berlin. The opportunities for hearing music are infinitely greater in Berlin, and I have friends there who might be very useful to you.

Emerson says in one of his essays something that resembles the Arthur Symons quotation: something to this purpose, 'A man who works with his whole soul at anything whatever will make it a success before he is fifty', and I believe this to be perfectly true. One's talent develops like muscles that you are constantly training. Trust more in hard work than in inspiration.

Besides writing this letter of sympathy and encouragement, Delius gave further proof of his affectionate solicitude by arranging an interview with Philip's parents, in which he strongly urged them to permit the adoption of a musical career. In addition he invited Philip to come and stay with him at Grez in order to discuss the matter more fully, which he did in March. In spite of everything, however, it was eventually decided that he should proceed to Oxford, if only for a breathing space, until a definite course of action should be decided upon.

An extract from a further long letter to Delius is moving and revelatory, confirming, incidentally, what was suggested earlier concerning his unusually late development. It is only after considerable hesitation that I have decided to print it, but it is obviously a document of such primary importance to the understanding of the boy he was and the man he was to become that to withhold it would, to a great extent, amount to a stultification of the purpose of the book.

PHILIP TO DELIUS

Didbrook Vicarage
Winchcombe, Glos.
Feb. 17th, 1913

. . . I never stood upon my own feet, never woke up to life beyond the nursery and my mother's apron strings until a year or so ago – that is, exceptionally late. I suppose I woke up comparatively suddenly, with a rude shock, so to speak, being quite incapable of standing on my own legs at all – as though all previous foundations had suddenly collapsed. They were thoroughly rotten, I admit. I am never thankful enough to be rid of them; but the unavoidable fact remains that I am, virtually, but three or four years old; my first fifteen years might almost as well never have been lived, and I find this lack of experience and accomplishments of living quite appalling. I struggle hard to develop now, I am trying my very best to live so as to redeem a part at least of the lost years, but I am constantly being dragged back – at least I am always feeling the drag, though I do think I really am becoming harder and a little stronger at last. At the present moment, I cannot but feel that I am an absolutely useless specimen in every branch of life – only fit, as I am, for a lethal chamber . . . But for you, and a very few others – just one or two – I should have slept through life until the last and final sleep. Now, I am just about as fit for life as one who has only just woken up in the early morning, at the period when one is, perhaps, more inert and incapable of anything than at any other time, is fit to begin the day's work immediately. Though, alas, in my case, it is not quite early morning – so much of that is gone. This mood, however, is very amply outweighed by a passionate hope that something – perhaps unknown and inconceivable to me at the present time – will happen or develop. My strongest joy lies in *expectation* – in looking forward to things, especially if they are unknown, mysterious, and romantic, full of possibilities. That is what keeps me going; perhaps it is but a vain illusion, a dream – but it is all I have. I have often felt myself to be a mere *spectator* of the game of Life: this, I know to my sorrow, has led me to a positively morbid self-consciousness and an introspectiveness that almost amounts to insincerity, breeding as it does a kind of detachment from real life. Lately I have tried passionately to plunge into life, and live myself, forgetfully if possible of this horrible aloofness. I believe I am just beginning to succeed a little, perhaps though I know only too well that complete success now will be long and difficult, if not impossible of attainment . . . Those fifteen years cannot be shaken off. I was formerly lonely, and shunned the healthy animalism of private and public schools, holding aloof, clinging to the

atmosphere of home. Now that I can no longer endure *that* –
though I have found, in part, a far better and more congenial
atmosphere, though I would not exchange the nature of the
typical English public-school animal even for my present
unsatisfactory state – I know that I have been too much, too
foolishly and fruitlessly alone, and at home now, I am far
more lonely than anywhere else. As a result of this I have
become morbidly nervous – even down to a physical 'nervous
stricture' – which fact is a terrible hindrance to my having
free, happy and healthy intercourse with my fellow-creatures
– especially strangers, and those of great 'accomplishment' (so-
called) in those rather trivial yet, from a social point of view,
important things – games, of various kinds, indoor and outdoor,
and an easy, natural, unaffected and unselfconscious manner in
general. Though I loathe athleticism, a mild proficiency in the
elements of certain of these games is of great use to one, in helping
one to opportunities of intercourse with others. Yet all this I
would gladly have sacrificed if I could fall back for consolation
to dreams which I felt one day I could create into realities.
But I have, at this present moment, nothing at all . . . I said
just now that I was three or four years old; in reality I have
only just been born. The great fact that Life is before me, to
make something of, is all that I have to live on – but surely it is
enough to begin upon, with all the bitter, though useful, experience of those other years to look back upon, as upon a nightmare.

. . . The long and the short of the matter, however, amounts
to this – that now, at any rate, I am determined to live my life,
to drain its cup to the very dregs, to live each day, each hour,
feverishly perhaps just now. I am absolutely ravenous for life;
what I do matters not so very much, so long as I live. . . .

The importance of this as a psychological document cannot, I
think, be over-estimated. Finally, the following extracts from
letters, showing the extent to which the music of Delius dominated
him at this time, may be of interest.

EARLY YEARS: DELIUS

Christ Church
Oxford
Feb. 11th, 1914

I have postponed answering your letter far too long – please forgive me . . . First of all, let me try and tell you, as best I can, what a perfect joy it was to me to hear your two pieces for small orchestra[1] at Queen's Hall on January 20th; the first piece is the most exquisite and entirely lovely piece of music I have heard for many a long day – it almost makes one cry for the sheer beauty of it. I play it often on the piano and it is constantly in my head, a kind of beautiful undercurrent to my thoughts. For me, the deep, quiet sense of glowing happiness, and the mysterious feeling of being at the very heart of nature, that pervades the piece, is too lovely for words. I only wish I could express to you a tithe of what the music makes me feel; it is simply perfect. Lately things have happened which have made me feel a new being altogether, and given me a deeper joy and a greater realization of life than I have ever known before; your music ministered to this mood in a wonderful manner – it seemed to have a new and intimate message to me, and strangely to express the very thing that was awakening in me. Forgive this confused attempt to express what mere words can never do, but I feel I must try and tell you, however feebly, what a wonderful message your Cuckoo brought me.

PHILIP TO DELIUS

Didbrook
Winchcombe, Glos.
July 10th, 1914

I must write you just a few lines to tell you, however inadequately, what a wonderful and overwhelmingly beautiful experience last Wednesday's concert was for me, and to contribute my tiny share – however futile – to the debt of gratitude

[1] *On Hearing the First Cuckoo in Spring* and *Summer Night on the River.*

57

the whole world owes you for such superb, such glorious music. No words could do it justice; it is too magnificent. It transcends everything – not only all other music. For me it is the greatest thing in life. Any attempt to express what it means to me in mere words appears weak and ridiculous, but I feel I must tell you, somehow or anyhow, something of what your music makes me feel; please forgive the inadequate means of doing so.

Also this from a letter written to Colin Taylor:

PHILIP TO COLIN TAYLOR

Cefn Bryntalch
Abermule
Montgomery
August 1st, 1914

. . . I spend most of my time saturating myself with Delius's music. I am sure there is no music more beautiful in all the world; it haunts me day and night – it is always with me and seems, by its continual presence, to intensify the beauty of everything else for me.

Altogether, as will be seen from the foregoing correspondence, the influence of Delius, both as man and artist, was of decisive and crucial importance in these critical years of his development. In many respects it was wholly beneficial. One would naturally have expected that in such a close spiritual relationship between a completely mature and unusually strong personality on the one hand, and an immature and somewhat unstable character – as Philip was at that time – on the other, the latter would have been completely submerged and become a mere ineffectual echo of the former. That this did not happen was largely due to Delius's passionate insistence on the necessity of developing one's own personality, first and foremost, at all costs; of following the dictates of one's nature in spite of all opposition and all possible consequences, of realizing one's own peculiar angle of vision –

what Cézanne called his 'petite sensation' – however greatly it conflicts with that of the rest of the world. 'Try to be yourself and live up to your own nature', we find him writing to Philip in one of the early letters, in 1912; 'whatever one's nature one ought to develop it to its utmost limits and not be constantly trying to become someone else. This leads to continual dissatisfaction and failure', and this is, in effect, the *leitmotiv* of all his letters to his young friend. There can be no doubt that his continual exhortations in this direction contributed largely to the building up of the self-confidence and self-reliance in which Philip was so gravely lacking in his early years, as we see only too clearly from his letters.

At the same time one cannot help feeling that such a complete absorption in the music of Delius as is indicated in these last letters was definitely harmful in certain respects; not merely because such a highly personal and idiosyncratic art must of necessity constitute a dangerous influence upon an aspiring composer, but also because its inner spirit and emotional content are fraught with perilous consequences to any who are insufficiently provided with the necessary antidote to it. It has always seemed to me to be one of the strangest of paradoxes that Delius, the avowed disciple of Nietzsche, the champion of the manly, pagan virtues as opposed to those of Christianity, should have written the music that he has done, which seems always implicitly to contradict the doctrines he so insistently proclaims. When one listens to the music of Delius one begins to understand what the old Greeks meant when they attributed to music a more powerful moral influence than to any of the other arts, and why Plato should have claimed for it an even greater subversive power than is possessed by any other. In his ideal Republic indeed, the music of Delius would have been sternly proscribed, for its prevailing mood of tender melancholy and wistful resignation is the most subtle solvent that exists of all the civic and manly virtues, and even of the very will to live. It is the final and supreme expression of the desire for annihilation first voiced by Wagner in *Tristan und Isolde,* and it is no mere coincidence that what is perhaps the culminating moment in all Delius's art, the closing scene of the *A Village Romeo and Juliet* should, like that of the other great swan-song of romanticism, the *Axël* of Villiers de l'Isle Adam, be directly concerned with the presentation of the act of renunciation of life and self-destruction. . . .

Philip passed his entrance examination to Oxford in the summer of 1913, and went up to Christ Church in the following October.

CHAPTER II

AT OXFORD: BY ROBERT NICHOLS

It was 'Jiggers' – let me so style him – who first informed me of Philip Heseltine's existence. 'Jiggers' and I were both in our first Oxford term in the autumn of 1913. We had been talking motor-bicycles, Jiggers' favourite and indeed sole topic, when, as he rose – some loose-limbed yards of him – to leave my gloomy digs, he said, 'There's a chap in the House you ought to know. An extraordinary chap – plays the pianola, the piano and all that. In fact, I think he's a what-d'you-call-it – a musician.' 'I'll go at once,' I said, 'I've been here some weeks and up to date I haven't met a soul who cares about that sort of thing.' 'I wouldn't,' Jiggers returned, 'he might not be in the mood. He's queer. I'd drop a note.' 'Very well, I'll take a note with me and, if he isn't in, I'll drop it.' Jiggers regarded me dubiously. 'I wouldn't,' he said. But I was not to be dissuaded.

When I entered Mr. Heseltine's room the occupier was not at first sight to be descried. He was in fact ensconced behind the sofa and his attitude betokened grief.

'Go away,' he cried, 'I don't want to see you. Go away.'

But I was not to be deterred and approached the pianola. 'So you compose,' I remarked; 'setting Yeats? I admire him very much. I compose poetry myself.' (I was intensely proud of the fact.)

'It's no good. Go away.'

'I'm not going away. I've been in this so-called home of learning and art for some weeks and I have yet to meet anybody of my own age who practises any of the arts. I have been trying to write poetry at a couple of crammers for four years now and have never yet met anybody of my own age who tried to create anything. Won't you play it over to me?'

'Are you fond of music?'

'Next to poetry I like it better than anything in the world.'

'Have you heard much?'

'Quite a lot' (a lie, but secure in a few Queen's Hall wallow-ings in Tschaikowski, Dvořák, and Wagner, etc., on winter Sunday afternoons, I didn't know it for a lie).

'Ever heard of Delius?'

'No. Who's he?'

'The greatest living composer.'

'I thought Strauss was the greatest living composer.'

'Strauss is a vulgar tune trundler who can write for the brass and doesn't allow you to forget it.'

His aspect had changed. He stood by the upright pianola. He was slightly above middle height, very neatly and quietly dressed (but not the least the dandy). His face was very pale and his hair, a little long, of an ashen blond. His blue eyes jealously regarded the manuscript on the piano. At the first opportunity he stowed the MSS. away.

'Will you play me some Delius?'

'He writes for orchestra, not for the piano. And in any event I couldn't give you any idea of him, for I'm a very bad pianist.'

I felt baffled. 'What nationality is he?'

'He's a Yorkshireman. He studied with Grieg. Do you know Grieg?'

'Very little.'

'I'll try and play you some. I only use the pianola for big works.'

He sat down, and, peering at the pages, played me some arrange-ments of folk-tunes by Grieg. As he did so his face grew gentle and that queer smile I was afterwards to know so well became fixed upon his lips. I had – I don't know why – expected something rampageous. This music was very quiet.

'I don't know anything about the technical side,' I said, 'but the way those chords move – I don't know if that's the proper expression . . .'

'The harmony, you mean . . .'

'The harmony is novel to me. It's sort of . . .' – I hunted for a phrase – 'it's unexpected and yet somehow just right. I mean that's what I find striking and beautiful in what you're playing.'

He glanced with some interest at me. 'That, as a matter of fact, my dear sir,' he returned, '*is* what is unusual and peculiar. Don't you play?'

'Not a note. I wish to God I could.'

'Well, Delius has developed all that. The usual music – the music you hear most of, especially here, Bach and so forth – is mostly contrapuntal: that's to say the interest is horizontal. One tune moves in combination against another. The interest in Delius is vertical: one chord melts into another. In fact you might call it a melody of chords. That's an exaggeration, of course, but perhaps it'll help you to see what I mean.'

By this time we had definitely got on terms and the longer I stayed with him the better I liked him. 'Liked' is perhaps too weak a word, for added to liking there was that admiration – yes, admiration is the word – one feels for any person who, taking one's weakness into account, reveals to one a new world.

'What a beautiful Egyptian bust,' I said, when at length he had closed the pianola, 'and what splendid brown beech leaves behind it. Did you buy them?'

'No. I got them in the wolds yesterday afternoon.'

'How did you get there?'

'Motor-biked.'

His grief returned. He appeared embarrassed.

'What's up?' I said.

'It's that long-nosed woman of Gloucestershire!' he cried.

Later I was to learn that nothing could have been more typical than this reply.

'In love?'

'I suppose so.' He seemed exasperated by the fact.

'I'm in love too.'

And I launched into an impassioned harangue upon the subject. The fact that the lady concerned was a musician seemed to afford him a slightly sardonic satisfaction – 'at least she's an artist'. The passion moreover had his approval because he had heard her play in Oxford earlier in Term. She played well, with much fire, and was also extremely beautiful in the 'Lady Hamilton as a Bacchante' style – what more could be wanted?

Such or some such was the substance of our first interview. I remember it very clearly, for the mere fact that my new-found friend – I felt from the first that we should be friends – was an artist gave him a sort of sanctity in my eyes, and, in fact, twenty years of contact with artists has not cured me of that sort of pre-disposition in a man's favour. It is a disposition Philip shared, provided he felt the object of this regard was a true artist and not a 'faker'. If in addition the artist concerned happened to be un-fortunate, suffering from the indifference of the public or empti-ness of pocket or subject to unjust attack, there were no lengths – no lengths whatever – to which Philip would not go to advantage him. Those who have blamed the harshness of his public exposure of such as he deemed *simulacra* are probably not acquainted with the reverse side of the medal. I persuaded him to come to my 'digs'.

We set out beneath an autumnal sunset – heavy coils of clouds laboured across wet heavens sufficiently tinctured with orange to kindle a subdued warmth of reflection in the damp and gritty pavement. Philip walked without a hat. I can see him now – for it was between Tom Tower and Carfax that I first saw and heard him whistle the penultimate variation for solo violin

from Delius' *Dance Rhapsody*. This variation was ever a favourite with him and the whistling of it – he whistled more sweetly than any person I ever knew – was usually a sign of recovery of spirits or of temporary consolation. Whistling it, his face softened and lighted and he seemed to attain to a state of distance and tranquillity. I had then in my digs a bottle of particular liqueur called *Crème Napoléon* which I have since sought in vain. Under its influence my visitor forgot his shyness and in exchange for the catalogue of my woes recited his. The evening ended in laughter and talk about Elizabethan poetry. Finally he said, 'Recite something of yours.' I needed no second invitation – had in fact been hoping this would happen. 'Why,' he cried when I had done, 'you really are a poet.' I do not remember what poems I recited, nor can I imagine how he arrived at this conclusion for which, I take it, the *Crème Napoléon* may have been in some sort responsible.

I was immensely bitten with him, but he was, at first, difficult to find, for love sped the wheels of his motor-bicycle upon devious paths. In fact, so I have been since informed, it sped those wheels during the Christmas vacation as far as a Scottish county in order that he might return with the lady's initials on the bicycle's official number-plate. But, if he was in a state of agitation, I was in like case, so much so that he christened me 'Berlioz' – we had discovered a common enthusiasm for that composer – and likened my aberrations and exaltations of mood – and they were many and vehement – to those occasioned by Miss Smithson. From these moods originated the first verse of mine that an indulgent critic might dub poetry, a happening that interested him and provoked his envy, for his passion had, so far as I was permitted to gather, no such effects in him but only 'put him off'. And here, perhaps, is the place to state that, in my opinion, desire, which ever trod somewhat closer upon the heels of love in his case than mine, was always a great perturber of his work until such a time as the fulfilment of that desire seemed sure and close, when it would prompt him to music often of a kind far distant from what those not closely acquainted with artists and their psychological processes would expect.

Later I was more fully to understand that love did not only perturb his work, but, while it lasted, transformed his whole being and

seldom, in my opinion, for the better. Persons in love are proverbially capricious and moody but in many the mere state of
being in love, even though the course of love be not smooth,
makes for something akin to happiness, a development probably
due to growth of magnanimity. Such a magnanimity was not
absent in Philip when in love but was offset by such violent
alternations of mood as to suggest a ballet of contrasted personalities. For love did not seem to integrate him as it does some,
but to split him up. Love, in fact, acted on him, if I may be permitted the metaphor, somewhat after the fashion of a bad wine,
particularly of that sort of bad wine which has been doctored and
'gingered up'. A sort of spiritual *malaise* overcame him. Now he
would be aimlessly excited and sally forth in a hurry to effect
some negligible purpose. Anon he would retire into a sort of
reverie which was perhaps the only true happiness he knew in love.
Next he would take love's name in vain and inveigh against particular circumstances that surrounded the object of his love or
even against the object itself. A period of dismalness (what he
called 'grisliness'), characterized by a sort of lackadaisical
cynicism, would ensue and this in turn give way to abrupt hilarity,
new hopes, weariness, irritability and finally dejection and exhaustion. And if to love was added – as it usually was and that
early – the sting of frustrated desire, Philip's condition became one
of impatience and of gloom not the less gloomy for the fact that it
was shot with flashes of saturnine jest. For myself I could but pity
him, since it was plain that he was not one of those fortunates who
has the gift to possess his love and not be possessed by it. Such a
condition is always dangerous to the subject, as it is frequently
dangerous not only to his intimates but to the object of love itself.
There was little that could be done to succour him. Perhaps the
most suitable course was to encourage him to throw up the affair
altogether.

Those who are sympathetically acquainted with the figure of
Stephen Daedalus in Joyce's *Portrait of the Artist as a Young Man* – a
novel Philip much admired – and with *Ulysses* will the more easily

understand Philip's malady, its nature and origin. It is significant to me that he more than once quoted to me two lines of poetry which were favourites with Stephen Daedalus:

> And no more turn aside and brood
> Upon love's bitter mystery . . .

He came often to my rooms where, with a bottle of wine, or, as the shillings grew scarcer – for I shared with him the inability to sew up the pockets – bottles of beer before us, we talked on every subject under the sun save such as occupied the majority of our fellows. He had read Havelock Ellis, Carpenter and Otto Weininger – of whom he had then a considerable opinion, later abandoned – and we discussed 'sex' after a manner now common among 'modern' flappers but in those days rare. Carpenter received more consideration than I thought (and still think) he deserved. From Carpenter we turned to Walt Whitman, whose rhapsodies upon sexual love and nature delighted us. We agreed that the course of honest passion did not admit impediment and we castigated Christianity with a fervour only equalled by our ignorance of all but its unpleasing manifestations as seen in our Public Schools and in parochial affairs. Our abomination of it was indeed extreme and was fortified by my soaking in Jefferies' *Story of My Heart* and our common admiration of Nietzsche. True we had – and I particularly – but a very patchy acquaintance with his works and had by no means understood all we had read, but we discerned in him – in *Zarathustra* especially – an attitude and opinions that appealed to us, expressed in a manner that exalted our spirits. Philip also enlarged on war and declared such views as would nowadays result in him being labelled a 'Conchy'. Little did either of us dream that but a short period was to elapse before he was to be summoned before a Military Tribunal, and I, an ex-soldier, was to volunteer to attest that he had held such opinions more than a year before the opening of hostilities, an offer of which he did not in the event avail himself – the more, from my point of view, the pity, for it would have given me much satisfaction, as one who had fought against a nation singularly confused on the subject of right and might, to tell that Tribunal exactly what I thought of efforts to coerce genuine conscientious objectors in defiance of Mr. Asquith's pledge. Myself I was steeped in Vigny's *Servitudes et Grandeurs Militaires*, a book which would not, I think, have appealed to Philip had he chosen to read it.

The grounds of his objection to any kind of service that would assist the prosecution of a war were threefold. First, he spoke of the existence in him of an unalterable instinct against the shedding of human blood and more especially the blood of those who had but just arrived at an age when life first declares its fullest and sweetest possibilities. (It was this instinct that later was to make D. H. Lawrence's theories of self-destructive forces, etc., for a time so attractive to him.) In those days I was a little shocked at Philip's downright and open expression of such opinions, though I did not venture to say what I felt. The fact was that I didn't understand them and considered he had a 'kink' on this subject as I held he had on the subject of food, for he displayed vegetarian leanings (in those days such as I grouped such opinions in brackets), though his objection to animal food was based on purely hygienic grounds. His second objection to service was psychological and ethical. He pointed out that youth was usually conscripted for a war that had arisen due to a collision of political ideologies of the interplay of which youth usually had no notion, for which it was not responsible and in which it took little or no interest. In a word, 'They bolt you into it and before you know where you are thousands are shot in a quarrel with other youths who have been bolted too.' This argument I endeavoured to counter out of a fathomless ignorance of the existence of such a pact as, unknown to me, then existed in the shape of the celebrated Belgian 'scrap of paper'. Philip's third grounds were personal, anarchic and religious: this is a democracy at least in name; let those fight who wish to fight and let those who don't wish to fight be subject to no pressure from a state whose authority derives

68

from a counting of heads; to some such heads to fight is almost a religious duty, to others not to fight is equally so. It is evident to me now that, considering his youth and surroundings, he must have brooded a lot on the subject. These arguments are commonplaces of youth to-day. They were very far from being so then.

Sex, literature (particularly Elizabethan literature) and music were our great subjects. On the first I suppose we divagated in about equal proportions. On the second I fancy I mostly took the floor, and on the third Philip. Then, as later, he much enjoyed 'juicy' words and I remember what pleasure he took in certain passages of Urquhart and Motteux's *Rabelais* on account of the abundance of such words. Russian novels he did not appear to have read. For Tolstoy he later in life conceived a lively antipathy. I never remember him mentioning Turgeniev. But I seem to recall, during Philip's latter days, a violent, lurid and somewhat Dostoievskian discussion of Dostoievski. Greek and Roman litera-ture had perished for us in the Public Schools which purported to teach them. I read after desultory fashion here and there in French literature. I don't think Philip did. Philip had one par-ticular attachment in English letters which is, I think, worth special mention: he loved George Borrow and, I believe, continued to love him when other idols had 'gone west'. In modern letters his poets were Dowson, Yeats and Arthur Symons. He sometimes mentioned poems from *The Shropshire Lad*. He did not appear to have read either Hardy or Conrad.

In music his chief subject of discourse was Delius, and not the music only. For he revered Delius with that sort of idolatry that is only to be found in the young and which, when informed, gives great masters perhaps more pleasure than any other save that of their peers. I am certain that this love of Delius and his works was, with Philip's love of nature, then and for several years after-wards by far the best thing in Philip's life. Delius' great stature as a composer, now recognized in England, was then (1913) but little realized in this country. Philip was fully cognizant of it. For though I doubt whether he had had opportunity of hearing more than a quarter of Delius' music, he had examined at the piano a large number of the scores and even then knew *The Mass of Life* to be one of the world's masterpieces. To what extent his musical opinions were influenced by those of Delius, to whom he had already acted (I believe) as amanuensis, I cannot say. Philip spoke rather of those he particularly admired, Grieg, Chopin, Wagner, Berlioz, than of those he disliked or of those whose music made little appeal to him. Of Beethoven he said, 'Of course he's very great but his music somehow doesn't move me.' (Some years later – during the war – we shared a score of the *Fifth Symphony* at a Prom. and Philip grew so excited that he lost his way in it.) Bach, he said, afforded him little pleasure, but he drew my attention to Bach's endless ingenuity and 'right copious invention'. On Handel he was silent. There was some talk of quartets by Haydn (a consequence, I think, of conversations with Dr. Walker). Mozart, to my disappointment, was passed over (I do not think Philip was then at all familiar with his music). Schubert's last two symphonies – 'the *C major* is better than the *Unfinished*' – were praised, but I recall no mention of the songs. My mother had sung some of them to me when I was a child, but I did not like to bring them up, my attitude being – and rightly in view of the extent of his knowledge as compared with mine – one of deeply respectful attention. I remember among foreign composers, then 'modern', the names of Busoni, Debussy, Ravel and Ladmirault, but not of Fauré. He had a lively admiration for *Till Eulenspiegel* (though Strauss' musical personality was repugnant to him) and asserted, 'I haven't heard much of his work and find it hard to get hold of the scores, but I doubt if he ever had done anything else as good as that and am quite certain he'll never do anything better.' (Strauss came to Oxford to receive an honorary degree at the end of the following summer term. *Till* was given. Philip was much excited about it but reiterated this opinion, with which, exactly twenty years later, many far more competent than myself will doubtless agree.) Philip had not only heard of Schönberg but had seen a score of the latest piano pieces. He couldn't make head or tail of them, 'they seemed like something gone rotten' (or words to that effect). The sextet however he approved (we heard it, if memory serves me, at the Oxford Music Club). Ornstein he had heard of. Dohnányi seemed to him only a belated Brahmsian, and he distrusted Brahms, feeling that Brahms was a sort of Schumannesque pastiche of Beethoven. Béla Bartók he approved, though whether it was then or a year or two later he showed enthusiasm for Zongaradarabia I cannot be certain. I don't remember Moussorgsky being mentioned, but Rimsky Korsakov was, and I recall a full score – heavy on the knees and bewilderingly pepperpotted with notes – in Philip's rooms. The title was in Russian, but whether the score was that of *Scheherazade* or a Borodin Symphony or of a work by Balakirev I cannot say. Balakirev's *Islamey* long stood on the piano defying determined if desultory assaults upon the easier passages. Only Raoul Vines, I was told, could play it. Later, in one of Philip's London flats, a pianola triumphantly and strepitantly disposed of these difficulties, as of those of some note-riddled, massive and occasionally impressive works of Max Reger. (Then it was that I advanced a plea for one of my gods – since somewhat fallen – César Franck and his *Prelude Chorale and Fugue*, but found the verdict go against me.)

In the afternoons we sometimes took a walk. Philip was not communicative on such walks and the autumn dismalness depressed us. None the less, was any fragment or ghost of beauty, whether in cloud-crag's edge or in stretch of vapour hovering between us and the willows, to be discerned, Philip would discover it and we would both stop and regard it in silence before continuing upon the roadside path. Indeed, I have never known anyone more sensitive to the more retired moods and fainter beauties of nature than he. This loving observance of nature was entirely poetical. He never in my experience showed the slightest interest in any branch of science with the exception of that of psycho-analysis, the findings (and still more the pretensions) of which he disputed.

I suppose he had faults – even intelligent and sensitive under-graduates, an on the whole delightful species, have them – but they were never such as conjure up in me a spirit of criticism. Indeed, throughout his life I never criticized him, though upon sufficient occasion I tried to place before him as sympathetically as I knew how my views for and against certain attitudes and courses. I recall but one serious quarrel and that was during the war when, out of exasperation with all things, he spoke (as I thought) insultingly of those who had volunteered. I took this 'insult' personally and in a Byronic huff left him in the middle of Piccadilly Circus. But a few days later we met again, all reference to the incident was avoided on both sides and our relations re-newed. To criticize him either to his face or in hopes that what one said would be passed on, above all to sit in summary judgment on him was neither fair to him – since his was a very complicated and subtle nature – nor expedient. He had great determination and a sharp and quick mind in which abstract theories frequently buttressed personal disposition, and those who argued with him were apt to find themselves suddenly in very deep water. In this he resembled a character from a novel by Dostoievski. When I knew him most intimately, namely at Oxford, the 'gentle' side of this character was most constantly in evidence, so much so in fact that, quite apart from less amiable Dostoievskian elements, even the English 'hearty' side of his character had not developed, save in so far as he loved earthy words for their own sake and was inclined to curious jests at the imaginary erotic eccentricities of personalities for whom he entertained or pretended to entertain no great opinion. I say 'pretended' to entertain for he had even then a rare eye for the components of personality, and while he could and did perceive what was admirable in a figure, his sense of fun provoked him to diverting and scandalous impromptus on the subject of such a figure's supposed or actual weaknesses.

I gathered that by and large he had not really detested his life at and the customs and institutions of his Public School as I had detested mine. On the whole he had been 'let alone' and one or two figures of masters remained sympathetic memories. Oxford he did detest both then and later in memory. But here, too, certain figures shone for him – the Dean of Christ Church in particular. Of Dr. Walker, as musician, he had a considerable opinion, though violently at difference with him on some musical matters.

Apart from music and discussion on such subjects as I have indicated, his chief interest was in motor-bicycles and the eccentricities of the aforesaid 'Jiggers'. He knew, I think, nothing at all of how a motor-bicycle functions and delighted in this minor mystery somewhat as he did in the major mystery of how 'Jiggers' 'functioned'. This interest in 'Jiggers' and his curiosities of conduct had no malice in it and was thoroughly characteristic of Philip, for all his life he took an amiable delight in the eccentricities of odd characters and the motives behind them. This amiable delight was much akin to that of a zoologist, 'Leave 'em alone. For heaven's sake don't touch 'em. Something curious is going to happen.' And if the 'something curious' seemed somehow to be hanging fire Philip would lovingly do his best to place the object of his interest in such a position as to ensure what was most individual in it doing itself justice. In later life such manœuvres might have as their ultimate aim the undoing and exposure of pretensions, ethical or aesthetic, in an object which he had come to consider required (in the public interest) such undoing and exposure. But when I first knew Philip, such doings were entirely 'platonic'. Though far from delighting in the diversity of all God's creatures, he often rejoiced in those in whom others had not the eye to rejoice, and the curious mixture of naivety and shrewdness in 'Jiggers' procured him much pleasure of a Shakespearian sort. The world of non-human animals, however, left him cold, albeit he liked birds and entertained a Shelleyan regard for snakes. Cats were in another category altogether. They were neither human – he seemed to like and respect them for their remoteness from the human – nor were they of the world of birds and snakes, much less of horses, cows, dogs and so forth. He kept – against rules, I believe – a little stray ragamuffin kitten, black as your hat and with a timid expression, in or about his rooms at the House. That first afternoon, ere we sallied forth, he placed a saucer of milk with some precaution and ceremony inside and behind his inner door. I was to remember that years later when I read the reports of another autumn evening's happenings.

January found us both again in Oxford. That term was full of trouble for me. I had got out of leading strings at last and proceeded to indulge in capers unpleasing to the academic authorities. I did foolish, but not I think reprehensible, things, and I did not know why I did them. Such capers Philip regarded with an indulgent eye, and indeed they signified no more than the ebullience of youth and the extravagances due to a passion which had created a condition of anarchy within. Philip's passion appeared to be in an elaborate decline and he sometimes busied himself holding an examination of the state of the patient, the causes of the decline and the probable intolerable consequences of the approaching death. I regarded myself as an expert and, on those rare occasions when I was permitted to approach the bedside, flourished my stethoscope with the more gusto in that the examination diverted my thoughts from my own passion which was weekly becoming more frantic. Here, I think, is the place to mention that he then behaved in very characteristic fashion, for when I was completely out of pocket he furnished me with the wherewithal for the presentation of a luxurious bouquet to the object of my affections at a concert in town which I could not attend. But it was ever so with us throughout our friendship. Whoever happened to be in funds paid, and it did not matter in the least on what the money was to be spent so long as the recipient needed it for a specific purpose. I do not imagine Mrs. Grundy would have approved some of the items of expenditure. Far from it. But the mere fact that her shadow fell athwart the scene was but an additional reason for forking out. Aesthetic fastidiousness more often, I fear, prevented us outraging that shadow than moral scruple. When Philip's passion in due course petered out

74

he did not take to riot as I did when mine suddenly collapsed. In connection with which collapse (during the autumn of 1915) I may, I think, make bold, not because it concerns my history but because it was so characteristic of his, to record an expedition he took on my behalf. The lady I loved had by this time been married for well over a year and I, lying in hospital, prostrated after service in France, was in a bad way, was in fact verging toward the condition of a borderline case. For such had been the exalted desperation of my feelings that I had at the front indulged in a piece of entirely useless bravado that should properly speaking have cost me my life. I told Philip of this when he visited my bedside and declared to him how much I desired to see the face that had occasioned so much folly and could, so I fancied, by one small kindly act help deliver me of that folly's consequences. I said, 'I know it is all over' – indeed I had spoken to the lady less than half a dozen times – 'and that she is married and happy and that from the first I have only myself to blame for my troubles, since never by word or look has she displayed any more interest in me than any beautiful woman does in the least of many young admirers. Yet for all that I think I should mend and rapidly, would she but stand a moment within the door and say, 'I hope you will get well'. I do not ask her to be sorry for me – I have no right – I desire but this small evidence of goodwill and will not presume upon it, if granted, or ever ask to see her again.' Philip immediately volunteered to approach her. He went home and wrote what was probably one of his more elaborate as it must have been one of his most difficult letters, to a married woman he did not know. In it he craved an interview. The interview was granted. In vain. 'I pleaded with her for over an hour,' he said, 'and she answered always that such a visit would do you more harm than good. I replied that I knew you very well indeed and that she hardly knew you at all. But it was all to no purpose. In the end I went down on my knees to her, literally went down on my knees. But she refused.' The tears stood in his eyes as he said it. They were my only alleviation. I still believe that had he succeeded in his object the whole course of my life would probably have been different and better, for to my desperation there ensued a state of complete and blank despair in which I no longer cared what I did. Yet she is not to be blamed. She decided for what appeared to her the best course and my consolation is that this incident served to demonstrate how well Philip knew me and understood my state that he should go to such lengths. Of a truth his determination in the cause of friendship knew no bounds and now, when the passion that gave rise to the occasion of those tears has long departed and Philip himself is gone, the memory of his face as he sat by the door obliterates hers. This is I think as it should be: the face of hopeless love in youth is taken from us but the face of youthful friendship recurs, since Nature has ordained that by and large we should have visions rather of what has been a blessing to us than of what has dealt us wounds.

Knowledge of such things was, however, very far from me in the spring of 1914. Indeed it was during these months that I discussed with a New College man, one Roper, destined to fall in battle, the possibility of a visit to Germany the following summer with a view to gaining some insight into the latest developments of the German stage. (In those days the possibility of a National Theatre was seriously considered in the country of Shakespeare.) In this theatrical preoccupation Philip showed not the slightest interest. Neither then nor at any other time did Philip, so far as I remember, show any interest in the stage and, though I occasionally attended concerts with him or more often happened on him among the audience, I never went to a theatre with him or even a music-hall, for the less sophisticated of which he had a certain partiality. As to Opera Houses, they were to him, I think, chiefly places where such works as *Euryanthe*, *Beatrice and Benedict*, *Les Troyens*, *Falstaff*, and *A Village Romeo and Juliet* should be performed and nine times out of ten were not. I don't think Philip, though he delighted in the dramatic in purely instrumental music (as found, for instance, in the *Symphonie Fantastique*), was ever much interested in the problem of the synthesis of the dramatic elements, explicit and textual or implicit in character and situation, with the music, which is one of the grand problems of this medium. That is not to say that, when this problem was successfully solved, the synthesis as such did not, whether he was aware of the fact or no, work upon him. Far from it. He was acquainted with the history of this problem, but, though I have heard him make exposition of the theory of Gluck, I never heard him express admiration for Gluck's solution of the problem of dramatic declamation. If he came to admire Gluck – as I believe he did – it was probably Berlioz's enthusiasm that induced him to listen and, of those elements which Berlioz has extolled, noble dramatic effect and elegiac tenderness, it was probably rather the second than the first that Philip remembered.

This would seem to be proved by the fact that when in later years he urged on me that I should write librettos for Sorabji and for Bernard van Dieren, each of whom happened to need a libretto in a hurry, he seemed to think that this hurry was of no account whatever, whereas to extract the full significance from a series of situations (not to speak of making up the myth to start with!) always requires, in my experience, considerable time. My librettos for *The Rider by Night* and *The Tailor* were (in Hollywood studio-slang) 'so gosh-awful they was jus' t'rrible'. There was, I hold, a genuine idea in each, but Philip, in tyrannic mood, only allowed me about a week (if that) for the first and something less than a fortnight for the second. None the less he appeared satisfied with them, nor when I ran through them with him pointing out what damage this haste had done and how particularly it had impoverished the strictly dramatic interest, did he seem to care a rap.

Whether he tended to feel dramatically as opposed to lyrically in *life* I cannot say – by which I mean I do not know whether, in addition to his undoubted appreciation in later years of a situation as a situation, he had a thrilling outside view of himself as a factor in that situation were he involved in it. I doubt whether he saw

himself lurking near the crowded bar for a critic he intended to
tackle publicly on some disputed subject, or waiting alone with
his shadow in the moonlight for some girl he loved. I take it he
simply lurked or waited, and that therefore he may be said to
have felt more lyrically than dramatically. It may be urged that
he was not as simple as this and it is undoubtedly true that while
(for instance) one part of his personality waited another analysed
his feelings with mildly sardonic derision. But the point is that
this second self *analysed a complex of feelings rather than contemplated
the fascinating relations of elements within the situation*, such, for instance, as the spectacle of himself, a living lonely figure in the
moonlight and the indifference of the grotesque, abstract shadow
springing from his feet, the stillness of the branches overhead and
the pounding of his heart, the contrast between the all-too-pro-
tracted passage of time as he felt it and its normal passage as
registered by the sound of the girl's train arriving at and departing
from the neighbouring station. I lay emphasis upon this distinction, for the difference between the lyrical and the dramatic types
of artist is, in my opinion, absolutely fundamental to the understanding of a given artist both as artist and man. Philip's nature
was, I hold, predominantly lyrical and analytic and it was the
interplay of these two which accounted for much that those who
did not know him intimately found puzzling in him.

While at Oxford he displayed no interest whatever in any kind
of opera. So far as he was 'tending' any whither, that tendency
was toward an increased interest in English folk-tunes. It was
during this Spring Term that the name of Vaughan Williams fell
more and more frequently from his lips. He came to have a very
great admiration for this composer. (I well remember once in
later years Philip pointing out 'V.W.' to me at a Prom., 'That
big man there, standing by himself, who looks as if he ought to
have straw in his boots!' On another occasion after a performance
of 'V.W.'s' *Pastoral Symphony* he exclaimed, 'A truly splendid
work!' and then, with a smile, 'You know I've only one thing to
say against this composer's music: it is all just a little too much

like a cow looking over a gate. None the less he is a very great composer and the more I hear the more I admire him.'

A late letter to me, however, discovers a very poor opinion of the *London Symphony*.

Philip's interest in folk-tunes took us on rainy evenings to a little public-house – much out of favour with academic authority – that hid itself between Carfax and the railway station. Here, ensconced in a dark cubicle, we shouted orders over a partition to the landlord and encouraged a certain old party to 'give us a song'. This lady's inspiration did not spring from Helicon but from liquor of less antique origin and it was always a gamble whether she would pass through her repertoire of 'The Soldiers of the King, my lads,' etc., to what we wanted to hear before the sound of Big Tom bade us depart. She sang, I remember, a folk-song that contained the words 'So we all sat down together, love, to hear the nightingale sing'. This was to her what 'Ah! fors' è lui' was to Melba and unless liberally encored in it she was reluctant to proceed. I was told that, as the night advanced and Bacchus and Erato prevailed over Apollo and Euterpe, she would burst into strains of priapian wording and of considerable musical interest. But, alas, I never heard her do so.

Term ended and I was not encouraged to return to the University till I had mastered the peregrinations of St. Paul and could display a working knowledge of certain authors of the antique world: a sentence due, I think, largely to the unfortunate trajectory of a mangel-wurzel which, thrown by me in an undergraduate 'rag' during Mr. Lloyd George's visit, knocked the episcopal top-hat from the head of His Lordship of Winchester. In this 'rag' Philip did not join, not because he did not approve of it but because both then and later politics and more particularly politicians were objects of mere indifference or disgust to him. There was, however, one exception to this disposition of mind. He took at one time a certain interest in Home Rule for India and sided with the Home Rule Party on the question. This interest did not, however, long survive, if memory serves, the non-return of cash and a pair of trousers loaned to a Bengali gentleman Londonward bound to prosecute a highly verbose if irregular passion.

Exiled from Philip and established with a clergyman near Warrington, I felt our separation the more keenly in that shortly after I arrived at the rectory he imparted to me the information that the woman I loved had married. This intelligence was contained in a brief postscript to his letter – a proceeding characteristic of him. I can imagine him worrying over a method and deciding that this, which might seem so cruelly casual in another, was the correct method for him to follow with me at that juncture. He was correct. It was the right method to impart news which he understood must occasion me the most terrible emotion I had till that moment experienced. His subtlety in such matters was extraordinary.

We met again toward the end of term when I came up to be 'ploughed' once more and, as the event proved, for the last time. I did not expect my father would allow me to return to Oxford even if the authorities permitted it. Our spirits were low. We walked out to a neighbouring hill and leaned upon a gate. We could not know how few of the undergraduates then in residence would ever return to Oxford, but we certainly felt that this was the end of an interlude for us since he was due to stay up and I only too probably to be sent to France for an unknown period in order to acquire the language. We did not talk much but watched the light lessening upon the fields. At length he spoke of art and of nature as perpetual refuges. Many years afterwards, during the last months of his life, we were to sit in a field above Eynsham and I was to speak to him much as he spoke to me then, without however being able to evoke a similar response. The doubt of his own powers, that existed in a mild form even at Oxford, had by then become the demon that at last destroyed him. For so long as our belief in our capacity to create works of art, of however limited significance, remains with us and we feel inclined to employ it, we can somehow consent to exist, but when we hold that that capacity has left us (if indeed we ever possessed it) and feel no inclination to make so much as one more attempt at the veriest trifle, even for diversion's sake, then the very foundation of our lives, that which in some cases alone renders life supportable, is taken from us. During the summer vacation we kept in touch and the outbreak of war occasioned an exchange of violently phrased epistles, I being indignant at this barbarous break-up of a so-called Christian Europe and he furious at the public prints which, then as now, grotesquely ignorant on the subject of Nietzsche's personal history and published works, ascribed to the German-Pole the philosophic responsibility for the conflict.

Toward the end of September Philip and I met again. We stood, I remember, awhile on Westminster Bridge, just below Big Ben, to gaze up-river at a quince-coloured moon, slightly veiled by a tawny skein of vapour, sinking its round head in deeps of fuliginous cloud. A curious calm overhung us. I had applied for a commission and, having a far sharper imaginative notion of what modern war was like than most of my contemporaries, did not expect to survive and had already accomplished one half of that act of renunciation which was to be completed, in so far as in me lay, almost exactly a year later. Philip has expressed what he then felt in the following poem:

WONDERMENT

I watched the moon set in a sea of golden gloom
  Like a soft horn-tone, merging in the twilight chord:
  Yet in the sickle image of the moon a sword
Lurks, and the horn but echoes trumpet shrieks of doom –
And men exult to drink the darkness of the tomb,
To pay the great price for the steely mastery,
And scorn to live and dream, and taste the ecstasy
The moon sheds, sinking in a sea of sable gloom.

        October 14th, 1914

The spell of that scene did not however endure. Later that night or some night closely consequent, he and I and my friend

Harold Gough (afterward killed in action before Ypres) and a blonde girl, a rather pretty streetwalker picked up in a Greek Street night club, boarded a taxi and set out for my father's country house in Essex. We drove through the small hours, I on the roof and the others within. Why we took the girl I cannot imagine. But the whole affair was a somewhat desperate and forlorn lark. Toward six o'clock we arrived at the top of the double avenue of elms that lead to the old house. We were then in a quandary, for the girl's profession was unmistakable, the Rectory windows all too close, and uncertainty prevailed as to quite who was at home at the farther end of the avenue. Philip was left with the girl while Gough and I went in and breakfasted, to emerge in due course with food for the stranded pair. We then drove back to London; a drowsy Philip and a somewhat fractious girl being dropped at Colchester railway station on the way.

This was our last fling and so ended the Oxford period of which Mr. Gray has requested me to give my reminiscences. I was to see Philip often again, but sporadically. Our affection for each other never diminished. When we met the old intimacy was re-established and we spoke freely, not only of art and so forth but of our private affairs. Yet were I to write that things were exactly the same as ever after that parting in the autumn of 1914, I should not write the truth. Nothing for me, as for myriads of others, has ever been quite the same since that autumn. But in so far as things could ever 'be the same' – having regard to the fact that I served out of conviction that it was my duty to do so and that for like reason he did not, and to the fact that I was (save for three months) continuously abroad from 1921 to 1926 – things between us were the same as ever. Here is the place perhaps to record that, since during the period from 1914 to his death I was able once or twice to be of some small service to him, he showed himself extraordinarily grateful. This is by no means always the case with artists and more particularly when so exasperated and dejected as Philip became toward the close.

Since Mr. Gray has requested me to do so, let me give my

opinion upon Philip as an author. Philip had all the feelings of a poet – he was peculiarly sensitive to the most 'poetical' poetry such as among the moderns that of Mr. Yeats – but at long last, though his verses were far better than many which obtain praise to-day, he lacked something, though I know not exactly what, of that which finally transmutes verse into poetry. The poem 'Wonderment', quoted above, is, I hold, the best of such efforts toward poetry as I have seen. Indeed, I think it is poetry, though poetry of the kind we call 'picturesque' and therefore not of the highest quality. Technically this poem is remarkable for two things: for the fine management of the vowels (probably, having regard to the date of its composition, a purely instinctive mastery) and for the ingenuity with which the return to the opening rhyme is effected. The subtle influence of orchestral music – I do not refer to its obvious influence as seen in the analogy of the 'soft horn-tone merging in the twilight chord' – is plainly perceptible in the movement, crescendo and decrescendo and final pianissimo of the poem.

He had another rhyming talent in the use of which he was a master. He could write better rigmarole, nonsense verses and limericks, Priapian and other, than any man I have ever known. I say than 'any man I have ever known', because such pieces often cannot by their very nature obtain a wide circulation.

Such of his prose as I have read – and I have read much – was always sound, frequently excellent and on occasion brilliant. If his pen was sometimes felt to flag, one could depend upon it that this was because the writer had been driven, as I know him to have at times been driven, by journalistic exigency. None the less his prose seldom flagged in even the toughest tasks. One of the toughest is exposition. The talent for it is by no means common. Philip was singularly felicitous in exposition. Where the matter in other and quite moderately competent hands would inevitably have tended to become so dull and complicated as to stultify all but those intelligences which can read *anything* (and usually show small profit for it) Philip knew how to render the brute intractable substance, if not entertaining, at least acceptable. In exposition – especially controversial exposition – of matter that fired his imagination he was quite wonderful and that imagination, set to work, soon communicated both the substance of the thing in all its ramifications and the enthusiasm of the writer. In the composition of such a passage, Philip's extensive and sometimes curious culture lent enormous aid. For he was as fertile in analogies as he was subtle in drawing them, and thus it was that his knowledge of painting and of literature (particularly its bypaths) enriched what he had to say about music. Persons more knowledgeable of music than I – Philip ever entertained an exaggerated idea of my capabilities as a music critic (and, I may add, as poet) – will assess the value of his judgments on the subject. I can only say they were and are of extreme value to me, not only because he was evidently a very competent musician with an original mind and great imagination, but because these judgments always, as we writers say, 'suffered themselves to be read' with lively interest and frequently were set forth in such flexible and vigorous prose as bears witness to the presence of a master, namely, a prose that conveys the maximum of accuracy and suggestion with the minimum of means.

My task draws to its close. First as to his 'attitude' to the 'public' and the effect of the public's on him. I have heard it said since he died that he despised public opinion in respect of his own music, the music of the past that he put into circulation and his own exertions on behalf of other composers. How could he do so? Such an opinion did not and does not exist. It could scarcely be expected to in a nation with our record. Edward Elgar was forty-two before he received any consideration whatever and, when he did, that consideration was chiefly due to the exertions of a foreign conductor (Hans Richter) and the homage of a foreign composer (Richard Strauss). Delius had to wait even longer, and, had it not been for Sir Thomas Beecham, might not for many years yet have attained the fame in England he now enjoys. Philip never had any pretensions whatever to be of the category of an Elgar or a Delius. None the less he created some beautiful music and exerted himself to the limit on behalf of masters of yesterday and of to-day, supposedly 'known', little known and unknown, who, he considered, had created beautiful music. Was he rewarded by any display of public interest in that music? In the case of his work for Delius and forasmuch as Beecham, superlatively gifted as musician and a man of ample means, was in the field long before Philip, 'yes'; in the case of Berlioz, 'just possibly'; in every other case, including that of his own, 'no'. I repeat, first, that Philip could not despise public opinion because we working English artists who are under fifty years of age deceive ourselves if we fancy that any public opinion upon our work exists. Philip did not deceive himself in this matter. He was far too sensible to expect informed judgment in the public. But I think the total lack of sufficient interest to prompt any judgment whatsoever did to some extent tell on him and the indifference or imbecility of supposed informed judgment still more, since it served but to emphasize the total hopelessness of the general situation. So much for Philip's 'attitude' to the public. Let me in conclusion touch upon some matters that concern his attitude not to an invisible public but to those immediately around him and my persuasions with regard to some aspects of his character.

Now that he is dead, I feel for him exactly as I have always felt. Though we do not love our friends for one particular quality but as a whole and because, in Montaigne's immortal phrase, 'he was he and I was I', yet there is usually some element which while the friend is with us especially appeals to us, and the memory of which we most cherish when he or she is absent for a while or for ever. For me that element in Philip was and is the extreme gentleness hidden in his heart of hearts. Those who knew him only as a combative spirit in the world of music may be astonished at that statement. Yet I hold this gentleness to have been absolutely fundamental in his character and that no few of his troubles were attributable to continued and exasperating outrage of it. D. H. Lawrence in his letters calls Philip 'a bit backboneless', 'empty', 'uncreated', and so forth. Lawrence 'gets' some characters, whom he and I have known, after a fashion. That is to say they are recognizable. But his focus is so warped and his lens so fuzzy that, though these figures have many of the surface peculiarities of the particular psyche, he seldom seems to me to pierce to the psyche's depth if depth it possesses. When Lawrence comes to the depths he interprets out of his knowledge of *himself*, especially the female part of himself, and in a manner suitable to his theories (were he able to assume the psyche's surface peculiarities) and not out of knowledge, consequent on careful prolonged observation, of the depths from without. Nor is the reason far to seek: that reason is his profound and everlasting subjectivism from which indeed he only completely escaped as artist in some short passages of *The Trespasser* and *Sons and Lovers*, in certain short stories and in some of his later poems dealing with non-human entities such as animals and plants. Philip was neither 'backboneless' nor 'empty' nor 'uncreated'. Just because he was gentle he could, his sympathy being aroused, exert himself to an extraordinary degree and sometimes after no gentle fashion on behalf of others, particularly artists. For the same reason he frequently could not properly exert himself on his own behalf. Gentleness, for instance, won't get you very far on your own behalf in business. Yet he could and did exert himself after a thoroughly businesslike fashion on behalf of others. So much for backbonelessness. He was not 'empty' – he was merely weary (weary to death at last) when that spring of gentleness, in which so much of his best art had its origin – examine the works and see! – failed him. He was not 'uncreated': his gentleness sometimes found for the time being nowhither to flow and was therefore formless. If by 'uncreated' Lawrence would indicate that the gentle spirit and the impartial intellect were not in such accord as to present a total harmony of form, I reply that 'createdness' in this sense in the early war years was scarcely to be expected of a young man of Philip's inner gentleness and with an intellect such as his, an intellect, in my opinion, of wider range, of sterner mettle, of tougher integrity, of more persistent energy and of more imaginative quality in the meta-physic sense than that of Lawrence. There was something very earthy, very literal about Lawrence's mind. He lacked imagination, as may be seen by the pitiable futility of his views on Shelley. That that synthesis, that 'createdness' was indeed never attained was, I hold, just because Philip's innate gentleness was so fundamental a thing in him and, being exasperated both by events and by his intellect's persistent commentary upon those events, became toward the close so utterly weary and exhausted that the capacity for synthesis was lost to it. For in these matters, certainly with regard to such a romantic nature as Philip's, the synthesis usually proceeds by the tenderness of the heart working upon the intellect to urge upon it some suspense of judgment and not by the hardness of the intellect working upon the heart and bidding it in reason's name to cease expecting to find things other and better than they are: the hearts of other humans more tender and their heads some whit less dense. I have not written thus of Lawrence out of malice aforethought but because Lawrence's estimate is supposed, especially in cases of persons with whom he was in close contact, to carry authority and these words are therefore convenient pegs on which to hang what I consider the correct explanation of peculiarities and obscurities in Philip which some find puzzling.

And now that Lawrence's name has found its way on to paper – as it must in any more than superficial account of Philip – I may as well proceed to some comments on their relations and such commentary is best approached, I think, by way of a consideration of Philip's 'free living' (as the phrase goes). To-day an unthinking licence prevails in many circles. If Philip's manner of life displayed 'licence' in this sense – which I deny – it certainly was not an unthinking 'licence'. Philip, from Oxford on, held theories as to personal freedom of thought and behaviour and dared to act according to them. Those theories may be wrong. That is a problem I have not here space to discuss. But that, believing in those theories, Philip acted upon them and did not reserve them for merely academic discussion, I hold to his credit. For, as

Goethe says, 'Thought and Action, Action and Thought, that is the sum of all wisdom, admitted in all ages, followed in all ages, not understood by all.' That Philip did others and himself damage in the process I admit and regret. But I have observed that many 'conventional' persons do others and themselves a great deal of damage without displaying a tithe of Philip's integrity and courage, since they act cruelly upon theories in which they no longer in their heart of hearts believe or contradict their theories in captious action for lack of courage to discover new theories. In addition, in Dryden's words, 'few know the use of life before 'tis past'. Philip died before he was forty, endowed with a temperament little calculated – if heaven calculates such things – to make easy the paths of true wisdom, paths which, I venture to suggest, often contradict the stereotyped notions of them entertained by those who – perhaps the majority of our contemporaries – are unwilling or unable too closely to consider the matter. To the difficulties occasioned by this temperament were added those contingent upon such a succession of particular circumstances as might well have weighed down and disconcerted a man tougher-fibred than Philip and better versed in this world's ways and in the less likeable peculiarities of men and women. As to general circumstances, the burthen of war and post-war years and their moral chaos have proved extremely difficult to men just as hard-minded as Philip and a deal less sensitive. To this must be added, since Philip was an artist and a propagandist on behalf of certain masters ancient and modern, the depressing influence of the vasty, nay unfathomable, indifference of the countrymen of Byrd and Purcell to art and to artists touched on above. I take it that I have said enough to indicate that such 'conventional' solutions as may occur to some readers were inadmissible in Philip's case, just as inadmissable in fact as they would be in a novel of Dostoievski. Offhand to 'do the right thing' – so often used (to borrow an image from motor-racing) in England as a mere 'escape-road' – was not the way to escape his difficulties. On the only occasion in which, being thoroughly muddled, he took to the 'escape-road', the consequences were, in my opinion, disastrous. I am far from blaming him and I am unwilling to take the responsibility of blaming others in this matter. In any event he paid to the end of his life for that mistake and I hold our duty is not to sit in judgment on him, whether we theoretically disapprove the use of the 'escape-road' or no, but to understand and, having regard to the penalties he paid, to forgive.

The subject of D. H. Lawrence is always a thorny one. I introduced Philip to his books. They had an immense influence on him. Later – that is during the autumn of 1915 – he brought Lawrence to see me and a certain degree of acquaintance was established between Lawrence and myself. That acquaintance was renewed about a year before Lawrence died. It was my ill fortune that these two periods should both have been periods when Lawrence was ill. In my opinion, during the first period, Lawrence was not only suffering from a 'bad patch' of the tuberculosis which eventually killed him, but from a nervous condition which did not permit him to display that balanced and good-humoured sense which Mr. Aldous Huxley and Mr. Koteliansky assure me strongly characterized other phases of his life. Knowing the genius of his early books, the shock that the destruction of his *Rainbow* occasioned him and having regard to his psychological and physical condition when I first met him and for some time afterwards, I find it impossible not to regret that, since it was decreed that Philip should meet Lawrence, that meeting should have taken place just when it did. The amazing qualities Philip discerned in those early books (especially the poetry) prepared him for capitulation to a 'genius' (Lawrence was certainly that); Lawrence's sufferings in connection with *The Rainbow* not only pre-empted Philip's sympathy but his rebelliousness, while, at the same time, Lawrence's psychological state passed at first for merely the normal state of one gifted with a seer's insight and a prophet's message. The results were, to put it mildly, unhappy; the more so in that both D. H. Lawrence and his wife then harboured – I know not why – a singular bee in their bonnets, namely that both Philip and I should each of us get married and that quickly. The Lawrences had indeed even been so benevolent as to select the girl – a very good-natured, capable and candid girl I may say – suitable to one if not the other of us. Thence ensued a comedy. We were each in turn asked up to Hampstead to meet the lady and in my case a pretty palpable hint was dropped as to the hopes entertained. I avoided this meeting. Philip, I believe, avoided his. Later we compared experiences and both met the lady, whom Philip had encountered somewhere else than in Hampstead, one late afternoon near the Embankment. She, too, had somehow discerned what was in the wind, and the meeting of the three parties most concerned dissolved in inextinguishable laughter. I do not say that either Lawrence or his wife took the project very seriously, did in fact do more than toy with it as a warm, pleasing project, but that he should have troubled with it at all, when neither Philip nor I nor, as it appeared, the lady had displayed the slightest inclination toward matrimony, bears witness, I think, to his peculiar state of mind. Some months later I had other occasion to mark another and more serious phase of his condition. The Lawrences asked me to spend an evening with them in, I think, Mecklenburg Square. The inevitable topic of the war arose, and, the discussion waxing somewhat intense, Lawrence declared that he was being 'shadowed' and requested me to fling the door open and discover the two men who had dogged his steps, so he asserted, during the latter half of the afternoon. I obeyed, little inclined to believe him, but in a mood entirely sympathetic to Lawrence and one that bade me demand these men's names and their business should they exist. There was no one on the landing. I know that just prior to this Lawrence had been forced by the fanatic imbecility of some local military busybody to leave Cornwall. Nonetheless I permit myself grave doubts as to whether he had been followed that afternoon and find it quite impossible to believe that there was the least likelihood of a couple of plain clothes men lurking ear to door on that landing as, to my amazement, on my return he assured me had occurred the night before.[1] Under these circumstances, I repeat, I count it very unfortunate that Philip should have met Lawrence when he did. The reader will do well to bear in mind that Philip was an admirable conversationalist and that in some respects he was better informed than Lawrence, both in some branches of particular knowledge and as concerns the behaviour of certain sections of the community. Furthermore, in analytic discussion Philip was distinctly able, and in contradiction, when an idol had in his opinion displayed all-too-human qualities – and Lawrence did, I hold, tend to be perverse in argument – relentless. I was never present at one of these controversies but, having some knowledge of both men as they were, I fancy that Philip, aroused, may have been very upsetting to the none-too-secure prophetic equilibrium and not less so because the offender had been taken to be both *in statu pupillari* and incapable of such ferocious dexterity. The prophet moreover had, so I more than once observed, an abnormally developed curiosity as to his friends' – and even his acquaintances' – private affairs. No doubt he meant well, but his habit of putting sudden and difficult questions – somewhat of the same cast as the following recorded by Gorky of Tolstoy: 'What do you think of yourself? Do you love your wife?' etc. – was disconcerting and rather calculated in the result to darken counsel than to aid those he had decided needed his assistance. Forced confidences have a way of being false confidences, and the sequent advice so urgently and persuasively proffered out of a full heart, a heated fancy, and a brain teeming with semi-mystical theories was not, however well intentioned, the more sound on that account. I hope I have made it sufficiently clear that I consider Lawrence's condition at the period in question to have been very far from normal, so much so in fact

[1] In justice to Lawrence I feel it necessary to say here that whether or not there had on this occasion been detectives lurking about his door, there certainly had been on other occasions. When he was staying, about this time, in my mother's flat in Earl's Court, I had myself to interview several. Needless to say, so far from contradicting Mr. Nichols' impression of Lawrence's abnormal state of mind at that time, it tends rather to confirm it – but there was good reason for it. C.G.

that he can hardly be held to have been responsible for many of his utterances. That fact, for I hold it for a fact, does not however render his influence less unfortunate. I can therefore only regret that in the interests of what I take to be truth I am compelled to write after a fashion that may appear harsh of one who was undoubtedly a genius and a brave man. But I do not see why I should sacrifice what I consider very necessary truth concerning the relations between Philip and one who so profoundly influenced him out of deference to Lawrence's memory. Both men are dead. During their lives I used toward each the utmost gentleness of which my nature is capable and, if I now appear to be gentler to Philip than to Lawrence, let the reader remember that much, though tardy, justice has been done to Lawrence and little to Philip, and that in writing of Lawrence as I have written I am not aware that I have done Lawrence anything less than justice.

I trust that the reader will not think that in writing of Philip as I have written I have made an attempt as regards the domain of sexual love to scatter soot on him or in emphasizing his gentleness to whitewash him. I can conceive that in his later days he could be cruel. Gentle natures of acute sensibility and strong intelligence, long exasperated by indifference and opposition to what they hold of sovereign importance in art and life, are apt to turn cruel and even vindictive at times. At least twice I observed Philip callous, as I thought and still think, to the pain he was causing one who certainly deserved better treatment of him. But I never witnessed vindictiveness or cruelty to anyone and I will not go by hearsay. What I have written is drawn *solely* out of my personal experience of Philip and out of meditation to which that experience gave rise during his life and has given rise since his death. To write in other fashion were to be false to the memory I have of him. I leave the whitewash and soot to such as like to splash about in such things and create striking effects. Myself, I am only an artist remembering his friend and accordingly I have written of Philip after a manner in which, were I dead and Philip alive, I not only hope but believe Philip would write of me.

CHAPTER III

THE WAR AND D. H. LAWRENCE

INTENSE though Philip's dislike had been for Eton, it was nothing in comparison with his loathing for Oxford – for the life of an undergraduate there, that is to say, not for the place itself which, I think, he always liked. The following letter to Delius expresses his sentiments eloquently enough.

PHILIP TO DELIUS

Ivanhoe Hotel
Bloomsbury Street
March 24th, 1914

. . . I am burning to find some means of escape from the appalling, enervating, and depressing atmosphere of Oxford; the place is just one foul pool of stagnation – I simply cannot stand it, and I am getting no good, and any amount of harm, from staying there. Yet nothing can I find to do elsewhere; I would do anything to get away from the place, and if possible make a little money. But it seems hopeless, and my people suggest nothing. Oxford leads nowhere, and it is fearful to wander on through life, aimless, objectless, and – what is worse – moneyless.

I met Ernest Newman the other day, and sought to discover what it was necessary to do to become a critic. Apparently there is nothing to be done, save to study scores, ancient and modern, on one's own account, and write articles in the hope of getting them accepted, and thus becoming known well enough to get a permanent engagement with some paper. He considers the ordinary academic musical training of small use, and he strongly advises taking up some other profession to keep the pot boiling till one is ready and able to stand on one's feet in the musical world. But as for other professions – this accursed public school and university 'education' (!!) fits one for nothing; at the age of 19, the product of Eton and Oxford is worth a thousand times less than the product of the national board schools. What, in the devil's name, is to be done? My case, really, is very akin to that of the unjust steward we used to hear so much about, who could not dig and was ashamed to beg!

Can you suggest anything – no matter what it is – that I could do now – or at least begin studying with a definite view to and prospect of doing in the near future? I simply cannot continue to drift along in my present aimless fashion. Could one get a job in the way of copying or transcribing music, correcting proofs, copying orchestral parts, etc.? I don't mind what it is, so long as it gives one occupation.

The catastrophe of August, 1914, eventually provided him with the opportunity to escape from Oxford and settle in London, whence he wrote to Delius a long letter of which this is an extract:

PHILIP TO DELIUS

54 Cartwright Gardens
London, W.C.
Oct. 18th, 1914

I have never been able to understand the sentiment of patriotism, the love of empire; it has always seemed to me so empty and intangible an idea, so impersonal and so supremely unimportant as regards the things that really matter – which are all the common heritage of humanity, without distinction of race or nationality. And in spite of the gigantic wave of patriotism that has lately swept over the whole world, I cannot honestly say that I feel it to be any more real – or less disastrous, even in its unreality – than ever I did.

It makes one's position very difficult, since unless one follows the line of least resistance and becomes a mere hypocrite, one is cut off, in one's sympathies and mental outlook, from at least nine-tenths of one's fellow-beings. Isolation, such as you can enjoy, is the only escape, but unless one has sufficient wealth of

PHILIP HESELTINE (*circa* 1915). ON HIS RIGHT
JACOB EPSTEIN; ON HIS LEFT HON. EVAN MORGAN
(NOW LORD TREDEGAR)

imagination and creative power within oneself, to absorb one completely, even this becomes intolerable. One feels oneself to be one of those who, as Dowson says, 'deem no harvest-joy is worth a dream' – though surely Dowson never pictured such a grisly harvest of flesh and blood as constitutes the joy of the war-fiends!

But for my 'nervous stricture', which of course renders me 'physically unfit for service' (thus runs the phrase – the crude mind of the militarist has never yet dreamed of the mentally unfit!) the general public pressure would probably have driven me to enlist myself; hideous though a soldier's life would be for me, it would be less so than a life marred by the cheap sneers and dismal attempts at wit of the vulgar, blatant and exasperating Jingoes, who at a time like this, carry all before them. Fortunately, in my present condition, I escape both courses; but there must be hundreds of other unfortunate beings who, not having the saving physical blemish, are bullied into a life which is a hell for them, and at the end of which is the possibility of the great and endless darkness – or worse, a dragging existence with a broken body and a bruised mind – all for an ideal which they have never felt. They have not even the consolation of thinking that it is sweet to suffer for their country's sake! And the conditions of military service must be far worse in Germany – or even in France – than they are here. . . .

I have left Oxford for ever! This step was facilitated by the financial panic which is the inevitable concomitant of war. My people, being thoroughly pessimistic, imagine (for no reason whatever) that they will be ruined, so, discovering that it would be cheaper to keep me in London than at Oxford, they welcomed my proposals! And as a matter of fact, I am very much better off on the reduced allowance than I was at Oxford – which is a most extravagant place, and gives one no return for one's money. I have decided not to concentrate entirely on music for the present. I feel that, in spite of all the years I have spent ostensibly being 'educated', I know scarcely anything about anything; my interests have outpaced my knowledge completely, and at the present time I feel very keenly the need of a somewhat wider education – as a kind of mental foundation. I have accordingly entered the University of London, as a student of the English language and literature, with Philosophy and Psychology as subsidiary subjects, for three years. The London University is a very good place, run on thoroughly sound, modern lines – a complete contrast to Oxford in every way. One has merely to attend certain lectures there, and for the rest one is completely free to do what one wants.

In a few weeks I hope to begin lessons in composition etc. with Gustav von Holst, whom Balfour Gardiner recommends as the best man in London for this purpose[1]; apparently the Royal College and the Royal Academy of Music are so effete and antiquated that it is merely a waste of time to study there.

In music as in other affairs, I feel very strongly the need of a master, and a thorough course of instruction, in matters of technique. In composition I am stuck fast; I simply have not the means to express what I want to – it takes me hours to evolve a single bar. During the whole three months of inactivity in Wales, I only managed to do four or five little songs – the making of which could not have occupied more than a week at most.

. . . I am living in a very jolly part of London – in a quite secluded square in Bloomsbury, near St. Pancras station. The neighbourhood is thoroughly alive – which is essential, for my liking – and unrespectable; at night the streets swarm with whores and hot-potato men and other curious and interesting phenomena, and the darkness which the fear of hostile aircraft has enforced upon the city makes everything doubly mysterious, fascinating and enchanting – for London is enchanting at all times and seasons. Music is, of course at a low ebb, and I fear it will suffer greatly during the next few years, though there will be some consolation for the flood of patriotic filth that will be poured forth, in the fact that those composers who resist the force of the mob's passion will stand out in the greater relief and pre-eminence. . . . I have been to various Promenade Concerts, but as a whole the programmes have been worse than

---

[1] This project never materialized

usual, and the audiences – as a result – proportionately larger. It is difficult to escape Walford Davies' *Solemn Melody* or Gounod's *Hymne à Sainte Cécile*, or some such tosh, which invariably gets encored. Whenever the organ is used the Britisher applauds, presumably because it reminds him of Church! Your two little pieces were mangled in the most execrable way; the strings played just anyhow, and the cuckoo came in at the wrong moment nearly every time – as for the rendering of the second piece . . . . . . ! !

For the rest, there has been nothing more exciting than symphonies by Brahms, Beethoven, and Dvorak, Macdowell's *Piano Concerto in D minor* (twice in a fortnight, and yours not once in the season) and *Tod und Verklärung*. The latter I heard for the first time, and was repelled, but I am grateful to it for causing me to enjoy the *Zampa* overture which followed it!

. . . In the absence of Colin Taylor I have become conductor of a little amateur orchestra in Windsor – 1 flute, 1 oboe, 1 clarinet, 1 horn, 2 drums, and about twenty strings. I took the first rehearsal last night; never having conducted before in my life, and knowing nothing about either the art of conducting or how the work (Mozart's *G minor Symphony*) should be played, I was very frightened, but managed to get through an hour and a half's stick-waving without a breakdown. My right arm, however, is dreadfully stiff to-day! It is very good experience for me, and I hope to improve with more practice. There is plenty of good material in the orchestra to work upon. When I know the scores better I think I shall be able to do a good deal with them. If it is possible to get hold of the material of the *First Cuckoo in Spring* without great expense, I want to make them do that; it would be so good for them, after many years' surfeit of Mozart, Haydn, and Beethoven.

Is there any chance of your coming over here this winter? *Do* come for a few days if you possibly can; I am longing for some walks in London with you. If you could come in December it would be great fun, as my term at the University ends about the second week of that month; but at any time my evenings are free, as a rule.

I have just read all the novels of D. H. Lawrence – three in number. They are to my mind simply unrivalled, in depth of insight and beauty of language, by any other contemporary writer. Shall I send you one?

In a letter written about the same time to Robert Nichols he gives further expression to this new enthusiasm. 'I am reading *Sons and Lovers* – quite magnificent. I know no modern prose style so perfect as Lawrence's. Every word is weighed, and its precise effect calculated to the minutest nicety. Every adjective hits the mark exactly; it is almost uncanny.'

Philip seems actually to have embarked upon a course of study at London University, for he matriculated in January (1915) in English, Latin, German, Mathematics and Logic. It did not last for long, however. Owing chiefly, I think, to the good offices and influence of Sir Thomas Beecham, whom he had got to know well at this time through Delius, he was offered the post of music critic on a daily paper, at the princely salary of two pounds a week. He accordingly abandoned his projected academic career and started work as a musical journalist in February.

To those unversed in the ways of Fleet Street in general and musical criticism in particular it might perhaps seem that he was unusually fortunate in thus obtaining an important post without possessing any credentials, previous experience, or any other apparent qualifications. Actually, however, there was nothing exceptional about this; the majority of such appointments were then, and still are, made without any reference to merit or capacity, but solely as a result of personal influence, especially when combined with the prestige of a public school and university education.

Any illusions he may have cherished on entering upon his duties were speedily dispelled. In the first place it goes without saying that artistic activities during the war were even more negligible in the editorial eye than now, even; in the second place, the particular journal in question has never been renowned exactly for its lofty idealism and devotion to the arts, and it was even less so then than it is to-day. It is not surprising, therefore, to find him, in a very short time, complaining bitterly in a letter to Delius of the impossible conditions under which he had to work.

PHILIP TO DELIUS

The business of musical criticism for a London daily is really a farce. Would you recommend me to continue doing this? It is quite evident that the cause of music cannot be in the least degree benefited by anyone who writes in such a paper. The people who control it and edit it dare not take the risk of offending anybody (except in political matters) and now even my painfully reserved and non-committal style – which it is exceedingly irksome and degrading to adopt – has been called too violent by the wretched news editor.

I see plainly that I am never going to be allowed to abuse anybody or anything – not even dead composers! My quite mild notice of a pianist who played some Debussy pieces in the most execrably vulgar manner, without either taste or feeling – was suppressed altogether last week. What can one do under such conditions? It is only doing harm to praise what one knows to be bad – and there are already too many critics engaged upon that perfectly hopeless undertaking.

Delius advised him to hold on until something better should turn up, and actually he seems to have done so for six months or more, which is much longer than one would have expected. In the meanwhile Beecham had conceived the project of bringing out a monthly musical journal, of which Philip was to be made the editor. A contract was drawn up, offices were taken, notepaper was printed with the name of the paper – *The Sackbut* – but the paper itself, in true Thomist fashion, did not materialize until some years later. In August he wrote to Delius, then in Norway, in a mood of great despondency.

PHILIP HESELTINE

PHILIP TO DELIUS

The Bungalow
Crickley Hill
Gloucestershire
August 22nd, 1915

There has never been a day in all the past seven weeks on which I have not determined to write to you, and all my intentions have faded away like smoke, or a dream, and each succeeding day I have thought 'To-morrow I shall see and say everything more clearly, more concisely', with the result that my letter to you has been deferred and, so far from my procrastination having the expected effect, my outlook has daily become more confused and trance-like until the difficulty of collecting and writing down myself has been increased to its maximum point. My mind at the present moment is fitly comparable to the blurred humming of the distant peal of bells, whose slow, monotonous droning seems to blend with the grey, listless sky and the still trees, and the far-off, shadow-like hills, in an atmosphere of intolerable dejection and lifelessness on this late summer Sunday evening. Over the wide landscape there hangs a false mood of peace – something seems to have died – or gone out – and there is no peace, but only a weary restlessness. My head feels as though it were filled with a smoky vapour or a poisonous gas which kills all the finer impressions before they can penetrate to me, and stifles every thought, every idea, before it is born. This is not the mere passing pessimism engendered by an English Sabbath; it is a feeling that has been enveloping me little by little for many months past and, although there are times when I think myself rid of it, it always returns after a while, more virulent than ever. When I left London early in July it was at its worst, but even these seven weeks in my beloved Gloucestershire have failed utterly to dispel its influence, save at fitful and transitory intervals. It has no definitely apparent cause, and when its power is strongest I have no antidote but must simply wait until it relaxes its hold. One lives thus perpetually behind a veil. I watch the sun go down behind the hills, flooding the broad valley with a glory of golden light that would in former days have made my whole being vibrate with its beauty – but I wait in vain for that old, ecstatic feeling. The colour and intensity of these pictures have become things external to me – they are no longer reflected in me, I can no longer merge myself in the Stimmung of Nature around me. I can only gaze wistfully, from afar, at her beauteous pageantry. I can no longer take part in it, and so I am debarred from the greatest – perhaps the only – source of joy, solace, and inspiration that life offers me. My brain is, at its best, merely receptive, and that but rarely and in small measure. Creative thought or work, or anything remotely approximating thereto, is entirely impossible, and the chances of their ever becoming otherwise seem every day more remote – yet without them existence, for all who desire them, is void and desolate . . . Hence those tears. . . .

This letter was broken off over a week ago by a nerve-shattering occurrence which drove me and my two Indian friends away from Crickley Hill altogether, and at the moment I feel even less able to write coherently than before ! However, I will try to be a little more terse and a little less depressing – for after all it is of no avail to whine and snivel, and I often feel when I write you that I am imposing far too much upon your long-suffering tolerance of my weak-kneed feebleness. Yet, however disgusting one's state of mind may be, one does feel the need of an emotional safety valve on occasions, though it is a little cruel that one should let off this malodorous steam at those friends one loves and values most of all. Forgive me – I have inflicted this kind of thing on you so often before, but as time goes on, I feel more and more that you are almost the only person I can confide in without the very smallest fear of a misunderstanding. And I can say so much more in writing than when I am with you. Often and often, words simply will not come out of my mouth, and this happens not only when I am indulging in tedious personal psychologics. It is a fearful feeling, and seems to erect an impassable barrier between one's self and one's most intimate friends – one doesn't feel it with ordinary acquaintances.

. . . Looking back, I believe I have not written to you at all since that June Sunday at Watford, when Beecham turned up unexpectedly . . . Nor, I am ashamed to admit, did I answer the very particularly kind letter Mrs. Delius wrote me a few days later, though it touched and cheered me more than I can say. I was tremendously disappointed when I heard you were not going to be with us this summer; if you had been, both this letter and the agglomerated moods that have prompted it would never have existed. However you are greatly to be envied, living amongst the mountains that will never re-echo with the sounds or even the news of war. Here the war-cloud looms over one like some great sinister bird, poised and ready to pounce upon its hapless prey. The black influence alone is enough to quench every artistic impulse in all but the very strongest. It is very hard to escape it – in London impossible. At the moment I am in Oxford – Oxford which, in its normal condition, I loathed and detested, but which now appears as a beautiful haven of peace and quietude. Of all towns this is surely the least affected – externally – by the war. This is, of course, vacation time, but even when all allowance has been made, the difference between the atmosphere of the place as it is now and as it was last year astounds me. Here in this tranquil old street, where even the passing of the baker's cart is an event, one feels as remote from the jarring elements of life as one does in the very heart of the countryside. More so, perhaps, since one's comings and goings are unobserved, whereas in a little village one cannot fail to arouse rustic curiosity and its invariable concomitant, suspicion. I would gladly live here with my two Indian friends, who are most kind and sympathetic companions, if circumstances permitted – and they may yet do so . . . My plans are very vague. It took three long letters, separated by intervals of a fortnight, and two reply-paid telegrams to extract from the elusive Thomas any information about the future of *The Sackbut* and, incidentally, my quarterly allowance. I dislike intensely taking money for nothing done, but under the present agreement I am neither completely free to do my own work, nor am I definitely given anything to occupy myself with, outside of my own studies.

The Sackbut is shelved from month to month – it is now postponed till next January at the earliest, and then, if we're all still alive, there'll be still another postponement – and I am given fearful operatic librettos to translate, and requested to coach singers for operatic performances at the Shaftesbury Theatre – neither of which tasks am I competent to perform – and in order to do this I have to remain in London, the one place of all others where the war-fever rages most violently and where its effects oppress and depress one the most. If one had some continuous, all-day occupation, one could live there, but that alone could make life tolerable in such a place at the present moment. The last two months might have been exceedingly profitable for me, as regards work, but for certain psychological accidents which could not be foreseen, but which nevertheless have been useful in providing cautionary experience.

This letter, incidentally, affords a good illustration of the danger, to which allusion was made at the outset, of supposing from it – as one might very well do – that its writer was perpetually enshrouded in the deepest melancholy. It so happens, however, that one of the Indian friends mentioned in the letter, whom Philip had come to know at Oxford, has given me a picture of this stay in the Gloucestershire village which, to put it mildly, does not precisely tally with the mood of this letter. For example, if one wishes to avoid arousing 'rustic curiosity' so very much, a good plan is to refrain from riding a motor-bicycle through the village streets at midnight at a speed of about sixty miles an hour, stark naked, and from having in the house attractive young persons of the opposite sex who could not, even on the most charitable assumption, be considered to be the lawful and wedded wives of any of the inmates – inmates, I think, is the right word, the Flaubertian *mot juste* for this occasion. The 'nerve-shattering occurrence' which drove them away can, I think, be guessed at without any very great effort of the imagination.

This is not to say that the letter is in any way insincere; on the contrary, no mood of depression is deeper or more real than that

which comes as a reaction from the opposite extreme. The rich
melancholy which exudes from this and many another letter of
Philip's is often recognizably that which characterizes the morning
after, or which the Greek physician Galen attributes to all
living creatures except women and cocks at certain moments,
which need not be specified.

The letter which follows, addressed to Colin Taylor, is chiefly
interesting in showing the inception of the enthusiasm for English
Tudor music which was subsequently to play such a large part in
his activities.

PHILIP TO COLIN TAYLOR

34 Southwold Mansions
Maida Vale
Nov. 12th, 1915

. . . I am recovering from a fearful, nerve-racking and entirely horrible three months, and trying to drown the memory of
this period in much musical work of divers kinds. Composition
is entirely impossible, but in December I am going to begin a
long and strenuous course of lessons with Goossens, in the hope
that I may be relieved of the fear which is haunting me, that I
have no musical bowels at all!

Meanwhile, I am delving deep into the origins of keyboard
music, and receiving daily delights and surprises from the
works of Byrd, Gibbons, Tomkins, Farnaby, and many another
astonishing master who preceded J. S. Bach by more than a
century.

I am also scoring from the old part-books in the British
Museum a quantity of early seventeenth-century chamber
music which is exceedingly interesting from an aesthetic as well
as an antiquarian point of view – a fact entirely ignored by most
of the old fogeys who have taken the trouble to do this in years
past.

There is an enormous amount of valuable work to be done
in this field. Apart from this I do occasional programme notes,
transcriptions, and make sketches for the Delius biography,

which is maturing. But the fearful gloom of the war makes the whole of one's life black, and often one simply cannot take one's mind away from it. I have never felt so consistently depressed and nervous and unfit for hard brain-work – except at lucid intervals which only come and go like little faltering gleams of sunshine on a November day. And every day – it is after all no good pretending to think and feel what one sincerely does not – I feel more and more out of sympathy with the general temper of the country. The agglomeration of horrors of all kinds that this war has brought about makes me so sick and fills me with so much impotent rage against the barbarous conditions of human life in this the twentieth century of the Christian era that I have absolutely no room and no use for any sentiments about patriotism, or nationality, or national honour or anything of that kind – which, indeed, I have never, in the pre-war days, felt at all. I only know that if there were no such thing as patriotism and no such thing as national pride or honour, the world would have been spared this unspeakable and soul-shattering devastation. And the self-righteous hypocrisy of England that muzzles every plain-speaking truth-teller and is ready to sacrifice not only the lives of all its inhabitants but also every conceivable tenet of a morality higher than that of brute beasts to these more than thrice damnable fetishes makes me green with fury. And yet one has to sit and look on at all this. One cannot even raise one's voice in protest – and such is the temper of one's countrymen, if one does, it only hardens their hearts in their own conceptions. Well did Blake say that unacted desires breed pestilence. For impotence is always a pestilential thing.

It was in this acute state of depression and repulsion engendered by the war that Philip met for the first time, a few days after this last letter had been written, D. H. Lawrence, for whose work, as we have seen, he had for some time past entertained the highest admiration. Lawrence himself was in a precisely similar state of mind, accentuated, moreover, by the prosecution and suppression of his latest novel *The Rainbow*, on the grounds of immorality.

Aldous Huxley, in his admirable introduction to *The Letters of D. H. Lawrence*, describes his own first meeting with Lawrence on a wintry afternoon in 1915, and how Lawrence announced his intention of building a new heaven and earth in Florida, and invited him (Huxley) to join him. This must have been about the same time that Philip met Lawrence, for we find him writing to Delius thus, in a letter dated November 16th, 1915:

PHILIP TO DELIUS

12a Rossetti Garden Mansions
Chelsea, S.W.
Nov. 16th, 1915

This evening I met and had a long talk with D. H. Lawrence. He can stand this country no longer and is going to America in a week's time. He wants to go to Florida for the winter, since he is, I am afraid, rather far gone with consumption. I write this hurried note to ask whether it would be possible for him to go and live in your orange grove. He has nowhere definite to go in Florida and is very poor. His last book – a perfectly magnificent work – has just been suppressed by the police for supposed immorality (!!).

He begged me to write you at once and ask whether anything could be arranged about living at the grove, but I told him that you probably had very little control over affairs out there now. However, it would be splendid if he could go there. He is such a marvellous man – perhaps the one great literary genius of his generation, at any rate in England.

To this letter Delius answered as follows:

DELIUS TO PHILIP

Nov. 24th, 1915

California is a far better climate than Florida; my orange grove has been left to itself for twenty years and is no doubt only a wilderness of gigantic weeds and plants. The house itself will also have tumbled down. Even if the house had been

inhabitable I should not have advised Lawrence to live in it.
The place is five miles from any house or store. Life is frightfully
expensive on account of the isolated situation. One lives off
tinned food, and a servant costs one dollar fifty cents a day.
In the south of California there are nice little towns; the climate
is divine and living far less expensive. I should have loved to
be of use to Lawrence whose work I admire, but to let him go to
Florida would be sending him to disaster.

Philip also, like Huxley, was one of those who had been invited
to join the 'colony of escape', whether in Florida or elsewhere,
and he was full of a naively youthful enthusiasm for the project,
as the following letter to Delius shows.

PHILIP TO DELIUS

13 Rossetti Mansions
Dec. 15th, 1915

. . . I feel that I am, and have been for years past, rolling
downhill with increasing rapidity into a black, shiny cesspool of
stagnation – and with every day the difficulty of pulling up and
reversing becomes more apparent. A big effort is needed – and
lately my eyes have been opened to a clear and terrifying vision
of this necessity, and I am filled with devastating fears lest it be
already too late to do so. Four years ago you warned me of all
this, and I was not ripe for understanding it and paid no heed.
Now I am determined to follow not only your advice but your
example too; casting all cautious fears to the winds I am going
away, to the uttermost parts of the earth, to *live*. Does this
sound wild and vain? I don't much care if it does, nor if I perish
in the attempt. This living death I can endure no longer. Here
I have been for years lamenting the barrenness of my life,
waiting for my seed to flourish in a desert soil – worse than fool
that I am. I have never yet lived at all, and that is why I am
going away – to Florida, Tahiti, anywhere – to have at least
a year or two of real life to try and make something out of.
The scheme originated with the writer I mentioned in my last
letter, who is keen that a small group of enthusiasts should

detach themselves from harassing surroundings and endeavour for a while to till the soil of their natures in a congenial atmosphere. There are some half-dozen confederates already, but innumerable difficulties beset the path. However, I myself have at last obtained from my late doctor a certificate of my unfitness for military service, so the passport difficulty will be considerably lessened for me. Of course all prospect of money-making vanishes, but my £3 a week remains fairly steadfast – that is to say, if my mother proves amenable.

Now do write, when you have time, and tell me more about Florida, and about Tahiti – which I myself favour personally, though the others are inclined to the west coast of Florida – Fort Myers way. Is the orange grove entirely impossible? Couldn't we by any means rejuvenate it with the aid of niggers? As a preliminary we are going to a farmhouse in Berkshire for January and February. God only knows (and he won't split) as to whether we shall ever get any further . . . This all sounds utterly wild, an irresponsible adventure, unthinkable to the cautious. But, good God, one must plunge, even if one never comes up again. I am in a state of flux – my mind is a whirlpool of alternating excitement and depression.

This is like Berlioz at his very maddest, as in the monologues of *Lelio*. Nothing came of the project, however. Difficulties in the way of getting passports and permission to leave the country in time of war, coupled with a lack of the necessary funds, entailed the abandonment of the scheme for the time being at least. A warm and intimate friendship nevertheless grew up between him and the Lawrences, and at the beginning of the new year – 1916 – we find him staying with them at the house in Cornwall which had been lent to Lawrence by his friend J. D. Beresford, the novelist. He stayed with them for a couple of months, part of the time together with an Armenian friend of his named Dikran Kouyoumdjian – later to suffer a sea-change into something rich and strange – but especially rich – i.e. Michael Arlen, the author of *The Green Hat* and other similar confections. From Cornwall we find him writing Delius as follows:

THE WAR

c/o D. H. Lawrence
Porthcothan
St. Merryn
Padstow
Cornwall
Jan. 6th, 1916

I have made five or six abortive attempts to write to you, but during these first days in a new environment I feel completely at a loss, mentally, and cannot write one coherent page. So you must pardon an apparent reticence, an apparent lack of enthusiasm and vitality, which I think and hope is only temporary and superficial. The past months have been full of anxieties and small nagging worries, each petty in itself individually, but en masse powerful and wearing to one's nervous vitality. At the moment I am completely exhausted, as though I had been dragged, insensible, out of the sea. And although I trust that with 1915 I have put behind me for ever a great deal of foolish and harmful stock-in-trade with which my life was encumbered, I have not yet gained enough positive energy to set out on the forward track again. Like the man out of whom Jesus cast seven devils, I feel 'swept and garnished' but empty, awaiting the arrival of the soul's new tenants (which in the case instanced were, I believe, seven more devils worse than the first! However, one can but hope for the angels!)

At any rate this is the beginning of a fresh start. Here on this stormy coast the winds blow through and through one from mid-Atlantic, and the waves surge and thunder and break right over the cliffs, and the spray falls on one's face with a chill, cleansing moisture. It is a wild, open country of vast expanses, giving a great sense of freedom and openness. The morning and evening twilights are incredibly beautiful. Yesterday, as I was walking home, into the sunset, I was haunted all the while by the Dance from the *North Country Sketches*, which seems most perfectly to express the Stimmung of Cornwall. . . .

I asked Lawrence to write you a few days ago, to give you this exposition of our plans. However, I don't want to identify myself with him in anything beyond his broad desire for an ampler and fuller life – a real life as distinct from the mere mouldy-vegetable existence which is all that is possible here. He is a very great artist, but hard and autocratic in his views and outlook, and his artistic canons I find utterly and entirely unsympathetic to my nature. He seems to be too metaphysical, too anxious to be comprehensive in a detached way and to care too little for purely personal, analytical, and introspective art. His views are somewhat at variance with his own achievements. But he is, nevertheless, an arresting figure, a great and attractive personality, and his passion for a new, clean, untrammelled life is very splendid.

. . . There are many other things I should like to talk to you about, but I feel too unclear to broach any of them at present. A few days will, I hope, bring both clarity and developments. I wish so much that I could have come over to you at Grez this New Year, but it appears to be quite impossible to get a passport. . . .

About this time he would appear to have sent Delius some music of his to look at, for we find Delius writing as follows:

DELIUS TO PHILIP

Jan. 22nd, 1916

. . . Your song *The Curlew* is lovely and gave me the greatest pleasure. Turn to music, dear boy, that is where you will find the only real satisfaction. Work hard at composition; there is real emotion in your song – the most essential quality for a composer.

. . . How are your other plans developing? I cannot understand Lawrence wanting to give up writing – what on earth for? Surely not for planting potatoes or tobacco? Just fancy neglecting the gifts one has: those most precious and rare and mysterious things coming from one knows not where or why! My most earnest advice to you is to turn to musical composition at once, and for good. Voilà.

The Curlew mentioned here, by the way, has no connection with the later song-cycle of the same name, but was merely an independent setting of one of the poems which was subsequently destroyed, although the germ of the music may have been the same.

PHILIP TO DELIUS

c/o D. H. Lawrence
Feb. 11th, 1916

Your splendid and encouraging letter cheered me immensely. It is hard to have faith in the progress of oneself when one's forward movement is so slow that it is almost imperceptible. Yet there is always the little smouldering fire of confident hope at the bottom of one's heart, and a letter like yours makes it leap into joyous flame. Oh, but this country is black and horrible – although, for me, things are tolerably easy. How right you have been to abjure humanity from your earliest days! But it is no good lamenting over one's fellow creatures – the more one thinks of them the more sick one feels . . . so to other topics. . . .

This Cornish coast is strange and sinister – one feels that there is nothing superfluous in the country (save the inhabitants, of course!) – it has been stripped down to its bare essentials. One could not deceive oneself in a place of this nature. The winds seem to search out one's very heart, and if one is weak and failing it is no good pretending to oneself – Christian-wise – that weakness is strength! There is a wealth of sombre colour in the landscape. The bare branches of the trees and hedgerows have all a kind of winter coat of a reddish tint which they put on to protect themselves from the excess of salt in the damp air. At this time of year, this dull red is the predominant hue; it is emphasized by the redness of the soil which is just now being ploughed up. And at sunset (on clear evenings one sees the sun sink right into the sea) everything becomes burning red – even the grass seems to have a layer of red over the green. On the greyest, dullest days, a faint bluish-red comes filtering through the cloud-masses. All the roads, for some curious reason, are cut very deep down in the rock, below the field level, and on the rock, at the level of the field, grows the high hedge of evergreen tamarisk, so that one is always overshadowed. On the uplands, there are scarcely any shrubs or trees; the hedges are replaced by stone walls built in an intricate and very beautiful herring-bone pattern. It is all stark and elemental, rather cheerless and repelling if one wanted to assimilate it, identify oneself with it, but for a while invigorating, cleansing – essentially a country for deliberation at a turning-point rather than for settled work. At least I find it so.

While this war lasts, one feels that 'sauve qui peut' is the only possible rule of life – if one does not want to throw one's life away. It is so difficult to keep one's head above water at all. But if one can weather *this* storm . . . !

References to Philip and his sojourn with Lawrence in Cornwall at this time are frequent in the latter's published correspondence, and Mr. Nichols has already dealt with some of them so perspicaciously that it is unnecessary for me to do more. Of more than usual interest, however, is a long letter written by Lawrence to Middleton Murry and Katherine Mansfield concerning a scheme for publishing books and music which Philip had conceived. The Murrys, who had already been associated with Lawrence in a similar venture, *The Signature*, seemed to resent the idea that he should become associated with anyone except themselves, regarding him, apparently, as their own exclusive private property. Mr. Murry himself, in his *Reminiscences of D. H. Lawrence*, ingenuously admits as much. 'Katherine and I were rather nettled by this sudden intrusion of Heseltine, whom we did not know, and of whom (perhaps jealously) we boded no good.' (Here, incidentally, we already see the initial stages of the ludicrous and undignified dog-fight for the possession of Lawrence's soul and for the title of chosen disciple which has raged so furiously since his death.)

D. H. LAWRENCE TO MIDDLETON MURRY AND KATHERINE MANSFIELD

Now don't get in a state, you two, about nothing. The publishing scheme has not yet become at all real or important, to me.

Heseltine was mad to begin it – he wanted to get *The Rainbow* published. I felt, you don't know how much, sick and done. And it was rather fine that he believed and was so generously enthusiastic. He is the musical one: the musicians he likes are Delius, Goossens, Arnold Bax, and some few others. I believe as a matter of fact they are good, and we are perhaps, outside ourselves, more likely to have good music and bad books, than otherwise.

This is what is done so far: a circular, or letter, is drawn up, and a thousand copies are being printed. It is to be sent to everybody we can think of. Heseltine pays for all this.

. . . He has gone to London, and I haven't yet seen a printed leaflet. When I get one I will send it you.

This is all. You see it is Heseltine's affair so far. I feel that he is one of those people who are transmitters, and not creators of art. And I don't think we are transmitters. I have come to the conclusion that I have no business genius. He is twenty-one years old, and I must say, I am very glad to have him for a friend. He lived here for seven weeks with us, so we know. Now don't think his friendship hurts ours. It doesn't touch it. You will like him too, because he is real, and has some queer kind of abstract passion which leaps into the future. He will be one with us. We must treasure and value very much anyone who will really be added on to us.

The preliminary pamphlet of the publication scheme, which was written and sent out by Philip, runs as follows:

THE RAINBOW BOOKS AND MUSIC

Either there exists a sufficient number of people to buy books because of their reverence for truth, or else books must die. In its books lie a nation's vision; and where there is no vision the people perish.

The present system of production depends entirely upon the popular esteem: and this means gradual degradation. Inevitably, more and more, the published books are dragged down to the level of the lowest reader.

It is monstrous that the herd should lord it over the uttered word. The swine have only to grunt disapprobation, and the very angels of heaven will be compelled to silence.

It is time that enough people of courage and passionate soul should rise up to form a nucleus of the living truth; since there must be those among us who care more for the truth than for any advantage.

For this purpose it is proposed to attempt to issue privately such books and musical works as are found living and clear in truth; such books as would either be rejected by the publisher, or else overlooked when flung into the trough before the public.

This method of private printing and circulation would also unseal those sources of truth and beauty which are now sterile in the heart, and real works would again be produced.

It is proposed to print first *The Rainbow*, the novel by Mr. D. H. Lawrence, which has been so unjustly suppressed. If sufficient money is forthcoming, a second book will be announced; either Mr. Lawrence's philosophical work, *Goats and Compasses*,[1] or a new book by some other writer.

All who wish to support the scheme should sign the accompanying form and send it at once to the secretary, Philip Heseltine, Cefn Bryntalch, Abermule, Montgomeryshire.

---

[1] This work, though it was never published, did actually exist in manuscript, and I remember reading it. It struck me, even at that time when I was under the spell of the prophet, as being Lawrence at his very worst: a bombastic, pseudo-mystical, psycho-philosophical treatise dealing largely with homosexuality – a subject, by the way, in which Lawrence displayed a suspiciously lively interest at that time. There were two typescript copies of the book. Lawrence himself destroyed the one, while the other, which Philip had in his possession, was gradually consumed by him some years later, leaf by leaf, in the discharge of a lowly but none the less highly appropriate function. But the world need not be unduly perturbed at the loss; it was assuredly no masterpiece.

It is no doubt easy, and perhaps difficult not to smile at such youthful idealism and enthusiasm, couched, as it is, in somewhat grandiloquent phraseology, but still it must be remembered that its chief concern was the publication of the work of a writer on the verge of penury whom no publisher then would touch and whom the whole world now rapturously acclaims as one of the greatest of his age, and that Philip was one of the few to see it. Nor was the project so entirely senseless and impracticable as it might perhaps seem at first sight. The private press to-day is a flourishing institution, and it might easily have become one then with a little support. Even if it had not been a success at the time, the mere fact of possessing the copyright of some of Lawrence's books would ultimately have more than paid for any loss incurred in publication. When will people realize that artistic idealism is, apart from any other consideration, a 'paying proposition', in the long run, though it may admittedly sometimes be a very long one?

In this respect, as in so many others, Philip paid the penalty of being ahead of his time. He himself, however, had no illusions, from the outset, concerning the likelihood of obtaining sufficient support for the undertaking, as we see from a letter to Delius, enclosing a copy of the prospectus.

PHILIP TO DELIUS

13 Rossetti Mansions
March 1st, 1916

Here is the tentative prospectus of a despairing project I have set on foot in order to discover whether there are any left in this country to whom life and its expression mean more than the lust for death and destruction. I fear that our small voice will be altogether drowned in the roar of the storm; one can but do one's small best to rescue from oblivion the things one values most. More and more I am convinced that Lawrence is one of the greatest writers we have had for generations, and yet only fifty pounds stand between him and starvation at the present moment. *The Rainbow*, a superb piece of writing and intricate psychology, was accorded (thanks to the Purity League!) treatment from which thousands of books of the filth-for-filth's-sake order are exempt – as witness the windows of certain shops in Leicester Square and Charing Cross Road . . . What has happened to your *Three Elizabethan Songs*? If I get a good number of applications for music, why not let them head the list? They would bring us good luck.

There is abundant evidence in Lawrence's correspondence at this time, apart from the letter of his already quoted, to show that he regarded Philip as his chosen disciple, together with Middleton Murry and Katherine Mansfield. When Lawrence moved over to Zennor on the north coast of Cornwall near St. Ives, in March, he conceived the fantastic project that the Murrys and Philip should join him and his wife, and that all five should live together as one happy family. As he wrote to Murry: . . . 'What I hope is that one day you will take the long house with the tower, and put a bit of furniture in it: and that Heseltine will have one room in your long cottage . . . I hope you will really like him, and we can all be friends together. He is the only one we can all be friends with. But if you don't want him to have a room in your house – of course he would share expenses – he could have one elsewhere. Of course he may be kept away indefinitely.' He was. By a curious coincidence, on the very same day that these lines were being written by Lawrence to Murry – March 8th – Philip was writing as follows to Robert Nichols:

PHILIP TO NICHOLS

I am not returning to Lawrence; he has no real sympathy. All he likes in one is the potential convert to his own reactionary creed. I believe firmly that he is a fine thinker and a consummate artist, but personal relation with him is almost impossible. At least so it appears at present.

And about a month later there is this letter to Delius.

THE WAR

PHILIP TO DELIUS

14 Whitehead's Grove
Chelsea, S.W.
April 22nd, 1916

After a long, long period of storm and stress, I have at last
attained to something approaching peace of mind and have
settled down, I hope for a long spell, in a tiny studio attic from
which I can gaze, over the roofs of South Kensington, at the
sun setting behind those architectural glories of which we
sturdy Britishers are so justly proud, to wit, the Natural History
Museum, the Victoria and Albert Museum, and the ultra-
phallic Imperial Institute (the Royal College of Music, though
adjacent, is happily invisible!!). A garret of one's own – however bare – is so vastly preferable to any furnished flat or
apartments that I am full of regret that I never hit upon this
place before. It is very light and cheerful, being on the top
floor of an old house surrounded with lovely trees just bursting
their green buds, limes, and a rare species called sumac of
which I never heard before; it is said to have long, drooping,
fern-like foliage. My 'flat' consists of a bedroom, facing east
for the morning sun, the studio – with a submerged bath
beneath the floor – and beyond, down two steps, a wee kitchen
with a gas stove and oven and water laid on, two windows and a
skylight facing north-west. The house is discreet and pleasant
quite un-English or at least un-Londonish with its queer-
shaped rooms, full of nooks and crannies and secret cupboards,
its casement windows and innumerable gorgeous cats who dine
with me daily. My furniture is scanty but sufficient; for decoration two Allinsons, a Tibetan devil, a West African carving,
and rows of books; my piano will follow me here . . . As for
my personal affairs the narration of them would be so complicated – and painful, also, to both of us, I expect – that nothing
short of a novel (which I hope some day to write) would convey
any sense of them to you. I hate bare, fragmentary outlines
of things that are full of subtle and vital details, for they invariably lead to misjudgments and misconceptions. I always
wait before writing to you – on whom so much has to be in-

flicted – for events, material and psychological, to assume some kind of recognizable perspective – but one might as well wait for a river to run dry before trying to cross it. So scrappets must suffice.

One still wastes much energy resisting and resisting, saying No to the sausage-machine which gulps down human individuals at one end and disgorges at the other a conglomerate mass of units organized for human destruction – though this vortex is an influence rather than an actuality, something intangible – one feels it in the streets, in the strangers who pass one by, but one cannot lay hands on it – all the while one must σκιαμαχεῖν, be fighting a shadow. There was never any real chance of my being 'taken for a soldier'; indeed, when conscription was proclaimed I put in an appeal before the local tribunal, and after a medical examination in a few days I received by post a certificate of complete and absolute exemption from any form of service enjoined by the Military Service Act. . . .

. . . The *Rainbow* scheme fulfilled your prophecy and died the death. I got about 30 replies to 600 circulars. But I will gladly lend you my copy of *The Rainbow* if you are keen to see it. My sojourn with Lawrence did me a lot of good, but not at all in the way I had anticipated. Lawrence is a fine artist and a hard, though horribly distorted, thinker. But personal relationship with him is impossible – he acts as a subtle and deadly poison. The affair by which I found him out is far too long to enter upon here. I will tell you about it one day, and we shall laugh together over it. The man really must be a bit mad, though his behaviour nearly landed me in a fearful fix – indeed it was calculated to do so. However, when I wrote and denounced him to his face, all he could say was 'I request that you do not talk about me in London' – so he evidently had a very bad attack of guilty conscience. So I replied with a page of prophetic reviews of a future book 'D. H. Lawrence, a Critical Study by P.H.,' of which the *Times* will say: 'Reveals the distorted soul of this unhappy genius in all its naked horror', and the *Spectator* will gloat over 'A monster of obscenity tracked down to its secret lair'; *John Bull* alliterates with 'Personified perversity pitilessly portrayed', while the *Christian Herald* is

'grateful to the author for his scathing indictment of the immorality of the present generation – the book is a veritable sermon
and should be in the hands of every Sunday school teacher',
etc., etc. Lawrence was quite comically perturbed at the
prospect of my revelations. He has practically no friends left
– the last one to drop off before me was an Armenian[1] who
published in the *New Age* directly after the quarrel a most
scathing and amusing satire on a 'brilliant young author, whose
work was too good to be published' discovering his subconscious
self in the middle of the night!!

I do not know exactly what the immediate occasion of the
rupture with Lawrence was – the 'affair by which I found him
out', to which Philip refers in this letter; it must have been something that occurred, or some discovery that he made, between the
time of his departure from Cornwall and the date of the letter to
Nichols, since it is obvious from Lawrence's letters to Middleton
Murry that he and Philip must have parted on the best of terms
and with the intention of rejoining each other in the near future.
Philip was always reticent about the details, but from certain
remarks that he let drop on various occasions, and from what I
know of Lawrence from personal experience, I have no doubt
whatever that the latter had been attempting to interfere
gratuitously, and to an unwarrantable extent, in certain intimate
matters concerning Philip's personal relations with other people,
into which it is unnecessary to enter here. The truth is that
Lawrence was always inclined to treat his friends and acquaintances as if they were characters in one of his novels, and sought
accordingly to mould their characters and direct their actions as
he desired. When he failed in this – and he invariably did fail –
he took his revenge by putting the said friends and acquaintances,
recognizably, into his books, and there worked his will upon
them. In this respect Lawrence's life and his art were curiously
intermingled. But whereas he was wont to claim that his art was
a kind of overflow from his life, it was, in fact, the precise contrary,

---

[1] Dikran Kouyoumdjian (later Michael Arlen).

a substitute for life: to such an extent, indeed, that it is exceedingly probable that he would never have felt the urge to write his novels – the later ones at least – if he had been able to have his way with living personalities. Practically all his novels are essentially a form of wish-fulfilment, an imaginary gratification of his desires. Throughout all the later ones he himself stalks, thinly disguised as the hero, surrounded by malevolent caricatures of those who, for some reason or other, had failed to respond completely or to submit themselves entirely to his will in actual life. This is what happened in the present instance; as we shall see later, a particularly offensive caricature of Philip is to be found in one of the novels, *Women in Love*, for no other reason than that Philip declined to allow himself to become a mere puppet or marionette in Lawrence's hands.

The fact is that Lawrence demanded more from a friend than anyone has the right to demand or anyone the power to give – a complete surrender of one's personality, which no one with any personality at all could make. As one of his greatest admirers, Mabel Dodge Luhan, admits, in her preposterous but sometimes clear-sighted book, *Lorenzo in Taos*, 'Lawrence had to have one or two people completely with him, with their attention undivided, flowing with sympathy along with him, backing him up, being there for him . . . He simply couldn't bear to have anyone question his power, his rightness, or even his appearance'. Philip, however, had not merely a very definite personality of his own, but also an exceptionally keen critical faculty and a lively sense of the ridiculous which inevitably precluded him from filling the role of disciple-in-chief for which Lawrence had cast him in the drama of his own life. No one, indeed, with even the faintest spark of humour could continue for long to be a whole-hearted admirer and follower of Lawrence, and it is a significant fact that the most fervid of his worshippers are those most completely lacking in it, all of them women, of course – Catherine Carswell, Dorothy Brett, and the ineffable Mabel Dodge Luhan, who is almost too good to be true – they are all as solemn as owls;

never does the glimmer of a smile traverse the pages of their panegyrics and apologetics. As for Lawrence himself, Murry has said truly that he was a mixture of angel and devil, and angels are notoriously deficient in humour, while devils only possess a malicious satirical sense which stands at the very opposite pole. This Lawrence certainly had in abundant measure; no one had a keener sense of the absurdities and weaknesses of others. But of true humour, the humour of God and man as opposed to angel and devil, Lawrence was fundamentally incapable – at the time of which I am writing, at least. Now one knows well enough all that there is to be said in condemnation of the standards of judgment set up by those who lay claim to the possession of a sense of humour, which is only too often a cloak to mediocrity, stupidity, and cowardice. It is more than probable, indeed, that Lawrence's incontestable greatness in some respects, both as man and artist, was directly due to his lack of humour; it is equally true, however, that this deficiency was also responsible for his frequent bathetic lapses into the grotesque and the ridiculous.

Such was the power of his genius and the magnetism of his personality, however, that so long as one was with him one was hypnotized into accepting him unreservedly. In the curious glamour that he cast around him, his dark gods, mystic underworlds, and all the rest, became actual living realities; it was only when one got away from him that one suddenly awoke, dazed, as if out of a dream which, however inconsequent and absurd it might seem on waking had, while it was in progress, a reality and a significance, which no one who had not the experience of coming into close intimacy with Lawrence could possibly understand or appreciate.

What ultimately brought Philip to break with Lawrence, then, was not, I think, so much his refusal to subordinate his personality, nor even his acute perception of Lawrence's absurdities and inconsistencies, though these certainly played their part; it is rather to be found in the phrase of the letter to Delius quoted above – 'he acts like a subtle and deadly poison'. This is absolutely true, at least of the Lawrence of these days, although it is difficult to believe that he could ever have changed greatly in this respect. The Lawrence that Philip knew, that Mr. Nichols knew, that I knew, was a very different one from the characteristically feminine idealization which is presented in the pages of Mrs. Carswell's *The Savage Pilgrimage* – the wise, kind, lovable, sympathetic friend and man of genius. That side certainly existed, and I too can gladly testify to its existence. Many were the wonderful and unforgettable moments I spent in his company, but there was another side to the picture, which was very much in the ascendant during that period of his life: dark, sinister, baleful, wholly corrupt and evil. I believe myself that this aspect of Lawrence was the real and fundamental one, and that those who were unaware of it or to whom he did not choose to reveal it simply did not know him.

However that may be, there is no doubt that Philip's close contact with Lawrence was definitely harmful to him. He still for a time retained a great admiration for Lawrence as a writer and even renewed friendly relations with him for a time, as we shall see, but in later years he spoke of him and all his works with a bitterness and a detestation that can only have been the outcome of a deep spiritual wound which never healed.

PART TWO

BOUVARD AND PÉCUCHET

'All through the years of our youth
Neither could have known
Their own thought from the other's,
We were so much at one.'

CHAPTER I

CHELSEA DAYS

ONE late spring evening in 1916, as I was sitting with some friends in the Café Royal, there came up to our table a young man of striking appearance and an indefinable charm of manner and bearing whom I had not seen there before: tall, slender, pale, with bright blue eyes and longish fair hair, dressed in a neat black suit, soft black hat, and orange-coloured shirt, in build and poise resembling curiously certain archaic Greek statues, and particularly that of a Boeotian youth in the museum at Athens. A common acquaintance introduced him to me as Philip Heseltine. The name struck me at once as being in some vague way familiar, and then I remembered suddenly that only a few days before I had come across a book dealing with some musical subject at a second-hand bookshop in Charing Cross Road, on the fly-leaf of which was inscribed this very name in a minute handwriting of such exquisite delicacy and perfection as to arouse in me a lively feeling of interest and curiosity with regard to the personality of the writer, and the possessor of such an unusual, attractive, and aristocratically sounding name.

He sat down next to me at the marble-topped table, and we soon fell to talking of music. Our conversation quickly revealed such a surprising identity of tastes and interests that on parting outside the café at closing time it was arranged that I should come to visit him the next day at his flat in Whitehead's Grove, Chelsea, where he was then living.

I still remember the occasion as vividly as if it were yesterday. It was a glamorous spring morning, a perfect counterpart to the music of Delius's *Village Romeo and Juliet*, to which I was then introduced for the first time by my host, who played it through to

125

me at the piano from beginning to end. He was by no means an accomplished pianist, but he had a remarkable talent for the playing of transcriptions of orchestral scores, particularly those of Delius, many of which he had made himself. He had no voice, and instead of singing the vocal parts he whistled them. Ordinarily I detest this accomplishment, but with him it was something quite different from what is usually so called, and deserving of another name altogether. The very tone-production of his whistling still remains a mystery to me; the unpursed lips were hardly parted, and the sound seemed to come effortlessly from the throat, like the song of a bird, with a sweetness and purity of tone, a perfection of phrasing, a power of dynamic gradation, and a rich, expressive quality such as I have never heard from anyone else.

I have since become well acquainted with *A Village Romeo* and still think that it is one of the loveliest operas in existence, but I have never experienced its poignant beauty so intensely as on that memorable first occasion, as played and whistled to me by this strange young man whom I had just met for the first time, in the attic of an old house long since disappeared, on that spring morning these many years ago.

After this we went to Hyde Park together and walked there, discoursing endlessly on every topic under the sun, and discovering in each of them further evidence of the singular affinity that existed between us. At length we came to the boat landing-stage on the Serpentine, where our eloquent discourse was interrupted by the apparition of an exceedingly attractive young woman, obviously waiting for someone to invite her to a row on the lake. Just as Philip was about to make the necessary preliminary advances, a vulgar lout, looking like a commercial traveller, suddenly appeared, boldly accosted her, and carried her away in triumph. As Philip watched them, ruefully and disconsolately, rowing away together, I remember quoting with exquisite felicity and appropriateness the lines of William Blake:

A traveller came by
Silently, invisibly
He took her with a sigh.

Looking back upon it now there seems to me to be something almost symbolically significant in this trivial episode, and anticipatory of much in his subsequent life. How often, indeed, was it to happen that just when on the verge of triumphant success in some venture or other, within reach of the eagerly desired goal, something or other would intervene and the opportunity would fade away, through no fault of his own, but through sheer adverse circumstances and the malignancy of fate! The symbolism, in fact, is almost too obvious, with the lovely girl as the embodiment of worldly success, the commercial gentleman as its unworthy recipient, and Philip as the deserving failure – so obvious that I may possibly be suspected of having invented it, or dreamt it in a d'Annunzian *sogno d'un mattino di primavera*. It did happen, none the less.

On that day began the close friendship that was to endure, with only brief and unimportant interruptions, for fifteen years, right up to the end of his life. It was, from the very first moment, as if we had always known each other; a case of friendship at first sight, one might almost say, and a rare phenomenon, since friendship, unlike love, is essentially a relationship of slow formation and gradual development. Personally, I have never experienced it before or since with any of the other persons who have honoured me with their friendship, and since many people besides myself have confessed to a similar experience with regard to him it is only natural to suppose that this immediacy of intimate contact was a faculty peculiarly his own. Philip, indeed, had a unique gift for friendship. No one ever gave himself in this relation more spontaneously, more wholeheartedly, more unreservedly; there was literally nothing he would not do for anyone to whom he was thus attached – no service, however great, however uncongenial, that he was not willing to perform.

His capacity for friendship was only equalled by his capacity for enmity. He hated with the same intensity as he loved, and he was never able to resist the impulse to make the recipients of his unfavourable sentiments thoroughly well aware of the nature and extent of them, not merely in speech, public and private, but also in writing – a propensity which frequently brought solicitors' letters down upon him, and more than once threatened to involve him in a prosecution for libel. How he succeeded in escaping it, indeed, I still cannot understand, for he always greeted warnings and threats of legal action with sublime indifference and generally with an intensification of the hostilities which had given rise to them.

The publication of that part of his correspondence which deals with these activities is unfortunately impossible at the present time, for obvious reasons. He generally kept a rough draft however, of such letters of the kind as he felt constrained to write, and many of them are to be found among his papers. I only mention this because I feel sure that their recipients, who have no doubt destroyed their copies, will be glad to know that what is probably their sole claim to the attention of posterity is in safe keeping and in no danger of lapsing. Some among them, indeed, are undoubtedly destined to figure in some future anthology similar to Mr. Hugh Kingsmill's *Invective and Abuse*, as having been the occasion of some of the finest examples of modern times in this category of literature.

Philip's affections and detestations, moreover, were reciprocal. Few people can have been so dearly loved by so many, and few so cordially loathed and detested; and it is a remarkable fact that this is as true to-day, now that he is dead, as it was during his lifetime – neither his friends nor his enemies can forget him.

After this first encounter we met almost every day. About midsummer, in consequence of some difference of opinion with his landlord – a Scottish metaphysician with a walrus moustache who lived, principally on Hegel, in a caravan in the small front garden of the house in Whitehead's Grove – he precipitately left

Chelsea and established himself in a queer barn-like studio on the Battersea side of the river, where I eventually joined him, the third member of the household being his gigantic neuter black cat which shared with its master a veritable passion for the music of Delius, to which it would listen for hours, sitting on the lid of the piano, in a state of beatific ecstasy. All other music, however, it hated. As soon as one started to play that of any other composer it would leap down from its perch and, with back arched and tail in the air, would leave the room with an incomparable gesture of disdain.

Flaubert, in his masterpiece *Bouvard et Pécuchet*, recounts the story of two glorious imbeciles who, meeting by chance and discovering in each other a kindred spirit, decide to set up house together, and proceed to embark upon a course of studies and enterprises embracing the whole of human knowledge and experience, all of which inevitably end in comic disaster; and looking back on these years I am greatly struck by the extraordinary resemblance between Philip and me and the protagonists in Flaubert's immortal satire, beginning with the very circumstances of our meeting. Unfortunately it would require the genius of a Flaubert to do justice to the fantastic existence we led at Anhalt Studios, and to all the crazy projects we conceived and sought to put into execution, always ending in the same invariable fiasco. I only remember a few of them. Firstly, the launching of a new musical journal; secondly, the formation of a society for the publication of pianola rolls of new and interesting works on the same lines as those of the present gramophone record societies; thirdly, the renting of a large studio or small hall where concerts of the best contemporary music could be given every week, free, also series of lectures; fourthly, the yearly publication of a musical anthology representative of all that was best in contemporary music; fifthly, the writing of a history of music on wholly new lines; sixthly, the inauguration of a school for the teaching of composition, and, lastly and most ambitious, the presentation of a full-fledged opera season at a West End theatre.

None of these projects materialized, though actually some of them came very much nearer to realization than one might have supposed possible, as a result chiefly of the demonic energy, enthusiasm, and driving power which Philip displayed in all his activities. He had great gifts as a propagandist and proselytizer, and a remarkable capacity for convincing sceptics and winning over opponents by sheer eloquence and the power of his convictions.

The scheme which of all these enumerated above came nearest to fruition was, curiously enough, the least practicable and the most ambitious, namely, the opera season. Neither of us, it need hardly be said, had the necessary capital for such an enterprise, but under the terms of a will trustees of mine were empowered to release from their control a capital sum, if it could be shown that the object to which it was applied would be of ultimate financial benefit to me. It speaks highly, I think, for our persuasive powers that we were eventually able to convince a few hard-headed business men and lawyers that the production of a season of opera, in war-time, by two completely inexperienced young men of 21, on entirely different lines from anything previously attempted, might be regarded as being quite a feasible financial proposition. In this astonishing *tour de force*, it must be admitted, we had the redoubtable aid of Bernard Shaw, who had very kindly interested himself in us and our scheme. Not only did he invite us to lunch with him at his flat in Adelphi Terrace, where he gave us valuable advice in a discourse lasting several hours without interruption, but he even went so far as to write a long and eloquent letter on our behalf to the principal trustee – a characteristically generous gesture which deserves to be placed on record as an example of Shaw's never-failing sympathy towards youthful enthusiasm and idealism.

Some of the basic conceptions of our projected season are set forth in a long and interesting letter which Philip wrote to Delius at the time.

CHELSEA DAYS

PHILIP TO DELIUS

2 Anhalt Studios
Battersea, S.W.
Oct. 11th, 1916

Another long silence! And I just recollected with alarm that since I moved from Chelsea some months ago you have not even had my address. Forgive my negligence. This time I have great news for you, so I will confine myself to the one important topic.

I have found an enthusiast whose tastes and aims in music are almost identical with my own – and he has money! So we are going to set about the regeneration of music in this be-nighted country in real earnest. Quite definitely, next March, we shall take a small theatre and give a four weeks' season of opera and concerts, with a definite artistic policy and no com-promise with the mob. Preparations are already being made, and I have an important proposition to lay before you concern-ing the *Village Romeo and Juliet*, which I have always longed to see staged in a manner that shall allow the full significance of the work to be clearly perceived, and not buried beneath a mass of stage properties and theatrical misconceptions.

I will try and explain in a few words the general principles which we have arrived at for our guidance in presenting musical dramas. Needless to say, they are diametrically opposed to those of Thomas Beecham, whose productions, as well as the choice of works, are becoming more and more inferior and artistically valueless. Your opinion in this matter will be of enormous value to us, more especially since the *Village Romeo and Juliet* is a work which has been presented in the traditional manner, and you will be able to judge whether it would gain or lose by being given in the way I suggest. Please forgive me if this statement of my own views appears a little dogmatic, but I am so tremendously interested in this problem which appears to me to be of vital importance and to open up, if satisfactorily solved, so many possibilities for future development, that I cannot help advocating it with a great deal of enthusiasm.

I am firmly convinced that the 'realistic' type of opera is dead, utterly dead; further than this, I believe that the realistic manner of presenting opera is dead also. Opera is essentially a *conventional form* (conventional, in the purely artistic sense of the word); it is therefore as futile to attempt to make it represent real life as it is for a painter to make his pictures merely represent nature photographically. Even the ordinary spoken drama is not used aright if it merely portrays the external aspects of life. And to opera, where the text is sung, this principle applies with still greater force.

In the drama of the present day, whether it is spoken or sung, the *action* must tend more and more to take place *within* the characters of the piece – in a word, it must be psychological and not physical. Representation and realism (in the theatrical sense) must be replaced by suggestion and symbolism; where music drama is concerned the idea seems so self-evident that it is astounding that so few modern composers have grasped it. Perhaps this arises from the fact that most musicians are, alas, pure musicians – that is to say they know nothing about anything but music, and even where music is concerned they have not got as far as realizing its true function or its connection with life.

In the pure drama, these principles have already been put into practice – in productions by men like Granville Barker, William Poel, and Gordon Craig, and in actual creative work by Maeterlinck, Fiona Macleod, W. B. Yeats and the Russians, Andreiev and Evreinov, though these latter seem more intent on returning to the old idea of allegorical dramas, so prevalent in the Middle Ages, by personifying attributes and qualities, than on making a drama of individuals and of character study.

Now to come to the *Village Romeo and Juliet*. Your work has always seemed to me to be immeasurably greater than Keller's story by reason of its greater universality – that is to say, its symbolical qualities. It is so much more important than the mere story it is woven around; in fact the story, the 'plot' in the theatrical sense, scarcely matters at all, and this should be realized. What you have achieved in this work – and it is a great and unique achievement – is a drama in which the various emotions, brought into play by various contingencies and circumstances, are the real protagonists. But they are not *personified* in the old allegorical 'morality' style. They are far too subtle. They are presented, typified, in certain individuals who appear on the stage. But it is not these individuals that really absorb us. The work grips one, entrances one and carries one away because these individuals are so shadowy, so unrealistic that they become symbols of the pure emotion they are feeling – so that one can project oneself into them and feel them. The attendant physical circumstances are nothing; the fact of the two fathers quarrelling over a piece of land belonging to a certain Black Fiddler is unimportant. But what is real and vital and magnificent is the way in which you have expressed for us the conflict of love and hate, and blind fatality – the poignancy of love thwarted by circumstance, and the tragedy of materialism. The fact that the suicide of the lovers might easily have been averted does not really matter; nor does it prevent the last scene from being one of the most supreme things in all tragedy. But of course, if the work is presented realistically, as a drama of facts, it falls flat. From what I have heard of the Beecham production, I should imagine it to have been an entirely naturalistic affair – as though one should hold up a landscape of Cézanne in a gold frame at the Royal Academy and expect people to appraise it with all the other colour-photographs hanging round it! Naturally, everyone accused it of being 'undramatic' – and I do not believe even Beecham himself realized that it was never intended to be dramatic in the stagy sense of the word.

I propose to have no scenery – i.e. no set pieces; only plain curtains – possibly a suggestive back-cloth or two – nothing more; costumes of extreme simplicity. Perhaps, in the old Chinese fashion, one might have the stage directions read out or thrown upon a screen before the commencement of each scene.

In any case, the stage must be free from disturbing elements – the curtains or back-cloth beautiful but entirely free from any elaboration. The interest must be centred entirely in the play and the music; and as regards the setting the imagination of the spectators must take an active part (this is, as far as I remember, Maeterlinck's idea, but it is a very important one, and seems to tend to break down the sharp division between stage and auditorium which so often prevents the audience from being entirely caught up and absorbed in the piece that is played) and one can set their imagination working by the simplest clues, the plainest suggestion.

. . . I have sketched out a little mime-drama (very short – about fifteen minutes – very intense and very grisly, a sort of prolonged strain. No one speaks, scarcely anyone moves; the atmosphere is charged with emotion, but nothing happens in the theatrical sense. This is the text (such as it is) written by one John Rodker. It is called *Twilight*.

'Columbine, Harlequin and Pierrot sit relaxed in armchairs in a wide, white room.

Columbine sits swinging her legs.

It grows gradually darker.

They sit as though waiting.

Creepers swing against the window.

It grows darker.

They sit as though waiting.

It grows darker.

Only the windows and the white linen of Pierrot can now be seen.

Harlequin now a faint blur.

It grows darker.

Pierrot and Columbine show faintly. The easy chairs are rocks of shadow.

They sit as though waiting.

The creepers grow larger and swing against the windows.

It grows darker.

The moon rises.

They sit as though waiting.

It is quite dark.

Columbine shudders, rises and walks quickly to Pierrot.

When she is close she turns from him suddenly and walks rapidly back to her chair.

Harlequin leaps across the room, then seats himself and stares intently out of the window.

The moon gradually fills the room and it becomes lighter.
Pierrot has let his head fall on his knees.
Columbine sits relaxed swinging her legs. . . .
Harlequin stares intently out of the window.'

The other stage works we propose to do are all very old and
very lovely: Monteverdi's *Orfeo*, Purcell's *Dido and Aeneas*,
Pergolesi's *La Serva Padrona*, Mozart's *Schauspieldirektor* (with –
this is a dead secret – the theatrical manager and the comic
actor made up respectively as Beecham and Baylis!) and
Gluck's *Orfeo*. No 'transition period' of nineteenth-century
music – it deserves a rest.

This elicited from Delius a series of letters which, apart from
their relevance, have enough independent interest to merit
reproduction here.

DELIUS TO PHILIP

Grez-sur-Loing
Oct. 15th, 1916

I was so glad to receive your news; not having heard from
you for so long I was beginning to think you had been conscripted. Your enthusiasm is always so refreshing. Now to your
idea of regenerating music in England, especially the music-
drama. I entirely agree that realism on the stage is nonsense
and that all the scenery necessary is an impressionistic painted
curtain at the back, with the fewest accessories possible. In
Germany this has already been tried with success.

I entirely agree with all your ideas about the music-drama –
they are also mine, and all my works are written in this spirit.

I don't think that anything ought to be undertaken before the
war is over and the people have calmed down a bit. In itself
the idea is excellent – wait a bit, prepare, gather works.

I believe in the English youth under 25 or 30. After this age
he is hopeless. The war will have changed much – people will
have suffered, many will have realized the rot that has been
going on – the hollowness of patriotism and jingoism and all

the other isms. Politicians and diplomats and experts of all kinds have been making and continue to make such fools of themselves that the wiser folk will perhaps look for a little truth in art and the artists, and perhaps find some satisfaction in that rare event – a really artistic and emotional performance.

You must be able to keep at it in order to form a public. One season is not enough; it must be followed up by another season equally good, and for this purpose you ought only to begin such an undertaking at a favourable moment. Why not begin by a series of concerts in a small hall with a small orchestra? When you start your scheme you must absolutely make it a success or it will again fizzle into nothing, like all artistic attempts in London including Beecham, and that makes the public more and more sceptical. Practise conducting if possible; take an engagement at any theatre simply to get a little routine even if you have to conduct musical comedy.

The music drama you sketched would only have an effect with three great artists who at present do not exist in England, and it might turn out simply ridiculous.

Nov. 6th, 1916

I want to lay before you, very precisely, my point of view with regard to artistic and particularly operatic enterprises in England. I am so fond of you and admire your whole attitude so much that I wish you thoroughly to understand my attitude. I know of no artistic musical-dramatical undertaking that has ever come off in England. The great success of the Russian ballet was, firstly, because it was boomed by a fashionable clique; secondly, no Englishman had anything to do with it, bar financing. It came to London entirely ready to ring up the curtain. Every other enterprise has been a failure, and often a miserable failure. Where there has been enthusiasm among the promoters there has been amateurism and inexperience and inefficiency which has just as thoroughly ruined the whole affair . . . The attempt to mount *A Village Romeo and Juliet* with English singers, chorus, and stage manager, was a miser-able failure – inefficiency and inexperience bursting from every crack. The only good point was the splendid English orchestra and Beecham's conducting. Every gesture of the actors in my work must be controlled and ordered by the conductor, for my music is conceived in that spirit. Only thus can the whole be made comprehensible to the public. An old actor stage manager will be no good whatever, for he will make the singers act from the stage and not from the music. . . .

Don't you see, dear Phil, that you are all going towards disaster with the best intentions possible, and that is what seems to me so hopeless in our country. With no experience whatever you are going to undertake the most difficult of tasks, and you want to begin with one of the most difficult works. It is the Dardanelles and Mesopotamia over again. I advise you to begin in quite a small way in order to gain experience. The Russian ballet did this; it began in a barn in the slums of Petrograd with old cast-off costumes, and gradually acquired the wonderful perfection we have all admired. Tell Gray he has the opportunity of doing quite a unique thing, and it would be a terrible mistake to spoil the whole affair by a too ambitious opening. Feel your way, and whilst you are doing so you will gradually be acquiring valuable experience. My whole heart goes out towards your undertaking, and for this reason I write as I have done. It would be better and less harmful for the future of art in England not to begin this undertaking than to do it badly and fail. There have been too many such failures in England, and already the public only really believes in what comes from abroad.

Feb. 10th, 1917

You can understand, I am sure, my timidity and scepticism *vis-à-vis* your new undertaking; I have had such a lot of disappointment in that direction, and do not want the *Village Romeo* to be given again except under the best and most favourable auspices. You see, you yourself recognize that the régisseur conductor is absolutely necessary; I only know of two in Europe and none in England. Where are you going to find the conductor with the artistic instinct and the necessary experience of the drama and the stage? I have seen many conductors at work and have noticed how helpless they are before the stage and the

137

singers. They themselves feel their inability to suggest or show the right gesture or expression, and therefore leave it to the old actor régisseur who is lurking on every operatic stage with his old clichés.

It was naturally an immense encouragement to us to learn that our conception of how the *Village Romeo and Juliet* should be given corresponded so closely with that of the composer, and that Delius was also in agreement with the aims and ideals of our season in general. The salutary douche of cold water, however, which accompanied his approval, would probably not have sufficed to cool our hot heads sufficiently to prevent us from making egregious idiots of ourselves, had not my trustees at the last moment fortunately recovered their sanity to the extent of deciding that the venture might not perhaps prove quite so successful at such a time as it might at some other, and insisted upon a postponement of operations until the end of the war.

This was a bitter blow, for our arrangements had already been largely completed. Estimates had been prepared, a stage manager and singers engaged, and an opera had been definitely commissioned from Bernard van Dieren, to whom we had been introduced one evening in the Café Royal by Jacob Epstein.

The impression that van Dieren's music had made upon us both on first becoming acquainted with it, one afternoon in June, 1916, was a veritable revelation, and was destined to exercise a decisive influence upon the development of Philip's talent. A few brief extracts from a letter written by him to van Dieren immediately after will show this clearly enough.

PHILIP TO B. VAN DIEREN

14 Whitehead's Grove
Chelsea
June 8th, 1916

Please forgive me if this letter seems mad and chaotic – yet I must write you; first of all to ask your pardon for my impertinence in suggesting that you might contribute to our poor little volume of so-called 'advanced' compositions, and also for the wild and windy manner in which I spoke about music to you a few evenings ago. Alas for arrogance! Before you I feel that it is only colossal impudence that permits me to call myself a musician at all; but you are, I expect, already painfully aware of the fact that in this country, where Sir Hubert Parry is the beau-ideal of a composer, no sort of pseudo-musical monstrosity is impossible.

I was so utterly overwhelmed by your music this afternoon that all words failed me. And as is usual with me on such occasions – in deliberate mockery of my real feelings, I suppose, just when they are most intense – forces upon me the mask of listless, unenthusiastic, stolid complacence which not even an earthquake or a sign from heaven could cause to drop from the average Englishman. (Hence also our Parrys.) It is always when I feel most deeply that expression is most completely denied me. And so I feel I have to write and tell you – inarticulately enough – what a profound impression my visit to you has made upon me. It has brought me to a turning-point, opened out a vista of a new world; it has brought to a climax the dissatisfaction and spiritual unrest that have been tormenting me for months past – in the last few days more acutely than ever. All this may sound extremely crude and childish, but I feel it so – though God only knows why I should inflict my paltry feelings upon you.

Your music – (those fragments of the Shakespeare Sonnets and the Symphony you played to-day) is nothing short of a revelation to me. I have been groping about aimlessly in the dark for so long, with ever-growing exasperation – and at last you have shown a light, alone among composers whom I have met; for neither Delius nor any other has ever so much as suggested a practical solution of the initial difficulties of musical composition. I know that it is as idiotic to flounder about, without plan or purpose in music as I have been doing, as to become Professor of Composition at the R.A.M. Rather than do either of these things, I could abandon music altogether. If I am not to do this, it will be necessary for me to begin everything anew, *ab ovo*.

The music he had written up to this time consisted chiefly of songs in which the interest was almost exclusively harmonic, with complex blocks of chords for the piano through which a mournful and sluggish voice part drifted, like the waning moon through a bank of clouds. It was, indeed, very moony stuff altogether: clotted dream music, the larger part of it set to poems of Yeats, and the predominant influence that of Delius. I must confess that, in spite of our close friendship, I did not think much of any of it that he showed me, but it is quite possible that if I were to see it again to-day I might feel differently. Under the influence of van Dieren a sudden complete change took place. He learnt to purify and organize his harmonic texture by means of contrapuntal discipline, and the thick, muddy chords which characterized the early songs gave place to clear and vigorous part-writing.

The first-fruits of this beneficial influence are to be seen in the set of songs entitled *Saudades* which were written at this time (in 1917) though not published until after many other songs written much later. The title, we are told in a note, is Portuguese, and expresses 'the haunting sense of sadness and regret for days gone by – a word which has no equivalent in the English language'. The first, *Along the Stream*, a setting of a poem translated from the Chinese of Li Po by Cranmer-Byng, is pure van Dieren, but also probably the best of the set. The third, a setting of the famous translation from the Greek of a lyric of Callimachus by William Cory, is also under the same influence, but much less so, and is on the whole less successful, though deeply moving. The second, a setting of Shakespeare's *Take, O, take those lips away*, is the least so influenced, but also the least interesting. Taken as a whole, however, they represent an immense advance upon anything he had hitherto achieved. It should be mentioned, incidentally, that Philip, so far from attempting to conceal the profound debt they owe to the older composer, openly proclaimed it by dedicating the set to him.

As a partial compensation for the abandonment of the opera

season I was enabled to give a concert devoted entirely to the music of van Dieren, which took place in February, 1917, in the Wigmore Hall. Seldom has critical and enlightened opinion achieved a more impressive unanimity than on that occasion. Practically without exception the representative leaders of musical opinion of every tendency and persuasion, from extreme left to extreme right, burst out into a simultaneous howl of execration, occasioned as much by the manifesto in the programme, for which Philip and I were jointly responsible, as by the music itself. Although this manifesto contained nothing to which I would not readily subscribe to-day, I can see now that the somewhat aggressive and pontifical tone of it was a mistake, and was responsible for much of the hostility which subsequently pursued both the composer and ourselves. The financial outcome of the concert, incidentally – expenses £110, receipts £5 – was hardly of such a nature as to increase the faith of my trustees in our business capacity, and from that time onwards the opera season gradually faded away into the vast limbo of forgotten and unrealized projects. Perhaps it is just as well that it did. As Delius clearly saw, as any reasonably sane person could have seen, the enterprise was bound to have ended in complete disaster. From a purely aesthetic point of view I still think we were on the right lines, and ideas and conceptions similar to ours have since been put into execution by others; but our youth, rashness and inexperience must inevitably have proved fatal to any chance of success, both artistic and financial, in an undertaking in which the scales are weighted against one to such a formidable extent as they are in that of the presentation of opera or music-drama.

The project, however, was not entirely without indirect fruits. Our programme had been dual: the performance of such operas written in the past as were in accordance with our aesthetic principles, or could be satisfactorily reconciled with them, and secondly, the writing of such works ourselves. And although the scheme failed to achieve existence on the executive side, it certainly provided the stimulus and incentive to the composition of one of the most admirable operas of modern times which might not otherwise have been written – *The Tailor*, by Bernard van Dieren, to a libretto by Robert Nichols, to which its writer has alluded above in excessively deprecatory terms. And, though modesty forbids me to claim as much for an opera I wrote myself which similarly owed its inception to this abortive season, I can at least say that I learnt a great deal from the writing of it which I would most certainly not have learnt otherwise. As for Philip, the mime-drama to which he refers in his foregoing letter to Delius was actually completed in short score. He was not satisfied with it musically, however, and since its success on the stage would have been exceedingly problematical, as Delius observed, it was never orchestrated and was subsequently destroyed. Another stage work that he wrote about the same time was a Chinese ballet, with scenario by Adrian Allinson, the painter, who was also to be responsible for the costumes and *décor*. This work still survives in manuscript. After being lost for many years it suddenly turned up, shortly after Philip's death, in Berlin, though how it got there I have not the faintest idea. It is of no significance, and was never intended to be anything but a pot-boiler. It failed even as such, for it was never produced.

Of more interest and value among his compositions at this period was an elaborate parody of César Franck's most noble symphony in D minor – a witty and sacrilegious production which has the effect of rendering it impossible for any one who has once heard it to listen again to the original with due and becoming respect. The themes of the symphony are only slightly distorted, but in such a way that the *Père Séraphique* of music is made to appear like a saint with his halo over one eye, a red nose, and a hiccough. It is a perfect little masterpiece in a genre too seldom practised: not only amusing but also, as the best parodies always are, a serious criticism of the artist's faults – a scathing indictment, in fact. Some years later he scored it for a jazz band, and in this form it was actually played in the restaurant of a famous West End hotel as a 'serious' piece of jazz music. A set of four pieces for string quartet, also in parodistic vein, and anticipating in many ways the manner of the French school of *Les Six*, also belongs to this time, but seems to have disappeared.

Altogether, up to the time when he wrote the *Saudades*, in 1917, his actual creative achievement was negligible, and I confess that I never considered him seriously as a composer until one memorable evening when I heard him improvising at the piano, literally for hours on end, completely oblivious of his surroundings and of the lapse of time, with such a wealth of poetic thought, such a profusion of harmonic invention, that I was held spellbound. It seemed to me then, and it still seems to me now, that I have never heard any music more beautiful in my life than what he played that evening; indeed, often afterwards he used to chaff me for what he considered to be a strange aberration of my usually sound critical faculty in praising so highly such random improvisations of his, but I have faith in my judgment and still cling to my opinion. In such moments he was truly inspired, and was probably quite unconscious of the worth of what he was playing, so much greater than that of any music that he ever actually succeeded in imprisoning in notes on paper. But it is perhaps the essence of improvisation that it cannot be notated, and I often think that the most beautiful music ever conceived has never been written down, and never can be written down; that the most exquisite thoughts wilt and fade like plucked wild-flowers when brought into contact with the rigid and artificial conventions of musical notation. It is sad to reflect that Philip's finest substance was thus wasted and dispersed, but nothing could be more characteristic of the man he was than that he should thus create for himself alone and for the passing moment only – in this very impermanence, perhaps, by a profound paradox, lies his surest claim to immortality.

Music, however, was by no means his sole preoccupation in these days, but only one among many. Like our Flaubertian exemplars, Bouvard and Pécuchet, we took all knowledge for our province and ranged freely over the entire field of art, literature and philosophy. Philip was the Pécuchet, the more active, volatile, and preposterous of the pair of us; I was the Bouvard who, as the name suggests, was the more solemn ass of the two. In music Pécuchet cared mostly for the very ancient or the very modern; Bouvard's chief predilection on the contrary was for the established classics. In the domain of the plastic arts Pécuchet inclined to the primitive and the exotic, and surrounded himself with Peruvian pots, Javanese puppets, African fetishes, and Tibetan paintings; the chaster and more conventional Bouvardian taste lay rather in the direction of the Egyptian, the Chinese, and the old Italian masters. In religion and philosophy Pécuchet was a mystic and a heretic, steeped in William Blake, Jakob Boehme, Thomas Traherne, Eliphas Levi, Hermes Trismegistus, and Aureolus Philippus Theophrastus Bombast of Hohenheim, better known as Paracelsus; Bouvard tended towards Roman Catholicism and saturated himself in the works of the orthodox metaphysicians such as Descartes, Spinoza, Kant, Hegel, Leibniz, and Berkeley. In literature Pécuchet delighted primarily in the Elizabethans and modern writers; Bouvard was most attracted to the eighteenth and nineteenth centuries, particularly French and Italian writers.

But in addition to music, literature, art, philosophy, and the rest, there was Life itself, with a very large capital L, and in this respect at least reality was superior to fiction; there is nothing in the pages of Flaubert's masterpiece that approaches the fantastic existence one led at that time. Philip always lived at a tremendous pitch of intensity; to live in his ambience was to live at twice the rate to which one was normally accustomed – it was to experience a heightening, an enhancement of ordinary values, as if one were continually breathing oxygen instead of ordinary air. In those days this natural inborn intensity of his was accentuated by the ever-present sinister background of the war, which made itself felt increasingly as time went on, and conduced to a folly and a recklessness of behaviour inconceivable under normal circumstances.

Among all the confused recollections of that time there is one that stands out vividly in my memory: an occasion when we were crossing over the Albert Bridge from Battersea to Chelsea, one summer evening, and saw on the right side, to the east, the moon rising high in a clear, serene sky over Battersea Park, the trees of which under its light seemed black as cypresses, while to the left, in the west, the sun was setting, wreathed in an angry nimbus of storm-clouds, behind the great chimneys of the power-house at Lots Road. It was like two entirely different worlds, one on each hand, and even then I remember thinking how curiously symbolical it was of the complex and contradictory character of my companion, of the duality of nature which even then had already begun to declare itself – the combination of an underlying sensitive, gentle, melancholy disposition with an ever-increasing tendency towards an outward extravagance and perversity of behaviour.

Somewhere about April, 1917, I think, our life together came to an abrupt end. The cause was Philip's marriage, which was not a success; that is all I propose to say about it here. There was one child, a son. Shortly afterwards he departed to Cornwall, alone, where he stayed for some months and incidentally re-established friendly relations with D. H. Lawrence. The letters to various correspondents, which follow, in contradistinction to most of those we have so far seen, are noteworthy for their exuberance and high spirits, and also for the passionate love of nature which they reveal. Few musicians, incidentally, can have been more intensely visual than he, or more sensitive to the beauties of landscape.

PHILIP TO ROBERT NICHOLS

Tinners Arms
Zennor
April 16th, 1917

O most excellent one! Greetings! How are you and when is the book coming? Write to me about yourself – not a word, though, about London, not a whiff of the old stench that still

hangs over the old dead past! Let us cut adrift and start anew!
This stupendous spring is going to blow my head clean off, I am
sure, and I shall have to go chasing it over the moors like a bit of
dandelion fluff, from one sea to the other! Come and hold it on
for me, do! It would be so good if you were here. The world
has been reborn at Easter – everything is new and wonderful!
This is an excellent inn and there is a furnished cottage to
let for about a pound a month right out on the open moor, 500
feet up, where one could live for tuppence ha'penny a week.
Come – one can work here as nowhere else. Miles and miles
of moor, two seas and a forty-mile horizon, right away to the
Scillies! Don't reveal my whereabouts or tell anyone you've
heard from me or tell me anything about any of the old stink-
pots. Let us have done with the past, once and for all. Oh, this
spring! My head is dancing all day long.

With the letter was enclosed the following curious poem, in
which the influence of D. H. Lawrence is clearly discernible:

A Delectable Ballad in which is set forth ye Futilitie of
Remorsefull Retrospection

A signpost at a fork o' the road –
Two white arms a-poise –
On a bank behind, up in the sunshine,
'A golden noise
Of gorse rings out aflame. . . .

On a cross set by the roadside
Hangs a dismal man,
While a lark above him, fluttering and twittering,
Asks how he can
Play at such a queer game.

'Alas, in the bridal bed, I
Slew my purple love,
For which I cannot sufficiently crucify myself,
Or remove
The black brand of shame. . . .'

146

Then up comes a black man
  And 'Ha' and 'Ho' says he,
'I see nothing half as black as the face
  God gave me,
    And that's a fine face, I claim!'

Over the sun-strewn heather
  A wild girl dances
And casts on the man hanging so glib and so glum
  Merry glances,
    And bids him tell his name.

Then on a sudden, what with
  The black man and the girl and the sun,
'Cripes,' says he, 'what the Hell am I doing?
  What's done's done,
    Whosoever's to blame.

'Do you suppose I'm Jesus
  Saving humanity,
Or Judas Iscariot, expiating himself?
  (What vanity!)
    For you know it's all the same.

'No, I'm only an ordinary
  Thief, and old Pilate
Never caught me, yet here I am! Now isn't that
  Something to smile at?
    Down with this bloody frame!

'We're three fine vagabonds.
  The wind and the rain
And empty purses don't matter a damn. Let's go
  Thieving again!
    (Oh, but it's good you came!)

'Now for the rest of time
  We'll wander over
Open country, lie in the fields of
  Sainfoin and clover,
    And sing ourselves to fame.

147

'And whenever we see a signpost
   With white arms a-poise
Like a blooming crucifix, trying to lead
   Wild girls and boys
     By the hard road to the town

'Of smoke and sacrifices, pretending
   Moors are trespassers' land,
We'll climb up the bank behind it, when
   it's not looking,
   Into the sunshine, and
     Pull the bloody thing down!'

PHILIP TO P. V. C.

Zennor
April 19th, 1917

. . . You ought not to have left Zennor at the very moment
spring was coming. The gorse is bursting into golden flame
and violets are peeping out of all the grassy banks. And in the
lingering, coloured twilight everything is so clear, so real, so
alive. The light never seems to die, but gradually the hills and
the fields, each wall, each house, each little bush, seem to become
clothed with darkness, as though they all put on dark cloaks –
has it ever seemed to you like that? The sky never grows dark,
but as the blue deepens it becomes more luminous, and the
first stars always peep out of a warm purple glow. And what
space and freedom there is, and what distances one sees! All
the coast along to Trevose Head, nearly forty miles off, and the
Scillies the other way, that always look so impossible – one can
never believe they exist like ordinary islands and are inhabited
by ordinary human beings. They are like a mysterious gateway
leading to a mysterious, unknown fairyland of impossible dreams
come true – like Hy-Brasil the old Celts used to see shining far
out in the western sea at sunset. Perhaps it is Hy-Brasil that
one sees, although silly Reason says it's the Scillies! I like to
believe it – no, not 'like to' but do believe it. And when I

suddenly thought of you like a fish out of water in London the other day and then looked up and saw the golden islands gleaming so clear in the evening sun, a real piskie came and whistled the two thoughts together in my ear. And this was his message: – (you must read it in one breath!)

'You'll never come to Hy-Brasil,'
   A piskie whispers through your hair,
'By bending to another's will.
   For picks and packs you may not bear
Across the sea to Hy-Brasil.
   And you may sweat and you may swear
And swink and think until you're ill
   And die before you're e'er aware
There's such a place as Hy-Brasil.
   So have a care, so have a care. . . .
From Trewey Down and Zennor Hill
   You'd ride a puffin through the air
And circle over Hy-Brasil.
   But now from city windows stare –
There's not a sign of Hy-Brasil.
   As if to drive you to despair
The fog sits on your windowsill.
   You take a map and seek the rare,
The golden land of Hy-Brasil.
   You cannot find it anywhere.
The faery isle eludes you still. . . .
   You say it simply isn't there,
And raise a monster you must kill
   (An' if you dare, an' if you dare)
And lay his bones in Hy-Brasil,
   Or he will hunt you like a hare,
Or grind you in his grisly mill,
   And eat you in his lurid lair.
So never dare to rest until
   You let the piskie in your hair
Whisk you away t'wards Hy-Brasil,
   By your desire, against your will.'

Philip, incidentally, wrote a good deal of verse in his early days, especially at Oxford, and in the eyes of many of the best judges he was regarded as being one of the most promising poets of his time there; his stay in Cornwall seems to have brought about a certain recrudescence of poetic activity for the last time. He subsequently destroyed all his poetry, and in later years confined his gifts in this direction to the limited but none the less exacting form of the limerick, of which he was an accomplished master. I have printed the foregoing poems, not so much on account of their intrinsic merit which is no doubt slight – the first, as I have said, is demonstrably Lawrencian in style, and the second is only an amusing feat of versification – as because they are practically the sole surviving specimens of what was at one time a considerable poetic output. The point is important because it is, I think, largely in consequence of his gift in this direction that his achievement as a song-writer stands so high. Not only was his taste in the choice of poems to set to music impeccable, but his invariable respect for the poet's intentions, and his scrupulous regard for the rhythm of the words, down to the minutest details, are without parallel in modern English song. And while we are on the subject I might as well print here an excellent little poem in Latin hendecasyllabics which he sent me about this time. To those who remember their Latin it will tell its story plainly enough. 'Prosdocimus de Beldamandis', by the way, the name of an eminent musical theorist of the Middle Ages, was his favourite pseudonym at the time – a kind of anticipation of 'Peter Warlock'. 'Amphora Bolsiana' is, of course, Bols gin, a beverage to which he was at that time exceedingly partial. The precise significance of 'Probinbalneum' in the title, as applied to me – 'Try it in your bath' – completely escapes me.

PROSDOCIMI DE BELDAMANDIS AD FRATREM PROBINBALNEUM PALINODIA

Vere insanus eram (negare nolo)
Qui propter mulierculam impudicam
Dilecto potui nocere amico. . . .
Detestabilis usque erasque erisque
Cunne, heu, tot scelerum nefasta causa!
Cunne, in te latet omnium malorum
Semen: to quoque litium est origo:
Te vaginam habet universus ensis! . . .
Tristis, Prosdocimus de Beldamandis
Luget se, subito furore raptum,
Excordem simul occupasse amicam,
Dilectum male perdidisse amicum. . . .
Jam solum sedeo ad focum (puella
Nequaquam esse viro potest sodalis),
Nec fert amphora Bolsiana pacem.
Cunctorum at mihi pessimum malorum est
Illo uno comite unicoque egere
Quocum 'desipere in loco' solebam,
De mundo et furibunda cantitare,
Res et commemorare saurianas
Docto colloquio bonas per horas. . . .
Quid prodest aliquid? dolere vanum est:
Me ipsum follibus irrumare oportet!

Nunc, en! hendecasyllabis Latinis
Formosam palinodiam peregi.
Peccavisse pudetque paenitetque. . . .
Nonne ignoscere tu potes amico
Quondam, Prosdocimo de Beldamandis?

PHILIP TO ROBERT NICHOLS

Trewey Bungalow
Newmill
Near Penzance
(No date)

. . . I am living now in a little wooden house on the highest point of the moor that separates the two seas, north and south – between Zennor and Penzance. All round, on all sides, nothing but open moorland and rock-strewn hills, mostly crowned with marvellous Druidic temples. Without leaving the house I can see the sun rise at five in the morning, and watch it sink at night into the sea. The sky never grows dark; the darkness seems rather to come welling out of the earth like a dye, infusing into every shape and form, every twig and every stone, a keen, intense blackness . . . In the twilight, bushes, walls, roofs, and the line of the hills all seem to become rigid and sharp against the sky, like dark blades, while the upper air remains clear and bright and the sky becomes more and more luminous as the blue deepens to a marvellous purple setting for the first stars. The hollows and lower slopes of the hills are covered with a dazzling profusion of gorse and blackthorn – I have never seen such blazing masses of gorse. Tiny lizards dart about among the violets on the sunny banks and splendid gold-and-black adders often cross one's path on the moors. The other day, looking down from the cliffs into a clear, green sea-pool, I caught sight of a lovely young seal, gambolling about under the water. Up here on the moor all the birds and beasts come so near one, not suspecting any human presence. Foxes lollop leisurely along the road, bunnies hardly take the trouble to hop out of the way when one walks by. A chorus of larks makes the air ring all day long, and there are cuckoos innumerable, piping from far and near with delightful variations of pitch and interval – sometimes two sing exactly together, on different notes. One cuckoo (I've actually seen him several times – a beautiful, bluey-grey person who bobs up and down just like the one that lives in a clock) is very fond of sitting on my roof or on the fence just outside the house in the very early morning before his throat's clear: and he can't cuckoo properly, but makes queer gurk-noises and then chortles with a peculiar laugh of which I could never have thought him capable! And on the edge of the pond near by an assembly of huge gulls holds colloquy (there is no other word for this strange croaking).

I wish you would come and live hereabouts for a bit. There is an extraordinary fascination about this little remote end of Cornwall . . . We ought to re-people this wonderful neighbourhood, for the indigenous man is vile. It is all very well to wax romantic about the Celt in the abstract (though I suspect most of the Zennor stock of being pre-Celtic Iberians), but your average Cornishman is a veritable savage – ignorant, suspicious and quite hysterically ill-tempered.

PHILIP TO DELIUS

Trewey Down
Newmill
Penzance
Cornwall
May 13th, 1917

This horrid silence of mine must have seemed very strange to you all these months. Forgive me – the fact is, unpleasant though it be to have to admit it – at the beginning of March I found myself on the verge of utter collapse, physically and mentally. Material and psychological difficulties combined with other things to produce a kind of climax, a decisive point at which it became imperative to break right away from old paths and choose a new direction – or rather to pull oneself out of the mud and regain the path one had slipped away from. The English capital, which our countrymen like to call the hub of the universe, is really a great cesspool – more especially where any kind of art is concerned; if one lives in it continuously for a year or so, one sinks deeper and deeper into the mire until one reaches such a pitch of blasphemy that one begins positively to enjoy one's wallowing. Then comes a horrible moment when the truth of one's position rises up against one

– and then there is nothing to be done except to clear out of all the muck, or else sell one's soul to Satan for ever and a day. There seems to be a fatality about our generation – I mean the generation born at the tail-end of the old century; those of us who are not killed off *sur le champ de bataille* are marked down for a big dose of death and corruption in an other than material form. In ten years the survivors amongst us will be as rare as first folio Shakespeares! However, Providence is kind to some of us, in letting us have our dole of death in the form of an inoculation, with the 'sure and certain hope of resurrection' to follow. The whole of the past year has been a nightmare to me – chiefly through my own imbecility – but it has also been a good cautionary experience. But now – in this wonderful country – this wild end of England which is not England at all – I feel a real regeneration, I feel the spring in me as well as around me; this is a new beginning – but only a beginning. You were quite right, though I hardly appreciated the truth of your words at the time – when you wrote last winter that we – Gray and I – were as yet unripe for a big enterprise. I have now thoroughly understood how immature, how really uneducated one is – in every sense of the word – and, most important of all, how necessary it is to *be*, fully, before attempting to *do*. For one can only create out of the fullness of being – of this I am sure; it is no good building on the patterns of the past, which is all that the musicians of the present day are doing – not one of them has any real individual *being*. You have always been so very right in your estimate of them; and now I know what patience you must have exercised in tolerating my absurdly exaggerated and ill-founded opinion of the value of present-day artists. Really, when I consider what myself and my opinions have been during the last four years I am quite overcome with shame and confusion. You have been so good and so tolerant, and all the while so right.

The collapse of the opera season, through the withdrawal of the promised funds owing to 'war economy' was a bitter disappointment. But the scheme was a good one in outline and no harm will be done by allowing time to mature its details. And, really, there are so few operas that are worth performing at all. When one tries to think out a reasonable artistic basis for the musical drama, one finds that no works yet exist which can possibly be said to conform to its canons – except, perhaps, a few very old works which do so by accident and the *Village Romeo*.

. . . The little book about your works which I partially wrote last year, I am re-writing (since a great deal of it was very crude and stupid) and expanding into an examination of the condition of music in general at the present day. I hope to have it quite ready by the autumn, and it will be mostly done before you come over in the summer. Do come soon. I have not as yet been troubled again by the military but one never knows what may happen from day to day. You must come and stay down here: the country is quite marvellous. My little cottage is on one of the highest points of the moor on the little neck of land that runs down to Land's End, midway between the two seas, north and south, and one can see them both from the cottage, since they are only seven miles apart at this point. For miles around there is nothing but wide, solitary moorland, with little grey stone farms dotted about here and there. My cottage stands quite alone, half a mile away from the nearest farm. The effect of living in wide open spaces is quite miraculous; I feel a new being. From Zennor Hill, two miles away, you can see 70 miles of the north coast, from Trevose Head to the Scilly Isles, which gleam in the distance like some impossible Hy-Brasil. To the south there is the long length of the Lizard Head and St. Michael's Mount, and inland, mile upon mile of rugged, open country. The hills are not very high, but they rise from the sea with steep, rock-strewn slopes; on many of them are to be found marvellous Druidic remains – huge boulders piled up – God knows how – one on another, immense cromlechs and logan stones of enormous size, poised so that they rock at a finger's touch! The cliffs on the coast are marvellous too, very high and sinister, of black granite, but the sea, at this time of year, is calm and of a quite Mediterranean blue. The other day I saw a lovely seal gambolling about in a deep pool! and there are birds innumerable – all day long a chorus of larks rings out over the moor, and cuckoos call and answer one another from far and near, all with different pitch and intervals – sometimes one hears two at once, in harmony.

Gray has taken a big, lonely house about three miles away in a very wild spot, almost on the cliffs. He is going to live there permanently and is moving all his belongings from London. We are keeping on the London studio between us, but I shall also stay on in this part of the world as long as I can. So you must come over and stay with us – there will be heaps of room for both of you – and even if Gray and I are swept away, there will still be the house and, I hope by then, a housekeeper waiting for you. So *do* come very soon – there is already a foretaste of summer in the air.

Much love to both of you.

DELIUS TO PHILIP

May 27th, 1917

I was so glad to receive your letter and learn that you are still in the land of the living . . . I was relieved to hear that your opera scheme is still 'in petto'; the idea is excellent, and perhaps when the war is over I shall come over and join you and Gray in trying to present something really artistically excellent to the English public. It is no good whatever coming with anything half mature and imperfect. But to attain perfection one wants a lot of experience and must work hard and a long time in training entirely new young artists who have not already been spoilt by the old clichés . . . The weakness of the whole English nation is 'amateurism' and inefficiency and old methods. Look how they are running the war; they never seem to wake up to realities.

. . . Don't think that the public is any more rotten now than it ever has been; it was always rotten and there never has been an artistic epoch. . . .

The chief thing for you to do is to develop your own personality to the utmost. Never mind if you make mistakes – we have all made the most stupendous blunders – but keep your soul intact. By soul I mean your real bedrock self: that which you really are and not the trimmings or the adopted.

Because a thing is new it is not necessarily good or bad. Don't
be misled by jargons and mannerisms. There is really only
one quality for great music and that is emotion. Look with
what ease hundreds of young composers are expressing themselves in the 'new idiom' – otherwise the wrong note system.
Hundreds of painters are seeing in cubes, but it all means
nothing more than a fashion, and merely intellectual when at
its best.

You must be living in a lovely spot. I should love to come
over and stay with you – but how to get across the channel
dry! Your descriptions of the country in Cornwall tempts me
mightily. I should just delight in such scenery. I have always
loved the far, wide distance.

It had been Philip's intention to settle in Cornwall for some time,
but during the summer of 1917 a rigorous revisal of all exemptions
from military service took place, in accordance with which
Philip's case automatically came up for reconsideration, and he
received a summons to attend for another medical examination.
In view of his nervous disorder and the unimpeachable medical
certificate he could produce in evidence, there was never the
slightest possibility that he could be called up for active military
service; but rather foolishly, though very characteristically, he
simply decided to ignore the summons altogether, and left Cornwall for Ireland, where he stayed for a full year, until August 1918.

CHAPTER II

IRISH YEAR

The year Philip spent in Ireland was one of the most important in his life, for it was then that he first found himself as a composer. The early songs, as we have already seen, are mostly ineffectual echoes of Delius, and the *Saudades* effectual echoes of van Dieren, but in the music written in his Irish year one finds, firstly, that the derivative elements in his work have been digested, assimilated, and metabolized into an organic style, and secondly, that a genuine personality makes its appearance.

The first work to show this development is the short piece for small orchestra called *An Old Song*. It was originally part of a *Celtic Triad*, together with a *Dirge* and a *Cornish Rhapsody*. These other two, however, no longer survive; they were destroyed some time later. Writing from Ireland to Colin Taylor about this little work he says, 'The tune is Gaelic but the piece, for me, is very much the Cornish moor where I have been living. The tune should emerge, as from afar, chiming in with one's thoughts while walking. The curious way in which it seems to end on the supertonic gives the impression that it fades away into the distance, unfinished. One stands still, attentive to catch another strain, but there is only the gentle murmur of wind – and only fragments remain in the memory, and a mood half contented and half sad.'

The scoring was revised later, preliminary to publication, in 1922, but the alterations are few and unimportant. It is an exquisite little miniature, written for flute, oboe, clarinet, horn, and strings, full of delicate atmosphere and haunting fantasy. Some wit has dubbed it, 'On hearing the second cuckoo in spring', and there is certainly sufficient of the Delian influence to justify the joke. But it is more than a mere pastiche or imitation; one feels a definite personality expressing itself, a trifle uncertainly and hesitatingly perhaps, in the language and vocabulary of the older composer.

I have not been able to identify the fragment of Gaelic melody on which it is ostensibly based, but the question is of little importance seeing that the theme itself, like the plain-song motive in sixteenth-century polyphonic masses, is only the starting-point of a train of thought, and after its appearance near the beginning, on the oboe, does not occur again integrally, but only in half-remembered snatches.

To the same period belong also the earliest published songs: *The Bailey beareth the bell away, My gostly fader, Whenas the rye, Lullaby, As ever I saw, Take, O, take those lips away* (a different setting from that included in the *Saudades*), and many others which he did not see fit to preserve. He was also engaged at this time on an opera in one act, as we shall see from subsequent letters, but whether finished or not it has not survived. The above-mentioned songs, however, are not merely among the best he ever wrote, but works of genuine originality, quite unlike anything else.

During this short period he was also exceptionally active in critical and aesthetic writings. In October, 1917, for example, he sent to Colin Taylor four completed essays of considerable length, out of a projected series of nine, 'The Function of Music', 'Criticism and Creation', 'The Scope of Opera', and 'Intuition and Instruction'. I do not know if the remaining five were completed; they were to be on Delius, van Dieren, the condition of music in England, music as number (in the Leibnizian sense), and on 'the employment of hypnotism for the direct investigation of musical thought-forms'(!). Whether completed or not, however, they were ultimately destroyed together with the earlier four, like so much of his work – music, poetry, prose. It is possible, of course, that much of the material embodied in these essays has survived in a different form in his published writings.

In addition he actually delivered a lecture, with musical illustrations, on 'What Music Is', at the Abbey Theatre in Dublin.

This must indeed have been a strange affair, and I would give a good deal to have been present. Clad in a sumptuous flowing African medicine-man's robe, purple with green facings, and adorned with a large and unruly beard which he had now grown for the first time, he delivered a long, erudite, and fantastic discourse on the whole theory and practice of music from the tenth century to the twentieth. This was succeeded by a group of traditional Irish folk-songs sung by a native singer in the traditional manner, and a group of traditional Indian folk-songs also sung by a native singer in the traditional manner, showing the fundamental similarity which Philip had imagined himself to have perceived, underlying the two traditions. Then an ordinary European singer contributed a song of Schubert in order to demonstrate the difference between the fixed scale of ordinary European music and the fluid scale of the Indian and Irish music, following it up with one or two of Moussorgsky, Delius, and van Dieren. After that Philip himself played some Béla Bartók, and another pianist a Chopin Étude and Scriabin's *Vers la Flamme*. During all this the platform, or stage, was lit with dim green and amber top-lights, with no foot-lights, and the auditorium was plunged in complete darkness. Finally, a peculiar person, with flowing locks and a beard eighteen inches long, called 'The Old Man of the Mountains' – formerly a prosperous commercial traveller who had suddenly turned hermit and had lived seven years of monastic solitude and austerity in a little round house which he had built himself with a domed roof so that the light might reach him at every hour of the day – got up and made a speech exhorting the audience to go out into the mountains and live with the sun and the fairies.

Dublin audiences are presumably more used to that kind of thing than audiences elsewhere, for the famous theatre seems to have been crowded and the audience enthusiastic – though what they can have made of these strange proceedings one cannot conceive.

In spite of all these activities he writes, again to Colin Taylor,

'There are long periods when music recedes quite away from me and I bury myself deeper and deeper in other studies, of necessity.' The nature of these other studies was characteristically extraordinary; firstly, a comprehensive, comparative study of all the various branches of the Celtic languages – Irish, Welsh, Gaelic, Breton, Manx, and Cornish. His notebooks of this period, which still exist, contain copious notes which would fill whole volumes, concerning grammar, syntax, vocabularies, and so on, which testify surprisingly to the exhaustiveness and depth of his studies in this direction. Gaelic and Welsh he never followed far, but he obtained as thorough a knowledge of Irish as any Englishman can hope to do, and was able to read, write and speak it with considerable fluency. This he acquired chiefly during a stay of two months either on Achill or in the Aran Islands – I am not sure which – during which time he did nothing else except study the language. In this connection the following letter to Colin Taylor may be of interest:

> *74 Lower Leeson Street*
> *Dublin*
> April 25th, 1918

. . . For over two months I was away upon an inconceivably desolate island in the west, studying the Celtic languages and Irish in particular – a hard study but one from which I have derived a great deal of profit; the subject is very much more comprehensive and illuminating than it would seem at first sight. Besides which, my visit afforded me a wonderful chance to observe a strange and absolutely foreign people, and their ways of life, which were vastly interesting. But I have never known such barrenness, such utter desolation; it reflects into one's very soul till one becomes chill and numb – such desolate lives in such a desolate region – black wintry weather and the full force of the Atlantic beating, always beating, almost at one's very door. The island was not a mile square, all told, and the greater part of it consisted of bleak, weather-beaten rocks. Yet nearly a hundred souls live on it, scratching the miserable

L

ground here and there, to eke out a meagre living with a few potatoes. My host, the schoolmaster, was a charming person, of great versatility and strange experiences – the very embodiment of enthusiasm – living only for the preservation of the Irish language. He is also a champion bagpiper, and almost taught me to play that wonderful instrument!

But the Celtic language which attracted him above all others was the Cornish, probably because it was entirely extinct, the last person to speak it being one Dolly Pentreath, who died in the eighteenth century. He actually set himself to learn this preposterous tongue, and set a Cornish text to music in one of the best works he wrote during this period – the *Cornish Christmas Carol*, for unaccompanied chorus. There was also a shorter companion piece, likewise set to Cornish words, which he never published, but it still exists in manuscript. An entertaining letter on the subject is one which he wrote me during this time. In explanation it should be said that I was myself then living in Cornwall, at the place mentioned in the letter – Bosigran Castle.

The Cornish language should be revived – nay, is being revived, for am I not myself reviving it? For many most excellent reasons: Bosigran as the mystic centre of a new culture, as in other respects it will be. All neo-Celtic nationalism is in effect anti-national, in the sense in which we detest nationality; it becomes almost an individualizing movement – a separating one, at any rate. What more effective protest against imperialism (in art as in other matters) could you or I make than by adopting, as a pure ritual, a speech, a nationality, that no longer exist – for you to make your dwelling the centre of a Celtic rebirth – the rebirth of a something that never was born? This truly is to become a naturalized Mazagan. Besides, at no far distant date, you are going to make a pilgrimage with me to Carnac, where to speak French were a blasphemy. I have a great deal to say on this surprising topic; these hints, as all ill-considered hints do, convey almost a contrary meaning. But to have a private language! What a luxury!

It was a luxury, however, that I was able to deny myself, by dint of exercising stern self-control. In any case, I hardly saw myself in the role of the creator of the 'mystic centre of a new culture', 'the centre of a Celtic re-birth'. I have imagined many strange things in my time: never quite that.

In all this, as in so much else, it may perhaps seem difficult to decide whether Philip was serious, or simply deliberately playing the fool. Personally I feel that here, for example, he was neither wholly the one nor the other. It was part of the fascination of his personality, indeed, that while he was often sublime and often ridiculous, sometimes consciously and sometimes unconsciously, he had also the curious faculty of being able to balance himself, like a tightrope walker, upon that narrow, precarious razor-edge which proverbially divides the one from the other. One half of him, I am convinced, firmly believed in these fantastic notions; the other half was able to see the absurdity of them just as well as anyone else. From the combination of the two he was able to achieve this half-mocking, half-serious, ironical attitude of mind which was so characteristic of him.

His other chief preoccupation apart from music at this time was the study of the occult, and a large number of his notebooks belonging to this period are filled with extracts from and comments upon works dealing with every aspect of the subject, from the most highly scientific and elaborately technical aspects of astrology to the method of divination by means of the tarot, and from the purely philosophic and theoretical side of magic, as found in the writings of Eliphas Levi, down to its actual practice according to the formulas, rituals, and incantations contained in such works as *The Book of Abramelin the Mage* and the writings of Cornelius Agrippa.

From these activities Philip undoubtedly suffered certain psychological injuries from which, in my opinion, he never entirely recovered, and in saying this it is not necessary to subscribe to any definite belief in the objective reality of the phenomena with which the occult sciences profess to concern themselves.

Suppose, for example, that one were to make use of a certain magical formula, believing implicitly in its efficacy, in order to attain an end which one believes to be unattainable otherwise, one's power of attaining that end is automatically increased to such an extent that one will, almost inevitably, attain it – provided that it is within the bounds of human possibility. And if that is not magic in theory it is in practice as near the real thing as makes no difference. Call it auto-suggestion if you like, but the fact that you are able to achieve by this means something which you would not otherwise be able to achieve clearly demonstrates its practical efficacy. The whole thing, in fact, depends on the faith and belief you bring to it; the formula made use of is in itself nothing, as even the most convinced occultist would willingly concede. And there is no doubt whatever that at this time, and for some time after, perhaps always, Philip was an ardent believer in the objective reality of the phenomena of the magical arts, and that he practised them assiduously during this period of his life.

In this connection a document found among his papers at his death is of great interest. It is a horoscope, cast for him by an adept in the art, in 1917 I should say from internal evidence. I quote the more salient passages. 'There are two things that strike one very forcibly in looking at your horoscope; the first is the overwhelming number of planets in the seventh house (unions, partnerships), and the other is the strength of Mars, for he is ruler rising in his own sign, and he rules also Scorpio, the sign occupying the seventh house by intersection. You have Aries rising, and this is the sign of the Pioneer. You like a good fight, particularly a battle of brains, and you don't care how many difficulties you find in your path, you charge straight at them and rather enjoy it all. You are neither shy nor pessimistic; you have a happy knack of forgetting any failures you may experience, and you carry through your undertakings with a confidence, dash and brilliancy that disarm criticism. You are enthusiastic and warm-hearted in your friendships almost to a point of rashness. You like a change of surroundings and acquaintances; in fact you like to dash about over the face of the world, here to-day, and goodness knows where to-morrow. Mars your ruler is in the twelfth house and is in opposition to Saturn. This is the fundamental basis of a Satanic influence. The conjunction (exact) of Venus and Saturn in the seventh house shows that the Satanic influence is interwoven with a Venus or love motive, that the two are inseparable, and that this was put into action early in 1916 or late in 1915 by the passage of the progressed Sun over the position of Venus and Saturn. In August, 1916, this influence would be at its height, then subside to revive even stronger this present year when Venus progresses over the same conjunction. Many planets in a house tend to accentuate that house, so much of your present life will revolve about the question of partnerships and associations with others. You will be a determined lover, difficult to turn aside in your affections and desires. A mental awakening in 1911 was the result of Mercury (the planet of intellect) measuring by primary directions to the ascendant at about that date. You naturally have an active mind and a good memory. You can be sarcastic when roused by any injustice, and you have a ready wit. Your Sun (representing the individuality) is also in Scorpio. This makes you very determined, gives you great magnetic power, and critical perception. Scorpio is a sign of extremes; its sons are either saints or sinners – they never do anything by halves. The conjunction of the Sun and Venus gives you a love of art and refinement. The trine with Jupiter gives you abundant vitality and you will need it all with your Scorpio accentuation. The nerves are inclined to be very tensely constituted. You are liable to meet with some danger in connection with electricity, so keep this in mind. You are at times pessimistic but this does not last for long. It is usually caused by a transit of the Moon over the position of Saturn radical. You can easily watch this in the ephemeric for the current year. When the Moon is in the 29th degree of Libra (which it is every month) you will feel the Saturnine influence. Watch: April 15th in the afternoon, May 12th (1918) in the afternoon, and see what I mean. Your Moon (or personality) is in the sign of Sagittarius.

This makes you often at loggerheads with convention. It also gives a gift of prophecy and a fondness for dual experiences. Neptune is in Gemini, and this is a good position for developing occult or inspirational faculties. It is the signature of genius in many directions, but it makes you restless, and makes it difficult for you to concentrate on one thing for a great length of time. You will be good at mathematics, and will succeed in any field of endeavour where mental ingenuity is essential. To make this Gemini influence even stronger, you have now progressed into, that double-bodied sign. You will have an irresistible impulse to do at least two things at the same time and, what is more extra-ordinary still, you will succeed in doing them.'

If one strips this of its technical jargon, and makes due allow-ances for a certain naivety of expression, the psychological portrait here presented is astonishingly accurate in almost every respect, and the tentative predictions were, generally speaking, fulfilled. But here again the vast and incalculable element of faith enters into the question. If you implicitly believe in the infallibility of a horoscope you will inevitably and insensibly allow yourself to be influenced by it into fulfilling its conditions and predictions. Nothing, in fact, is more certain than that if you sit down on the afternoon of April 15th or May 12th, expecting to feel a Saturnine influence, you certainly will feel it; if you implicitly believe that there is something in your fate that makes it difficult for you to concentrate on one thing for a great length of time, the conse-quences are obvious – you will not be able to, but probably only because you will not try. Finally, if you believe implicitly that there is a Satanic influence connected with your sexual life, one shudders to contemplate the possibilities that this might bring in its train. The fact that the horoscope proved indisputably accurate on these two last major issues only raises the question whether the horoscope was a faithful mirror of Philip's personality and destiny, or whether to a certain extent at least he acquiesced unconsciously in what he believed to be true, and therefore inevitable. Personally, I believe that the former is the correct explanation, namely, that the horoscope constitutes a remarkable example of accurate divination,[1] but it would be a great mistake to minimize the extent to which Philip may have responded to its suggestions, and acquiesced in what was not necessarily inevitable.

In the horoscope quoted above reference is made to Philip's possession of a certain degree of occult power, and I can certainly testify to his power of divination by means of the tarot. On many occasions, indeed, I have known his predictions to be verified with quite uncanny accuracy, and I could quote several definite instances of this were it not that such things, however interesting in actual life, make very dull reading to those not personally concerned. In the actual practice of magic, on the other hand, he was spectacularly unsuccessful: not in the sense that he obtained no results as that the results he did obtain were so disastrous and catastrophic. A hint of this is conveyed in the following letter to Robert Nichols:

PHILIP TO ROBERT NICHOLS

Ireland
Dec. 14th, 1917

I break a long silence, but save for yourself and perhaps two others let it remain unbroken. I am dead to all the old environment – don't dig me up. . . .

I wrote you an idiotic letter some four months ago – believe it or not as you like, I was suffering from the reaction that inevitably overtakes those who tamper prematurely with the science vulgarly known as Black Magic. But a new environment has, I think, quite cured me; it is always good for one to dwell, periodically, in a quite quite foreign country, as this is.

Did you read D. H. Lawrence's recent essays in the *English Review*? At my instigation one of the partners of a big publishing firm here has secured the MS. of the whole book

[1] Even down to such a detail as 'danger in connection with electricity' – see, for example, the anecdote recounted by Mr. John in his Foreword.

from which they were taken – and it is, in my opinion, as also in his, the supreme utterance of all modern philosophy – This is a big phrase but it is impossible to exaggerate the book's importance. Lawrence can't get it published in England (of course not) and the other partners of the firm here are commercialists and bigoted Catholics who'll find it unintelligible and 'shocking' respectively. But we must get it printed and we want to make a big thing of it – that is, advertise it very extensively and work up all the excitement that a work of the prophet Ezekiel *redivivus* would arouse – 'for behold, a greater than Ezekiel is here!' I have suggested that several well-known people – writers and others – who know Lawrence and know the value of his work, should write letters to the firm expressing a hope that the work be speedily published, and pointing out the credit that will ultimately reflect upon the firm that is enterprising enough to take it.

. . . If you have my Eliphas Levi still, you might send it over to me. A great book, isn't it?

. . . I've found an ideal subject (and on an almost ready-made text too) for an opera, on the old Irish legend of 'Liadain and Curither'. I'm beginning work with great enthusiasm.

We see from this letter, incidentally, that in spite of personal differences in the past which, so far as he himself was concerned, had been composed, his admiration for Lawrence's work and his anxiety to be of service to him in any possible way, were unimpaired. The book in question was called *The Reality of Peace*. I remember well reading it in manuscript but it has never, so far as I am aware, been published. I do not know whether it still exists or whether Lawrence eventually destroyed it. Philip, I think, grossly overrated it as a contribution to philosophy – Lawrence was assuredly no thinker – but the sumptuous and impassioned prose in which it was written might well have turned a stronger critical head than his. However that may be, the fact remains that while Philip was thus altruistically busying himself in the capacity of literary agent to Lawrence, the latter was putting the finishing touches to his novel *Women in Love*, in which, as I have said already, there occurs a particularly venomous and offensive caricature of Philip. More than that, it appears from the dates given by Mrs. Carswell in her *Savage Pilgrimage*, the accuracy of which I have no reason to doubt ('Lawrence had now [July] finished *Women in Love*, all but the title and epilogue chapter') that he was actually engaged in writing his disgusting libel while ostensibly on the most friendly terms with Philip, and seeing him practically every day, during the spring and early summer months of 1917 at Zennor.

Here follows a series of interesting letters belonging to this Irish year, written to Delius, Colin Taylor, and myself:

PHILIP TO COLIN TAYLOR

28 Upper Fitzwilliam St.
Dublin
June 13th, 1918

I am grieved to hear that you have been ill, and labouring again in the toils of the fiend dejection – for this fiend is really more deadly than real physical illness – how well I know him too! He has treated me lately to a much longer spell of his society than I had any wish for. I think there are few influences more wearing than his: the inactivity, the consciousness of being void and sterile that he inflicts upon one, these things and the dark, brooding thoughts they engender are more dangerous than many diseases – more tormenting, even.

. . . As for me, I cannot write a note of music. I am utterly desiccated; I shall have to shut up entirely for a good while in this department, though I have a good deal to do in others . . . I have no illusions about the value of such little works as I have already done; and I do know that the work I hope to do some day will be of such a very different nature that I would rather preserve absolute silence towards the world at large until I feel myself ripe for a real achievement . . . The little orchestral fragment which you have does not displease me except in so far as it remains a solitary fragment in a heap of ruins; it is too frail to stand alone and it is impossible to companion it. I do not really believe in this tenuous kind of art; when one is really ripe, all is superabundant. At present I like the second of the Cornish carols, but it would prove a stumbling-block to most choirs and chorus-masters who imagine there is a thing-in-itself called 'choral technique', fixed and inviolable, and are always talking of what will or will not 'come off' – that which will not do so being anything that presents any kind of new difficulty to be overcome. The policy of extenuated laziness is almost universal among choral societies; and, furthermore, they would raise imaginary difficulties in the matter of singing in Cornish – though it is just as easy to sing one set of sounds as another, provided they are clearly and phonetically transcribed. The music of these carols is inseparably associated with the actual Cornish words; any translation would pervert the whole character of the works. A limited language like the Cornish has a very particular connotation, as a pure language-idea apart from what is said – and this language-idea had a large share in the conception of the music. A literal translation might be supplied – not to be sung, however – but the actual sense of the words, rendered in English, does not materially differ from that of many other carols.

Incidentally, within two months of writing thus, that 'I cannot write a note of music – I am utterly desiccated,' etc., there is another letter to the same correspondent in which he says, 'I have written ten songs in the last fortnight'.

PHILIP TO COLIN TAYLOR

July 19th, 1918

. . . Do tell me if you like the second Cornish carol; I should be greatly interested in your view of it. It seems to me a very simple and unpuzzling composition, but I sent it to Balfour Gardiner and he seemed to think it was a kind of essay in the style of the 16th century. I was flabbergasted: Is there anything 16th centuryish about it: and first of all what is 16th centuryishness in music? I suspect always the people who speak of music by century labels, and one knows that when they come to the 20th century they would explain themselves by adding: 'Oh, like Debussy and Strauss, you know the kind of thing'. – And, incidentally what is style? Is there any such thing? For myself, I am convinced that, as such, style does not exist, it simply does not exist, save as a disembodied fetish in the minds of people who, having no ideas of their own, imagine that they can strike them, like sparks, off this said fetish. 'Technique' is its twin-brother fetish. One knows that Monteverde proceeded from the chord of the dominant seventh to that of the tonic; one knows that Handel did too, and even a few others – why Strauss himself has done it! But what essential similarity in the various composers does this stupendous fact bear witness to. Oh, Lord, what a lot of work there is for a good pair of bellows!

P.S. The fungus is cultivated for a purely talismanic purpose; as such it works, and this is more important to me than mere appearance. I can't help what I look like, and after all I haven't got such a jaw to boast of! But quite seriously, it does have a certain psychological effect on me; and seeing that now for nearly ten years all my best strength and energy has been used up negatively in keeping out the tide of the world which wants to swamp me and prevent me from doing the only kind of work I can do with any success (and, just now, more than ever, everything is against me, and more than ever I want my whole time and strength for my work) – in view of this fact, it is necessary for me to make use of any little magical energy-saving devices that suggest themselves – and this is one of them.

The 'fungus' alluded to in the postscript is, of course, the beard, which he had now grown for the first time. The explanation he gives for its adoption is extraordinarily revealing and, indeed, of crucial importance to an understanding of the man; it is, in fact, the first decisive step towards the assumption of the elaborate mask which he was ultimately destined to adopt permanently, as a defence against a hostile world.

BOUVARD AND PÉCUCHET

PHILIP TO COLIN TAYLOR

August 9th, 1918

. . . It is not the mere neglect or negation of art that is art's worst enemy; it is as Blake said 'a pretence of art' that destroys art. This is the monster we are out to slay – the perversion of the very function of art. Art being the means of communicating spiritual realities to the world of material semblances, it is obvious that in a materialistic world-conception it can have no place and no function, seeing that to the materialist there is no realm of the spirit; matter is the real and the things of the spirit mere illusion. This at least would be the consistent attitude involving the complete negation of art, complete unconcern with it. It would not prevent house decorators from handling paint-brushes nor restaurant orchestras from assisting the diners' digestive organs; these and kindred things would also be perfectly consistent so long as their real purpose was kept in view and understood. It is when this true purpose is forgotten, when such things as these are done in the name of art, in the name of a spiritual principle of which they are themselves the embodied refutation, that the supreme blasphemy takes place, that – relatively speaking – evil arises, for even when we have overcome the initial duality of apparent values we still find discordant elements wherever there is an unbalanced conflict of absolutely opposed forces – unbalanced in the sense of causing a kind of reversed polarity, as though something were artificially arrested in its course and turned back upon its own path.

The spirit of the present era is materialism; it is everywhere rampant and, despite all seeming contradictions, as yet still dominant everywhere. It is a necessary phase for humanity to pass through. Materialism negates the things of the spirit, denies to such an extent that it is driven in the end to what practically amounts to a denial even of itself – for it is only through realization of its own essential non-existence in any absolute sense that it can cease to obsess the mind of humanity and dwindle to the nothingness from which the new light of the spirit will shine forth. The fact is that humanity's interest in things purely material has very quickly exhausted itself, the material world being particularly limited and narrow compared with the potentialities of the human soul. Hence universal boredom supervenes which nothing can relieve save sensationalism, a series of sensations each more startling and violent than the last. Humanity in the cage of materialism is like a child with a toy of which the normal interest has long been exhausted. In desperation he tries what can be done with the toy upside down, whether any fresh possibilities are revealed by turning it inside out; finally there is nothing left but to smash it to bits – Look round the world to-day: what is there but sensationalism, a frantic beating of the bars of a cage in silly disregard of the open door that lies behind . . . All is sensation, a frenzied effort of despair in the darkness. The inevitable outcome is universal death – for death is the last and greatest of all possible sensations. This is the real truth about the war.

. . . The extremist embodiments of any tendency usually wear the masks of their opposites, so cleverly sometimes 'as to deceive, if it be possible, the elect'. Thus it is among the Church Christians that we find the most complete materialists, and in the ranks of the 'atheists' we discover the rare surviving examples of true Christians.

. . . Music has nothing to fear from the Chappells, the Francis Days and Hunters and the music halls; there may be opposition but there is no confusion, that is the point; opposition is an ordered relation and thus in the higher sense essential harmony, confusion is chaos and discord.

PHILIP TO DELIUS

Dublin
May 15th, 1918

You will have thought this long year's silence very strange – some day I will explain it altogether. At present I can only tell you that I have passed through a year of dark and critical vicissitudes, metamorphoses of various kinds, follies and their consequences, from which I am only now fully extricating myself – and something, perhaps shame of my own stupidity, has kept me from writing you about these things, for you are never long out of my thoughts and I have time and again begun a letter to you and continued it at great length only to destroy it. But for years my letters to you have been too full of petty personal complaints, for all the world as if you were some old father-confessor priest in an ecclesiastical rabbit-hutch! Now, however, the skies are clearer, and I am no longer tempted to dilate upon the mere circumstances that have lately hedged me round – after all, one is always *free* the moment one ceases to *imagine* one's difficulties!

. . . I suppose, in view of the rigidity of the censorship, it is still necessary to act upon the old Greek adage which, though literally meaning 'Speak only words of good omen', resulted in enjoining complete silence, owing to the immense difficulty of complying with it! Nowadays one never knows what innocently intended remark may not get one's letter consigned to the official waste-paper basket, and one's name to the official black list, so it will be best perhaps to stick to music altogether in this correspondence.

In your last letter – almost exactly a year ago – I remember you detailed a long list of new compositions, and I envied, as I do still, the tranquillity of mind that enabled you to work on steadily amid the turmoil of the world, producing even more prolifically than in the old days of calm and quiet. How I long to know these new works! I have neither heard or seen any work of yours since the *String Quartet* was raped by that lecherous party of players in London – the *'Cello Sonata*, *Violin Concerto*, *Dance Rhapsody*, *Once upon a Time*,[1] the *Requiem* and the wordless choruses – all these will be new to me. And I suppose there is no chance of my seeing them for some time to come. I feel that I shall like *Once upon a Time* best – the title sets one dreaming, and all your loveliest music comes from the once-upon-a-time mood, I think!

I have not been in London for nearly a year, and have heard no music whatsoever – a great blessing, when one considers the utter poverty of nearly all the music one hears to-day. Most

[1] Eventually called *Eventyr*.

modern art is what Blake called 'A pretence of Art to destroy
Art' – for where there is no art the great man, when he comes,
will be reverenced; it is only where there is abundance of bad
art that he is despised and rejected. For this reason I distrust
all this frenzied awakening of so-called artistic interests in the
world at present; the first principles of art have been lost sight
of, and the herd is fantastically chasing something of whose very
nature it is entirely ignorant . . . I have not written much
music during the past year – a few small works which are, I
know, immeasurably better than the very paltry productions
I have sent you from time to time – but I am still in only a
very experimental stage, and do not expect to do anything of
real significance for another seven years. If I cannot come
forward before the world with something I know to be better
than anything of any of my contemporaries, I will not come
forward at all – and, good heavens, one hasn't much to eclipse,
anyway! At present there is only Bernard van Dieren who can
even share the name of composer with you; Béla Bartók has
done some very fine small works, but I have seen nothing of his
that is less than ten years old. I hope the war has left him
unscathed; he might become a very great man. But who else
is there? Schönberg still shows a cold, white light, but he will
never escape from the toils of his self-imposed originality – I
cannot think of a single other name that does not seem to belong
to a barrel-organ grinder or his performing monkey rather than
to a composer. Van Dieren, however, is a man of miraculous
genius for whose music my love and enthusiasm grows by what
it feeds on.

. . . It is wonderful how much more clearly one can think
about music when one is right away from it than one possibly
can do when in the whirl of a concert-season. I have done a
great deal of work at the philosophy and history of music while
I have been in this country. The wilderness is the best place
for meditation, and I have spent a considerable time in the
most desolate and solitary region of the West coast. I believe
it is so necessary to be sure of one's first general principles
before proceeding to formulate any ideas about particular
examples in art that I have spent most of my time lately in

attacking the most comprehensive question of all, in music – namely, *What Music is* – in all its aspects; and I really feel I have arrived at results which – at any rate as a beginning of new discoveries – are of some value. Last Sunday evening I made my first public appearance and gave a lecture at the Abbey Theatre, taking simply 'What Music is', as my title. It was certainly of a startling and revolutionary nature, but it was listened to with attention and even enthusiasm by an audience of nearly five hundred, which was encouraging for a first attempt.

DELIUS TO PHILIP

May 19th, 1918

I need not say how welcome your letter was; I was beginning to have serious misgivings about you and was splitting my brains to imagine what could be the matter. It would interest me enormously to hear all about your experiences and troubles, as I can assure you that there is no one who takes such an interest in you or is as fond of you as I am. So you have been in the wilderness – a wonderful place – and the only place to find oneself after a prolonged sojourn in towns; one gathers such a lot of dross that ultimately it smothers one's real self. I was also in the wilderness in Florida, and have since never been able to live long in a crowd. I was immensely glad to hear that you are writing music, and also that you had lectured in Dublin. What you say about art is so true: where there is no art whatever there is a chance for an original artist, but none where there are crowds of mediocre thrusters. This general interest in Art is deadly – example, America. In England it is not really so bad as there is very little interest in art.

. . . You know my opinion on contemporary music. For me music is very simple: it is the expression of a poetic and emotional nature. Most musicians by the time they are able to express themselves manage to get rid of most of their poetry and all their emotions. The dross of Technic has killed it; or they seize upon one little original streak, and it forthwith develops into an intolerable mannerism – Debussy and Ravel.

I am seriously thinking of going to New York in the autumn to have my new works produced, and then go to California until the war is finished. Will you come with me? – seriously. You might lecture on music; you will find a better public than in London. I want also the *Requiem* produced; I don't think I have ever done better than this . . . Do write soon and tell me all your troubles, and don't keep your friend again so long without news.

PHILIP TO DELIUS

Dublin
June 19th, 1918

It was a very great joy to me to receive a letter from you again; there is nothing in the world I prize so much as your sympathy and interest and kind thoughts for me, without the help of which, I need hardly repeat, I should never have emerged as far as I have out of the Cimmerian darkness which for most of our race constitutes life! How gladly would I confide everything about myself to you if we could but meet again for a short while! But these personal difficulties, these psychological complexities are so difficult to set down on paper with any degree of coherence and intelligibility; and although I think I may thank heaven that I have at last managed to extricate myself from the particular network of complications to which I referred, I am still too near to the old circumstances to be able to write about them with that complete detachment which alone could frame them into a consistent narrative. And, as I said in my last letter, I think it is better to confine oneself in one's correspondence at present to matters musical, or at least to things remote from the filthiness of the world at large. I should dearly love to come with you to America; indeed, were it possible, there is nothing that would be at once more delightful and beneficial also to me than to make this trip, but alas, I fear it would be impossible for me to obtain a passport despite the fact that I am completely useless for military purposes. The atmosphere of these islands becomes more and more stifling and putrescent to anyone who cares for art above all things. To get away altogether, to be with you, to be able to hear and study your new works and to be able to carry on my own work, writing and lecturing, in surroundings which gave it a chance of having some influence – this would indeed be joy and a new impulse of life to me. Oh, what a curse has fallen on the world – and when will it be removed?

. . . It is the musical profession that is always the greatest enemy of music, chiefly because, in listening to music, they cannot view it as pure utterance, pure expression: they regard as real the purely verbal, and so – in cases of true expression – non-existent, differentiation between the thing expressed and the mode of expression, with the result that instead of giving their attention to what is being expressed, they concentrate always on the manner – the 'how' – and thus is perpetuated the dismal superstition that technique, as a separate entity, exists as a thing apart from expression. It is this fallacy that lies at the root of all the rottenness of modern music. It is responsible for the prevailing view of music as mere sound-for-sound's-sake – a kind of aural equivalent of sweet scents, and it is to this fallacy also that one must attribute the fact that certain sounds have come to be regarded as 'beautiful' and 'ugly' in themselves, quite without reference to their context or to what they are used to express; and so we have arrived – so far as the musical trade-unions are concerned – at a kind of static musical diction which one may fitly compare with the formal 'poetic diction' of the eighteenth century – a tyranny which was only destroyed after a long and bitter struggle by Wordsworth, Coleridge, Keats and the rest. To us of to-day it seems incredible that the general appreciation of these poets was impeded by an obstacle of so ludicrous a nature. But it has always been so – in poetry, music and painting: almost every great manifestation in art has had to be forced upon the public like a disagreeable medicine, against their will – I say their will, but what will of their own have they? They have surrendered it long ago to the hypnotic influence of the 'recognized profession'.

PHILIP TO DELIUS

Dublin
July 22nd, 1918

. . . I cannot tell whether we shall meet in England or not, but I think you know me well enough to understand that it will not be through lack of effort on my part if we do not. You can imagine how hungry I am for a talk with you after three long years. But there are considerable difficulties in the way of travelling and, quite literally, if I were to set out with the strongest will in the world to see you, I might still never reach my destination. It exasperates and maddens me that one's life is circumscribed with so many petty and idiotic restrictions in these evil times. For ten years now all my best strength and energy has been dissipated by the mere effort required, in these islands, to keep the flood of national bilge-water from surging in upon me and engulfing me completely; and when one bungs up one hole, it begins at once pouring in from another quite unexpected quarter. Just now, when I am bursting with fresh schemes and enthusiasms after my long sojourn in the wilderness (for artistically the whole of this island is a wilderness) there is no outlet for them or for any activity on my part. However, you may be sure that if it is anywhere within the bounds of physical possibility I shall come and see you at all costs: and I am longing for a sight of your new works also – there are so many now that I know nothing of. The past three years have been a real nightmare to me – not, perhaps, unbroken by flashes of light which, added together, do no doubt mean real progress, yet for their very brilliance the general gloom has only seemed afterwards to deepen and grow more intense. I have sunk to the very lowest depths, stuck fast in the mire and only lately realized, when on the very point of being wholly submerged, the supreme necessity of getting out of it even if I left my own skin behind – of throwing over the whole wretched past at all costs; and this, thank heaven, I think I have now succeeded in doing once and for all, though perhaps the costs are not all paid yet. Still, I believe in Destiny: one does what one does because one is what one is – and it is often necessary for the general plan of one's existence that one should have the most apparently absurd and profitless experiences. I have long ceased to imagine that anything one does has any connection with praise or blame, intrinsically, save in the minds of fools. You may hear all kinds of unpleasant things about me in England, but I know you are too good a friend to listen to these things before you have heard the whole truth from myself – for nobody else knows the whole truth. I have my sojourn in the wilderness to thank for the impulse that finally extricated me from the morass . . . and no two experiences in the wilderness are the same. . . .

How one grumbles and moans over circumstances and yet how little they really matter! After such a little while one is roaring with laughter over things that one formerly wept about. If only one has the courage to make no compromises and to be ready at any moment to chuck anything and everything that becomes a nuisance overboard, then not much harm can happen to one. And it is surprising, after a little practice at clearing the decks, what strength and dexterity one acquires in the art of throwing overboard one's lumber – people, things, ideas, superstitions, fears, fetishes – the whole cargo, lastly perhaps the old creaking ship itself! then one develops wings! But enough of this: and by the powers of Kether, Chokmah, Binah, Gedulah, Geburah, Tiphereth, Netzach, Hod, Jesod and Malkuth, I swear that it will not be my fault if we are not talking face to face, if not pacing the moors together, before many weeks have passed.

The following letters to myself are undated, but they all belong to approximately the same period – the spring and summer of 1918:

This morning has nullified months of monstrous imaginings; I cannot tell you what real joy I had at seeing your hand again – for I thought that my extreme madness had passed the limits of even your toleration and understanding, as in clear retrospect it passes utterly my own. I'm not equal to writing another word

— on this subject at present – and you will not misconstrue my reticence I think. . . . It is strange and satisfactory how, when one is abruptly cut off from an old life or an old surrounding, and a definite gulf, of sickness or madness, is set between present and past, all things fall away and all persons, into utter nothingness, save two or three persons and one or two things – and these emerge, clearer and clearer lights, in relief as the darkness grows deeper – but I have become mistrustful of words and will say no more lest I seem to repeat an old cycle and provoke your mirth.

Lawrence has written a stupendous book – for me it is one of the greatest utterances – and utterance is a big word to use of a modern; but Lawrence has become the mouthpiece of someone incredibly great. The real authors are, no doubt, in eternity. The book will be published here, to the glory of God and the honour of Eirinn.

I wish you would come over here for a short while . . . I have met a hermit in the mountains who, though he has never delivered himself on paper or platform, is a far greater man (than Æ) – living without money in a round domed house, symbol of the cosmos, and thinking thoughts in the dark mist like Synge's tramp.

I have been thinking for some time past of migrating to an Irish-speaking district but always when I make plans for departure I am detained by a silly mania for writing more music – very little comes of it, but it is insistent. I have begun to sketch an opera, which is practically a monodrama, on the tale of Liadain and Curither – a lovely subject, wholly admirable for music, with an almost ready-made libretto.

I have quite definitely decided to have an opera season here at an early date; a good deal of the money is practically assured already. . . . I believe this country is ripe for music; in utter contradistinction to England it is spiritually alive – intensely alive – and I think one feels this unconsciously from the first moment when one is struck by its intense foreignness to England – I think that is the true solution of its foreign-ness . . . Irish music has never emerged from the melodic stage – the plain-chant in the churches, the fiddle and bagpipe elsewhere;

on this account I believe one would have little or no 'harmonic prejudice' (this for lack of an adequate phrase) to contend with. (I was much interested the other day to hear an Irish folk-song and Gregorian enthusiast describing a performance of Schön-berg's five orchestral pieces to which he had evidently listened with a comprehensive alertness of mind quite impossible to an English musician – not that this man is a 'musician' – thank God I have met none here save a pleasant bagpiper.) The narrative ballad – sometimes running to fifty or sixty verses – is a great institution in Ireland; and, when you consider the matter broadly, you will see many points of similarity between the narrative ballad and opera as we should give it them – chief of which is the engaging of the imagination of the hearers so that it pictures fully all that mere words, in a ballad, can but briefly suggest.

. . . A few nights ago I met W. B. Yeats and his wife. . . . He talked for several hours about the moon, and the talk was as illuminating and beautiful as the moon of the fourteenth night itself. He is taking up the story of Michael Robartes again – you will remember this character in the wonderful tale *Rosa Alchemica* and in *Ego Dominus Tuus*, and preparing a study of the varying manifestations of the Spirit in Art seen in the light of a new and strange symbology (new to the West, that is) springing from the twenty-eight phases of the moon. . . . Do you know, by the way, his brother's pictures of life in the West of Ireland? They are very remarkable, very far removed from the spirit of W.B., at once real and utterly fantastic. If you have it not, I will send you his picture book for a birthday present – you still have a birthday, I think? Plotinus would never tell anyone when his birthday occurred, deeming it a folly to commemorate so trumpery an occasion as the mere entry of the soul into the mortal husk, but that was perhaps carrying philosophy a little too far. It would, in my opinion, be a pity to let slip by un-noticed this festive occasion, if so be that the soul-stirring beer which we quaffed together one memorable day at the sign of King William the Fourth in Madron is still procurable . . . You are seventy-times-seven times blessed in being able to see spring in Penwith. I have no memories from all my life so wonderful and so pregnant as of those first months I spent there last year; and although for the hideous blasphemy and profanation of my last visit the Spirits of the Earth and Air justly banished me from their domains, it will be an unending sorrow on me if I may never return, contrite, to do them my penance and receive their absolution. It is a strange thing, and a thing you will mock at, but a thing that I know very certainly, that for the last twelve months my life has been in the hands of elemental spirits – and if they have not actually been the controlling powers, they have at least been the instruments of a higher agency. On this hypothesis alone are certain events explicable in that positive manner that transcends mere ratiocination. Some day I shall write an exhaustive analysis of their operations; and perhaps after all you will not laugh, for did you not, once at least, speak with their voice when you caught the smell of the moon, and the cuckoo shouted at us, a strange definite message, out of the thicket in the marsh, although night had long fallen . . . *Errabant taciti per amica silentia lunae* . . . What am I to say now and why say anything at all, why write letters, impotent and inarticulate, weakly endeavouring to express something in particular (which is only some silly illusory aspect of nothing at all, in all probability) instead of launching on a floodtide – as though by accident, or if you like, instinct – the supreme generality which can only be conveyed by hints that are as far as possible from the point? – This method is very tedious, that however is pure joy.

Lord, answer prayer!

I am writing with great enthusiasm two Cornish hymns; it is probably the first time the old language has ever been musicked deliberately (assuming that the folk-songs – of which Cornwall seems to possess practically none – generated spontaneously) but it is wonderful for singing purposes, containing many sounds almost unknown in English (except in Cornish-English dialect) which have a real musical value of their own. The hymns, which are set for *a cappella* chorus, bear no resemblance to the clotted and sepulchral works of which I was guilty some eighteen months ago, being for the most part *vierstimmige* – as

are also certain songs with string quartet, not so wholly unsatisfactory as not to give me an irritating sense of what might
be achieved under decent conditions. But here, for one week
when composition is possible, there are ten wherein it is out of
the question and at least one nightmare of a week when it does
not seem worth while. Perhaps the just critic in you will approve
the nightmare . . . I have lately made a great many experiments with Celtic tunes without approaching a solution of the
problem of their adequate – I had almost said legitimate –
treatment. As far as I can see at present, it is unsatisfactory to
use more than fragmentary quotations from them in a composition; they do not seem suitable as 'themes' for treatment – they
are somehow too proud as well as too perfect, complete, and
rounded for that. But on the other hand, any attempt to
make little works which coincide with the structure of the
melody – extending nothing, curtailing nothing – formally
analogous in method to Grieg with his Norse tunes and Bartók
with the Hungarian – seems foredoomed to failure. There
seems to be nothing between the reticence of, for example,
Moffat's *Minstrelsy of the Highlands* (an admirable collection of
songs, as such, with Gaelic texts) and the lamentable arch-
pelican methods of Mr. Boughton and others . . . I myself
wrote a piece on the *Seagull of the Land-under-Wave* which was so
bad that I could never play it in the fading light without
exuding brine most copiously! One thinks one is hypercritical
as regards one's self, but relax the screw only a little and, Oh
Lord, the things that come out! I finally presented the *Seagull*
and a number of other pieces to Colin Taylor to move the
bowels of the old ladies of Newhaven with. He did; and his
own also. . . . If it is a sin to profane the scriptures, it is still
worse to profane what never ought to have been written down
at all – for it is only decadence that justifies or even renders
necessary the pencil and notebook as adjuncts to the ear and
the understanding. And oh, how miserably we have gone
astray! Irish folk-music is a glaring and horrible example.
Take up Petrie or any of the big notated collections – it is like
wading through a bog. It is not until one hears a native speaker
of the Irish language sing that one realizes that all Irish music

(except the imbecile reels and jigs) is simply an exaltation of Irish speech – only that and nothing more. The sounds of the language – of the spoken language (and there are, I believe, 41 primary sounds as against 29 in English) form such an integral part of the music that a tune in the abstract is nothing but a corpse, and a decayed one at that. A notated Irish tune bears much the same relation to Irish music as a phonetician's graph of the rise and fall of a voice bears to a rich dialect speech. And it is very curious to note how, in listening to an Irish singer, one is reminded, not even vaguely of any other European folk-music – to judge, if one may, from a musical standpoint for a moment – but, vividly, of an Eastern singer, Indian or Persian. And there are, I believe, quite fundamental analogies between Ireland and the East in this respect. I do not know if they have ever been worked out – I very much doubt it, but they offer a wide and profitable field for speculation.

. . . Do let us hear from you; a letter comes as a boon and a blessing to me from you at all times, and especially now when life is more than usually stagnant and depressing. . . . I would say, 'Give my love to Lawrence and Frieda' if I did not anticipate too clearly that he would fling it back at you; and oh, how horrible it is to be bespattered with flung love!

May 30th, 1918

Interrogatum est a Prosdocimo: – 'Ubi est ILLE Timpany?' Et responsum est, non sine cachinno: – 'Scilicet ventriloquitur pro imagine quadam!'
(Thus the oracle: and now Prosdocimus himself takes his pen in hand while I, in duly chastened mood, watch, without power to restrain, the rushing in of this obscene, irreverent pachyderm. But – (finger to nose) – 'You must not mind Prosdocimus – he is somewhat peculiar'. With which Apologia I yield him now carteblanche.')

Your letter brought me a double meed of pleasure inasmuch as I was beginning to fear lest the boredom – and worse than boredom – which, as I am only too well aware, emanates from my person had coagulated into an impassable wall of murk between us: and this, were it finally to happen, would cause me more real sorrow than you probably imagine, since, as you justly remark, one's friends become fewer and fewer in number, but one's need of friendship does not, I think, decrease proportionately. To me, at least, it seems as though the capacity for friendship remained always undiminished; it may diffuse itself about a number of individuals, and as these fall away and are lost, it concentrates, so to speak, upon the two or three that still remain . . .

I wonder what I wrote about poor Yeats to provoke so bitter a diatribe! Actually, I cannot remember – it must be quite two months now since I wrote to you. I should feel much inclined to dispute your judgments with you, had not the mode of their presentation roused an uneasy feeling in me that you do not yourself altogether agree with them. . . . Perhaps you are right; but you seem to me to be in danger of conviction by phenomenal diversity, and that you, of all people in the world, should seem thus convinced is to me a thing so incredible that I am uneasy and perhaps unduly curious of its cause. Does a painter 'believe in' his subject – that conglomerate phenomenon two stages removed from reality? Why should he – yet it becomes a stimulus towards the truth – and *this* is neither subject, canvas, paint nor painter. Symbolism in literature – in the special sense ulterior to that wherein all words are symbols – has its roots in the mystical and magical writers from Hermes Trismegistus onwards; it is a little part of a great tradition which has been followed alike by the French Symbolists, by Yeats and by countless others who are not indebted to one another so much as to the central tradition itself. There are only the great tendencies; all these smaller classifications of literary schools and sects are unprofitable and misleading. Strictly speaking, *Axël* (for example) is a far more literally derivative work than *The Wind among the Reeds*. And as for subject-matter, the vehicular matter so to speak, what does it matter – intrinsically? Does it even exist, intrinsically, as subject-matter? Mythologies, symbolic systems, old forgotten far-off things and battles long ago – these are no better and certainly no worse as matter than, say, marine botany or the alligator as a source of pure design.

. . . I am driven day by day towards a purely mystical conception of the nature of art; I believe that creation is a wholly spiritual act for which this or that faculty may or may not be employed as a tool. The means and methods are matters of indifference. To some the intellect may be of use, to others it is a clogging impediment. If one has something to say it will get itself said, sooner or later, whether one be mad or sane, willing or unwilling, conscious or unconscious. If one wants to assist, that is to accelerate the process, one can only aim at the realization of the central peace subsisting at the heart of endless agitation – for this is the condition of central being which, I think, is not a 'thing' one has or has not but a state to be realized and attained – though God knows the path is difficult enough at Time's present stage; our generation is overlaid and shackled and half buried by intellectual chains. Our first task is to resolve complexity and still our endless agitation. Graphically delineated, the history of the artist is a line perpetually oscillating between the pure mystic and the artisan, and one cannot strive for a golden mean without cancelling oneself out – why, are there not enough counteracting forces in the world to militate against one, that one should wish to militate against oneself? There is another symptom of the real 'hidden plague' of our time! How barren and stale is to-day's conception of art – the very meaning of the word spirit seems to have been forgotten and pedantically re-interpreted. Witness Benedetto Croce with his *Philosophy of the Spirit* and the wonderful treatise therein on *Aesthetic as Science of Expression* which leads one so far and raises one's hopes so high, only to bring one up against a bare brick wall which, good God, turns out to be the very point one started out from!

I have done a considerable deal of work lately in connection with problems concerning the function of art, and I actually went so far as to deliver a lecture in the Abbey Theatre some weeks ago on 'What Music Is' (though it was primarily concerned with art in the abstract). It was a startling and necessarily sketchy discourse to which – as also to a fine Indian singer and some piano pieces by Bartók and van Dieren – some 400 persons listened with respect and – as I discovered from certain questions put to me at the close – scarce a grain of understanding! However, I propose to persist in this possibly quixotic course, with lectures on the function of art, the possibilities and limits of musical education (which I am endeavouring to work out very fully), musical history and a few – very few – individual composers. These discourses may ultimately see the light in book form but I shall keep them back until they have been given out in what I really think is a more efficacious manner.

I cannot myself at this distance of time recollect clearly the substance of my alleged 'bitter diatribe' against Yeats, which is the subject of this last letter. I only remember having said something about what seemed to me to be the artificial, deliberately and calculatingly picturesque, and fundamentally insincere form of mysticism adopted by him in some of his writings, as part of his poetic equipment, without really 'believing in' it, as all genuine mystics, such as Blake, Boehme, and Swedenborg, do. In reference to the succeeding letter, I seem to recollect having said that in order to become a musician one could learn more from Fux and Albrechtsberger than from all the mystics who ever lived – a palpable absurdity, as I thought even then, but only thrown out as what I conceived to be a salutary corrective to his unduly mystical and unpractical bias at this time.

It is verily an admirable correspondent that answers one's letters by return of post, and I should have shown my more than common delight in this virtue by putting it into practise, had there not intervened one of those black periods when all thought, all feeling and all desire are relegated to the outermost darkness. And since this gloom is not yet wholly dispersed, I hope you will pardon such shadows and heavinesses as may obscure the sense of this communication.

The first retort that leapt to my mind on first reading your letter was the image of a human hand which, folded save for two digits ithyphallically extended, seemed to have been set in a peculiar and jerking motion by some ironic and unseen agency. And then I reflected; by you I would as soon be convinced as be acknowledged convincing. In our private and confidential correspondence we are twin seekers after the truth – both, perhaps, as yet far off from her – though maybe in our public or non-mutual utterances we might seem to be conflicting champions of rival dogmas. It is an effective method of argument, to adopt a dogmatic position – even though it be but a hypothetical one – and invite a siege thereof, standing one's ground until one's last defence is swept away. This is a good test of a position which need not necessarily be one's only position, since in its defence one may quite possibly be compelled to argue against one's own convictions. But between friends, in secret colloquy when there is no risk of misinterpretation by malicious eavesdroppers, it is more profitable, I think, to pool the arguments in one centre, rather than to fire them off at each other as from opposing camps.

. . . It is my conviction that the success of externalization in art depends solely upon interior clarity. I do not believe that it is possible for utterance to be impeded by 'lack of technique', or whatever you may call the mere craftsmanship. I believe that those who imagine themselves thus obstructed simply deceive themselves because the truth is not in them; that is to say they have not yet focused that truth they would utter aloud within themselves. Their cry is simply an excuse (quite unconscious as a rule – I would not impute deliberate falsehood to them) to cover their inability to conceive clearly. They want to grasp something firmly and bring it to light, but it eludes their grasp – it is the initial grasping, not the bringing to light, which baffles them. If only the vision can be held fixedly enough, its externalization becomes a puny process. But the securing of the vision and the retaining of it – the interior processes – *hic labor, hoc opus est!* As for the modes of expression, just as Art is subdivided into the various arts, so each of the arts may be almost infinitely subdivided, and one is impelled towards one of these subdivisions by a part of that same intuition that impels one towards one art rather than another. There is no one thing called Technique – it simply does not exist. How a thing is done is absolutely unimportant; what matters is to get it done, e.g., the Elizabethans played the virginals with three fingers only, and persons without any skill in pianistic technique can be hypnotized to perform works of the utmost difficulty – this is a point of great importance, if you will reflect upon it. I do not say that the conscious intellectual processes have no part in artistic creation – far from it; but what I do say is that the intellect is one tool among several, and a tool that may be dispensed with in many cases. Methods vary in varying ages, even in varying individuals. In an age of extreme materialism it is necessary to insist on the things of the spirit rather more strongly than would be needed by a more enlightened epoch. We, I think, can take the material processes for granted. Art, we are agreed, is pure utterance, but I would add, at this point, an axiom that if we cannot acquire and use the language of art as naturally and spontaneously as we acquire and use our mother tongue, we had better leave it alone altogether until we can. If we must learn the language of art laboriously like a foreign tongue, we shall only speak it as foreigners and our utterance will be at best artificial . . . Oh, you who would exchange for the Divine Poemandres – Fux and Schytte, not to mention MM. — and — ! What will become of you? An idle question, perhaps, for me who have deep-rooted and unshakable faith in your ultimate destiny; but if that faith could be shaken by a passing wind, your last two exhalations would have almost uprooted it. But it stands firm – for all winds pass away and are gone.

June 15th, 1918

'*Inde Trimalchio ad lasanum surrexit*' – which is to say that I feel decidedly less strictured in the presence of the Timpany[1] who is gradually emerging from the mask that has of late so effectually distorted his features into frightful shapes. Indeed, save for such psychopathic twitches as necessitate three O's and two U's in the word soul, one half of your letter voices my view entirely . . . The quotation from Flaubert is admirable –

[1] Timpany was his favourite nickname for me, the origin, presumably, being the familiar orchestral indication 'Timpani in C and G'.

as is too the one from *Religio Medici* which, curiously enough, I made use of in my lecture. As for the butterfly net – a figure I myself employed in the lecture – such similes are illuminating enough when used with accuracy and precision; but when the image becomes interesting or amusing on its own account your exposition is done for. Now I am sure you found exquisite humour in the mere picture of Prosdocimus frantically chasing monstrous moths with his immense black hat in hand. But, my dear Sir, do you not realize that the picture is in itself a conceived work of art, rounded, complete and absolute in itself without relation to any point of mere logic? On utilitarian grounds – which are implied in your simile – what is there to choose between a gauzy net and your hat stuck on the end of your walking stick? All that you want is a net, or something that conforms to the dictionary definition thereof. All our difficulties in this direction can, I think, be traced to that necessity of the normal plane of consciousness to regard a relation as two separate things joined together, and not as an essential unity. (I say necessity, but perhaps it is only an initial tendency; it can certainly be overcome.) And worse than this is the tendency to note relations where none exist – the fallacy of *Post-hoc-ergo-propter-hoc*. When we say that technique as such has no separate existence, we postulate that unity – but when we proceed to speak of objective butterfly-nets and the works of Fux and Albrechtsberger to boot, we straightway deny our proposition. Assuming this objectivity I ask what possible connection is there between the fixity of Fux and the fluidity of Timpany's thoughts? Your proposition in its final form bids me believe that you seek to attain interior clarity by study of what is not only entirely exterior but – what's more – what never in the beginning sprang from any interior impulse. I ask again, what is the connection, what relation could ever exist between two particulars of contrary species? And if you argue from precedent and tell me that great men of the past have followed a similar course, I would ask you to point out a single essential (i.e., truly expressional) feature in any work of art that can be attributed to this theoretical study, as distinct from the study of actual works of art – to say nothing of what intrinsic genius has itself created. . . . Mathematical exercises have, no doubt, their beneficial effects towards clarifying the mind, but then (I) musical composition is not a merely mental process (II) text-book counterpoint is not an exalted branch of mathematics, so that for this purpose it would be much better to confine one's attention to the differential calculus. I say nothing here – though much there is to be said – of the positive dangers incurred by excessive zeal for Fux.

Conception – that is the whole point, we are agreed. *A propos* of which another passage from Sir Thomas Browne is illuminating: 'In the seed of a plant to the eyes of God, and to the understanding of man, there exists, though in an invisible way, the perfect leaves, flowers and fruit thereof; for things that are *in posse* to the sense, are actually existent to the understanding. Thus God beholds all things, Who contemplates as fully His works in their Epitome, as in their full volume'. There is, too, a somewhat mystical utterance of Mozart, of whom one would hardly expect such a thing, to the effect that he frequently conceived instantaneously a whole symphony in all its parts and detail, after which vision its composition was only a matter of unrolling, so to speak, into terms of Time. And I remember van Dieren showing me one day a small sheet of paper on which were a few little pencil jottings, and saying that the whole work to which they related (I think it was the second string quartet) was now already composed – a statement which points to a similar conception or instantaneous vision having taken place in him as in Mozart. Furthermore I believe that the logic and structure of van Dieren's works are not due to conscious musical thought at all but to the structure of his mind and the logical conformations of his purely abstract, interior, and intuitive thought of which they are the perfect and infallible expression. I use the word infallible – I might have said automatic – in connection with van Dieren's process of externalization, to imply as nearly as a word can that sense of absolute unity in a relation to which I have made reference above. . . . I am fairly certain that if there is a philosopher's stone for creative art, it is simply this faculty of conception-in-a-mathematical-point – but the acquiring of it – there's the rub. However, I am going to curse you with great vehemence for writing one sentence of a superficiality I can hardly credit you with. 'Above all,' you say, as though obsessed by some superstitious terror of the Unknown, 'beware of becoming automatic – the method is that of stupefying oneself with drugs, drink or women, or mysticism', etc. This is, to put it mildly, balls . . . One evening, a little over a year ago, we walked together from the Chinese Restaurant to a bench in Hyde Park and thence, after long sojourn, homewards. Just as we were passing the Victoria and Albert Museum you said to me, retorting to some remark of mine which I have forgotten: 'You know, you really haven't the faintest conception of what the word mysticism means'. Maybe I had not, have not – who knows? But if the author of the words I have quoted were to repeat the accusation to me, I should be compelled to remind him of what I wrote well over a year ago in connection with a composer named Williams who, I remarked, is one of those for whom mysticism means mistiness and vacuity rather than exceptional clarity of vision – implying, I suppose, the latter as my provisional definition thereof. To instance Cyril Scott as the horrible example of what one comes to through taking to mysticism is much the same thing as to instance Alma-Tadema as a proof of the futility of the whole art of painting. There is good art and there is bad art – mystical or otherwise – but the enormous preponderance of bad art in the world is not an argument against art in general. But mysticism is a two-edged sword; in proportion as it enables the good artist to attain to greater conceptions than he would otherwise be capable of, even so does it cause the inferior artist to make a far, far bigger fool of himself than he would be able to do by any other method. But it is idle to close your eyes to all but its fools, in spite of their enormous preponderance. Do you imagine that —— is a bad artist because he stupefies himself with drugs, drink, women – or mysticism? This is surely *Post-hoc*, etc. We have two propositions: —— is a bad artist; —— stupefies himself. Neither proposition is the cause of the other; both spring from the central fact that —— is —— which would not be so without the bad art or the stupefaction. The case of —— which I would not mention if you had not dragged in his name, is slightly different. If he stupefies himself, it is with his own tinklings as he makes them. He is the pure sound-for-sound's sake improvising composer. All his music tinkles (in this connection it is interesting to note that the harmonica – a kind of celesta – was largely used in the early experiments in mesmerism); it is not so much the result of stupefaction as the cause of it. He evidently hypnotizes himself with the first few bars of his composition – one can almost see the sickly sounds he produces rising like heavy clouds of incense in the air – and so sets himself spinning on his own axis. . . . But I have digressed considerably. The taking of drugs may also exalt a man so that he surpasses himself (i.e., his normal self) and proportionately they enable him to sink to a lower level than his normal self could descend to. Everything depends on the man's nature. We have opium to thank directly for all the finest passages in De Quincey – and mysticism for the master-work of an English prose-writer who is the equal of any of the three you mention – Thomas Traherne. . . . One great thing that a mystical view of the processes of life brings with it is the ability to dispense with the dichotomies that ordinarily beset one on all sides, the ability to know things not in relation but in their essential oneness. This at any rate seems to be a constant and unvarying faculty common to all the very diverse and varying types of men whom we have come to regard, broadly if somewhat vaguely, as mystics. We poor struggling flies are continually obstructed by sharp dualities, rigid dividing lines which prevent us from wholly realizing. We apprehend, for example, Being and Doing in a sharp differentiation, irreconcilable almost – that is our common difficulty – while dimly we feel, and we can see it in the works of great men, that there is no such rigid division between the two, but that utterance or action is simply the exaltation and crown of Being, Being surpassing and thus realizing itself – and only thus for, though it seem a paradox, I think there can be no fulfilment without overflow. Under the sway of our tyrant dichotomies, we must need call pure utterance translation, and spontaneity automatism – a sorry tale. Another barrier is the arbitrary boundary-line of mental consciousness, the Known and the Unknown separated off like sheep and goats and generally regarded with corresponding approval and mistrust. Your sentence which I have quoted voices a very common attitude – and it is significant that in writing it you began 'Do not' which you then stroked out for the more emphatic and emotional 'Beware': fear of the dark, my child, and little faith! All art is simply the making known of the unknown. Most of the art of to-day, consisting of the making known of what is perfectly well known already, is verily the 'pretence of Art to destroy Art'. The modern cry of 'self-expression' – when one examines what its criers mean by the term – proves this beyond shadow of doubt. The self is carefully partitioned, and when the surface portion has become absolutely static and completely cut off both from its own roots and from everything that, in its drunken diplopia, it considers the not-self, it proceeds to strut about before a mirror and call its vain reflections works of art. The true self can never be static; it is grisly to think of 'the depths of our soul' as an old well at whose bottom a certain limited quantity of stagnant water may perhaps be found and laboriously hauled up in buckets out of a fixed darkness over a rigid dividing-line into a fixed light – it is grisly, I say, to think thus, because in thinking thus we may make our thought actually so in real earnest. This boundary-fence between the conscious and the sub- or super-conscious is an arbitrary and artificial thing; to continue the image of 'the soul's depths', we should know, if only as an act of faith, that they are perpetually creative, that in them is a spring that is joined with all the waters under the earth, a spring that will ever be bubbling fresh water up to the surface of its own accord – if only we can let it. 'We carry with us the wonders we seek without us', and that interior clarity which you seek is no more than the free flow of this living spring in the passage of whose waters there is no sharp transition from darkness to light, from the unknown to the known, but a ceaseless becoming and intermingling of the one with the other – which is the unity we call mystical – why, God only knows. It is this free passage through the *whole* of our being, this being-*not*-divided-up-into-compartments, this being open to the infinite (which is within, not outside ourselves) that alone can make one ἔνθεος (a term grossly and almost universally misunderstood thanks to the dichotomizers), and this rightly interpreted is the only true synonym for creative . . . All of which things, my dear Timpany, you already know perfectly well!

One of the most vital preliminaries to creative conditions – more necessary than ever in this peculiarly self-conscious age (in the worst and most strictured sense of the word) is the clearing away of surface weeds that have power, if left to accumulate, to choke down one's utterance altogether; amongst the most deadly of these are certain almost automatic inhibitions, though springing from reason primarily, and in a lesser degree from emotions. It is astonishing to reflect upon the enormous influence the merely reasonable, or practical, idea of difficulty, of danger, or of actual (apparent) impossibility exerts over us: remove this idea and nine-tenths, if not all, of the difficulty or danger will vanish with it. This can be, and frequently has been, tested by a simple hypnotic operation which could with very great advantage be employed more extensively. Suppose one wants to do a certain thing; one's desire begets a command in the mind but the command, in travelling from the brain to the hand – or whatever the executive agent may be – is intercepted, short-circuited by an accursed *douanier* of an inhibition who says, 'You can't, you mustn't, you daren't'. And it is useless to set your mere will against him and say I can, etc.; he has to be slain once and for all. Mere contradictions are of no avail, being but verbal resolutions and thus unreal. Every time one of these inhibitions is slain (no matter what weapon is used for the slaughter; one is as good as another, you have your choice to suit your own convenience and taste) you gain courage and confidence and the formidable bulk of the enemy gradually dwindles to a pale shadow which one can ultimately walk through without a thought.

Forgive me if my last letters have seemed cold and curt and remote. I was in a state of nervous tension and irritation most of the last fortnight and this made me unduly cantankerous. But beneath these superficial moods all is so admirably clear now that it were a thousand pities if the delicate adjustment of our own personal relations, which is so necessary for the inter-change of important matters from mind to mind, should be disturbed but ever so slightly by such trivial annoyances as come from hasty or imperfect expression. And despite your frequent eulogies, I am really a very bad hand at writing letters, and lately I have become more painfully aware than ever of the wide gulf that yawns between my real attitude, my real thoughts, and the prettiest and most polished piece of prose that would fain express them. It is largely because I am so disgusted with the futility of correspondence that I feel so strongly the necessity of coming over at this particular moment to see you. I am totally incapable of speaking directly in writ-ing; whatever efforts I make to do so, it seems inevitable that when I try to speak intimately through my pen I must also talk through my hat – and a very old, worn-out hat, too. The grotesqueness of this situation has been slowly dawning on me for some time and it has now become quite unbearable – per-haps because for the very first time in my life it seems to me that I have a few things to say. And since all subtle and not-quite-matter-of-fact communications depend for their being brought to light upon a sympathetic interaction between the speaker and his listener, I am full of anxiety lest the succession of fan-tastic masks that circumstances have clapped upon my funda-mentally unwilling person should have interrupted that fine current of mutual understanding along which whole chapters may travel at the utterance of a single word; and that this instrument should be in perfect working order is at the present moment more necessary (and as far as I am concerned more easily possible) than ever it was. (Incidentally, I have also dis-covered the true nature of those masks I referred to, and if I can put *that* into words that are intelligible, you will be con-siderably astonished and not a little amused. I shall reserve this anecdote for a cosy corner in the Admirable Duncan[1] over a creamy pint – if such can still be had.)

I am quite sure that the moment has come for the linking-up of a broken circle – if you can see what I mean; I can express

[1] The 'Admiral Duncan', a public house in Old Compton Street, which was one of his favourite resorts in these days.

it in no other way. As to what may follow upon *that*, who can tell definitely? I have my own speculations, but the one thing that is absolutely clear is that I must come over to you immediately. This is far more definite and clear than any idea as to the exact nature of the affairs whose instrument I am. All this will read like the most grisly gibber, so I had better cease, begging you as I do so to realize my miserable limitations of utterance and to be swayed rather by what I have not written than by what I have.

And grisly gibber it certainly did seem to me, all these mysterious references to affairs of which he was the instrument, broken circles which must be linked up, and so on. The explanation, I discovered eventually, was to be found in certain occult experiments in which he had been engaged at the time, in accordance with which he had received what purported to be communications – astral, celestial or demoniacal – to the effect that he and I were destined to be closely associated in some epoch-making, earth-shaking activity or other. I do not mention all this merely in order to show how deeply immersed he was at this time in the quicksands and morasses of occultism, but because, under the surface absurdity of the whole thing there lurked a certain element of truth. It was not only that we were in fact to be associated with each other in various enterprises – though assuredly of by no means so important a nature as the other-worldly revelations would have had him believe – but also because we were in a sense two complementary aspects of one personality, two halves of one whole. Alike in many respects, with many, perhaps most, things in common, we differed in others, but in such a way that each supplied the deficiencies of the other. We were in fact, born collaborators, and I believe that we could have achieved very much more in working together than we did separately.

I laughed at it all then, but now I see that the oracle – or whatever it was – spoke more truly than I knew.

Ostensibly in order to realize this chimerical project of a collaboration with me in some important enterprise, but just as much, I think, and perhaps more, because he was weary of Ireland and had exhausted all its possibilities as an environment, he decided to return to England, in spite of the equivocal position in which he stood with regard to the military authorities. He was, in fact, technically a deserter although, as I have already made clear, there was never any question of military service where he was concerned. The worst that could have happened to him would have been that he might have been ordered to do some uncongenial clerical or menial work, and if it had come to this I have no doubt that he would have been prepared to go to prison rather than comply. The alternative did not present itself, however. When he returned, in August, 1918, the war was self-evidently as good as finished, and the authorities were already becoming listless and negligent. Philip certainly did everything he possibly could have done in order to attract their hostile attention. When I met him at the station early in the morning of a hot August day he was wearing a thick fur coat with the collar turned up, a large, sinister black hat, with the brim turned down, dark blue spectacles and a huge unkempt beard which, though real, looked as if it were false. He looked, in fact, like an exaggerated caricature of a Bolshevik and a German spy combined, but no one paid the slightest attention to him.

I have no very clear recollections concerning Philip during the next few months, and as soon as the war was over I left England for Italy, where I stayed until the spring of 1920. There is thus inevitably a slight hiatus at this point in my narrative.

CHAPTER III

THE SACKBUT

Up to this point the subject has for the most part spoken for himself, through his letters, in a kind of monologue or soliloquy. From now onwards it will be necessary to adopt gradually a more objective method of presentation, if only because Philip, like most people, tended as years went on to write ever fewer and briefer letters, until in the end there is very little correspondence of any interest or value to consider – or if there is it has not been placed at my disposal by those to whom it was addressed, which amounts to the same thing.

It happens, however, that this unavoidable change of method, dictated by circumstances, coincides with a definite change in the nature of the subject as well. Indeed, those readers who only knew him in his later years, or only by hearsay, must already have found it exceedingly difficult to reconcile the foregoing picture, presented principally in his own words and therefore unimpeachably authentic, with the Peter Warlock with whom they were acquainted, or as they had imagined him to be. It must inevitably seem to them that they have been reading about some entirely different person; and so, in a sense, they have – Philip Heseltine and Peter Warlock are, ultimately, two entirely different persons. While it is no doubt true that we are all of us up to a point dual characters, in that what we actually are is one thing, and what we seem to be, or would wish to seem to be to the world is another, this dichotomy was more highly accentuated in him than in most people. The real, the fundamental personality is that which we have seen; from now onward we are chiefly concerned with the personality which, partly consciously and partly

PETER WARLOCK *(circa* 1927*)*

unconsciously, he adopted, cultivated, and imposed upon the outside world.

It is highly curious and absorbing to study the way in which Peter Warlock came into existence, gradually took shape and form, and finally became more real than his creator. He began simply as a pseudonym and nothing more, and that merely as a matter of convenience and practical policy. The world distrusts versatility above all things, and anyone who distinguishes himself in one direction or other has always a formidable prejudice to contend with if he takes to some other as well. Even such great masters as Liszt and Busoni have been denied serious consideration as composers for no other reason than their superlative eminence as pianists, and even stronger, naturally, would be the prejudice against a mere critic setting himself up as a composer – and especially one who had made himself so heartily disliked. Consequently, when Philip decided to publish such music as he had written which did not too greatly displease him, he very wisely adopted a pseudonym. When the first songs duly appeared and were enthusiastically received by the entire musical Press he justly observed, in a letter to a friend, 'It gives me great satisfaction to reflect what they would have said about these same compositions had they been signed Philip Heseltine.'

It was perfectly true. The world had repeatedly and resolutely refused to have anything to do with Philip Heseltine. Whatever he attempted seemed foredoomed to failure. The latest fiasco had been another desperate effort to launch his old conception of a new musical journal, which was to be called *The Sackbut*, just after the war in the spring of 1919.

As usual no material support was forthcoming, and we find him writing despondently to Delius later: '*The Sackbut*, I am afraid, will never materialize – the same fate overtakes all my enterprises; lack of funds, for which no earthly amount of good intentions can make up.' Delius, as we see from his reply, was more inclined to lay the blame upon Philip himself.

BOUVARD AND PÉCUCHET

Sennen
Cornwall
July 17th, 1919

. . . I am sorry about *The Sackbut*; your circular made such a good impression everywhere. You would have done better if you had followed my advice and waited until you had the funds. Don't begin to think, dear Phil, that luck is against you, because the real reason is that you do not push your ideas to their materialization with sufficient energy and *suite dans les idées*. You would succeed at anything you take up if you would concentrate on it and not diffuse your energies in so many things. Stick to one thing just for two or three years and see if I am not right. I think you are admirably gifted as a writer; you would succeed either as a writer on music or as a composer if you stick to it and push it through regardless of everything. I vouch that you would have the most influential paper in London if you started one and stuck to it. – Don't think I want to preach at you, but I am so fond of you that I would like to see you become something and assert yourself, as I know how gifted you are and what possibilities are in you. It annoys me to see fools succeeding all around us.

Delius may have been right, but whatever the reason, whether lack of *suite dans les idées* or of mere material support – probably a bit of both – the plain fact remained that Philip Heseltine was, in the eyes of the world, a failure; nothing he had attempted had ever succeeded, and everything that he attempted thereafter would inevitably lie under the cloud of these preceding failures. In view of this, what could be wiser and more natural than to have done with Philip Heseltine and start afresh under another name? The decision was further confirmed by another and more characteristic incentive. Only a short time before he had submitted some of the music of van Dieren which, as we have seen, he greatly admired, and to which, in fact, he was deeply indebted for the unfolding and development of his own talent, to a certain publisher named Winthrop Rogers. These works had been rejected in terms of such offensiveness and stupidity that Philip thought it would be an exquisite form of revenge to have some of his own accepted which were clearly written under the influence of the music that had been so contemptuously rejected.

The plot worked perfectly. He submitted a batch of songs to Winthrop Rogers under the pseudonym of Peter Warlock, which were duly accepted and published. The secret was not kept long, however. A common acquaintance of Philip and Winthrop Rogers, on seeing the manuscripts, was able to identify at once the highly personal caligraphy, and it soon became known that the greatly admired Peter Warlock was none other than the despised and cordially disliked Philip Heseltine. But it was too late; the enthusiastic reception accorded to the songs by the unsuspecting leaders of musical opinion and the Press generally was such that none of those responsible for it could creditably change their attitude on learning the real authorship – they had perforce to accept the position and the deception with as good a grace as they could summon up. Incidentally, it is this initial rapture and subsequent disillusionment that explains the tone of the official attitude which still exists with regard to Peter Warlock, and might be summed up as follows: 'Charming stuff, charming, and I said so from the first; but after all, you know, it doesn't amount to much, does it? I mean to say, such a slender output' (*vide* list of works at the end of this book, occupying seven pages) 'and no large works – you can't really say that it is of any real importance, can you?'

I remember well my astonishment and delight at seeing those first published songs on my return from Italy in 1920 – astonishment, not because I had ever doubted his potentialities or their ultimate efflorescence, but because they represented such a sudden and decisive advance on anything of his that I had hitherto seen. I still think that he never wrote anything better than these early Winthrop Rogers songs, particularly *As ever I saw*, *Lullaby*, *Take*,

O take, but above all, these two exquisite miniatures, *My gostly Fader,* and *The Bailey beareth the bell away.* In addition to the songs he also wrote at the same time the beautiful little choral work *As Dewe in Aprylle,* with its subtle and sensitive changing rhythms, and the original version of *Corpus Christi,* one of the finest things he ever achieved.

The peculiar quality which distinguishes these two choral works and the two songs specially mentioned from all other music that I know lies in the union of a vein of medieval mysticism with an acutely modern sensibility. The spirit of the ancient poems is perfectly caught, but there is never a trace or suggestion of archaism.

All the works mentioned above were written during his Irish year with the exception of *Corpus Christi,* which was composed in 1919. The other works – all songs – which he wrote during this latter year show no advance; on the contrary, I should say they are quite definitely inferior, with the exception of the enchanting *Balulalow,* especially in its later arrangement for solo, chorus and orchestra in the *Three Carols* – a perfect gem, this, in the same tender, wistful, mystical vein as the works already singled out above for special mention. But certain of the other songs written in this year are even quite definitely bad in my opinion, such as the *Dedication* and *There is a Lady.*

In the following year (1920) there comes a break in his musical productivity, the chief reason being the realization of his long-cherished project of a musical paper, after so many years and so many abortive efforts. The way in which this came about is told in a letter to Delius.

PHILIP TO DELIUS

35a St. George's Road
West Hampstead
April 16th, 1920

I hoped to see you again before you left England to tell you – or try to tell you, for words are very inadequate to convey such things – how utterly marvellous the *Village Romeo* seemed to me. I can honestly say that no music that I have heard has ever moved me more profoundly or given me such a satisfying sense of absolute perfection of expression. Ten years ago it was the piano score of this work that really opened my eyes to what music could mean but, although I have studied it constantly in the meanwhile, the actual hearing of the music was a revelation . . . I was amazed at the way in which the whole work came off dramatically – it is such a wonderful whole, as finely balanced and proportioned as a symphony, unrolling inevitably from the first bar to the last.

I had no idea, from merely reading the libretto, that it would play so marvellously (even with the handicap of bad acting and misconceptions of character) and that it would convey such a sense of cohesion and unity.

. . . However, I will not go on babbling my enthusiasm here, but you shall read, if you care to, much more of it in an article I am writing for the first number of *The Sackbut* which is in active preparation and will positively appear on May 15th! Winthrop Rogers has taken up the scheme with enthusiasm and I think we shall be able to make a big thing of it.

He took over, when he bought out one of the numerous small firms of which his business is compounded, a very miserable paper called *The Organist and Choirmaster* which – as it was, by some extraordinary chance, paying its way and making a small profit – he continued to run, rather unwilling, as it was a most uninteresting production. Early this year it occurred to him to reorganize the paper and try to make it into something better and of more general interest, and a few weeks ago he suggested that I should take it over and edit it. I was against this policy from the first and after many discussions I succeeded in persuading him that nothing could be made out of this rotten corpse of a paper, and that it would be far better as well as more profitable to start a new paper on quite different lines. Accordingly *The Sackbut* will absorb *The Organist* next month, but will start off with the advantages of *The Organist*'s existing circulation, subscription list, and organization – the latter including a very able and efficient business and advertisement manageress who has worked with Rogers for years and knows everything about the commercial side of running a paper, a very valuable asset.

It will not take long, I feel sure, to make this the best musical journal in England. Rogers has given me an absolutely free hand in the matter of contributions (save for the fact that a small section of 'organist news' is to be retained at the end amongst the advertisements!) and in no way wishes the paper to be associated in the public's mind with his publishing business. I feel very elated about the project, for it is now on a very much firmer financial basis than it could ever have been if I had started it on my own account, and I am actually getting paid for running it.

I want the first number to be very first-rate, to drop like a bomb into musical and pseudo-musical circles.

DELIUS TO PHILIP

April 19th, 1920

Your letter gave me great pleasure and I am astonished that you see so clearly what I tried to do when I wrote the *Village Romeo*. In *Fennimore* I think I have realized it still more; when you hear the performance you will yourself become much more conscious of this. As far as I can see (I have only seen two or three criticisms) no one in London realizes what I am driving at, and they have constantly the old music drama as their model before their eyes.

. . . I am delighted about *The Sackbut*, and I am sure you are just the man to edit such a paper. I am so glad that Winthrop Rogers has had the wit and intelligence and perspicacity to seize hold of this most excellent occasion. There is really no first-rate, unbiased musical periodical in England . . .

April 29th, 1920

. . . The chief feature of *The Sackbut* ought to be independence and real criticism. The old clichés of fault-finding as a subterfuge for one's impotence and incapacity ought never to figure in your paper. Only then will it become a real live paper, and only then will it be read by the real music-lovers and enthusiasts.

You have now a wonderful opportunity. I hope you will grasp it; I am sure there is a wonderful field open to you waiting to be cultivated. What is wanting in England, what is wanting in British music, is idealism and enthusiasm. Up to now when the British composer is sincere he is generally dull, and when he tries to be original he nearly always adopts the latest foreign mode – nearly always belated. Twenty-five years ago it was German; now it is French or Russian.

The first numbers were well received and the prospects for the future were bright; characteristically, however, Philip lost no time in becoming involved in a violent controversy with Ernest Newman which had unfortunate consequences. The subject of the controversy was the reluctance of Mr. Newman to interest himself in various manuscript works to which Philip had called his attention. Mr. Newman, quite reasonably, contended that he was a busy man and could not be expected to spend any of his valuable time in reading unpublished scores of composers of whom he knew nothing; and that in any case he was more than usually busy at that particular moment. Philip simply could not see this; having always been willing and ready to lay aside his own work in order to interest himself in that of others, he quite honestly and genuinely could not believe that anyone could possibly think or act differently. He was unable to see that it was he who was abnormal and exceptional in maintaining that it was a part, and an important part, of the duties of a critic to be perpetually on the look-out for new and promising talents, even if this should occasionally necessitate some sacrifice of his own interests or convenience. His whole conception of the critic as one who has a duty to perform and a service to render is, of course, so remote from actuality that one cannot resist a smile at such naivety. Besides, how can one blame a man for not devoting his time to the discovery of new talent when he is probably incapable of recognizing it when he sees it? In the *Journal* of the brothers Goncourt the eminent French literary critic Taine is compared with a dog which belonged to an acquaintance of theirs. 'Il quêtait, il arrêtait, il faisait tout le manège d'un chien de chasse d'une manière merveilleuse; seulement il n'avait pas de nez.' The simile always reminds me of Mr. Newman, who knows everything that there is to be learnt about music, but is generally quite at sea wherever a purely aesthetic issue is involved. He has no nose, in fact, like the Goncourt dog. Philip, on the other hand, as a critic, frequently behaved in a most odd and disconcerting fashion; he was perpetually starting hares and dashing off on the wrong scent, but the hares were there and the scent was real. In a word, he had a nose; he had flair, and several composers who are now well known were discovered and helped to recognition by him before any other critic was even aware of their existence.

His quixotic generosity and altruism in the cause of art, indeed, knew no bounds, and I am glad to be able to add to my possibly suspect testimony that of an independent witness, Mr. Vere Pilkington, who wrote as follows in the *London Mercury* of January 1931. 'I knew him only slightly,' but 'when I was in difficulties over the transcriptions of early tablature or of early keyboard music, he would take endless trouble to help me. I remember once asking him if he would help me over the transcribing of an early pavan and galliard in the King's Library at the British Museum; the next morning I received the two pieces carefully transcribed in full in his neat and beautiful handwriting' – and this, too, at a time when, as I happen to know, he was overburdened with work of his own. But Philip was like that in everything and, as I say, he could not understand that anyone could be otherwise.

The immediate upshot of the controversy was that the publisher, Winthrop Rogers, took fright at what I suppose he imagined to be an unwarrantable attack on a national institution, and decided to withdraw the issue in which the offending article appeared. Eventually, however, a compromise was reached by which Philip and I took over the proprietorship of the paper from Winthrop Rogers, and publication was resumed. This was highly satisfactory; we were now our own masters, and although the paper was not yet paying its way, the circulation was increasing and we had many promises of practical support. Everything went on well for several months, until December (1920) when Philip went to Paris, ostensibly for a few days, after having promised to be back in time to prepare the issue of the paper which was due to appear on the 15th of the month. On the 6th I received a letter from him, saying: 'I can't come back. A calamity has befallen me which has made me even less capable of thought or action than I was a week ago – if that is possible. I feel utterly annihilated, broken up. I leave for Naples to-morrow, hoping never to return. For heaven's sake try and sell the paper for as much as one can get. If it was worth buying two months ago it is still worth it.' There followed a few hasty, ill-conceived directions for bringing out the impending number, and a cheque was enclosed to pay for the printing.

I found myself placed in a very awkward position. Firstly, he was the registered proprietor of the paper, and I could not possibly have disposed of it over his head even if I had wished to do so. Secondly, there were practically no contributions in hand for the coming number. Thirdly, the cheque came back marked with the ominous letters 'R.D.', for it seems that he had slightly overestimated the amount standing to the credit of the paper, and the bank would not allow an overdraft. The deficiency, I believe, was only one of a few pounds, but it was enough to dishonour the cheque. Consequently, if the paper was to be saved I found myself faced with the necessity of writing practically the entire number single-handed, personally guaranteeing the eventual payment of the printer's bill (for I had no ready money at the time), and making-up the paper and seeing it through the press – a technical job of which I knew nothing, for Philip had always attended to this – all in the space of a week.

I managed it somehow – exactly how I do not know – and having thus temporarily saved the situation I was considerably relieved, but none the less exasperated, when he suddenly reappeared on New Year's Day at my place, as if nothing had happened, and seemed mildly surprised at my chilly reception. After he had precipitately retired I sat down and wrote him a letter in which I told him quite frankly what I thought about him, concluding with a refusal to be any further associated with him in any activity whatsoever; to which I received a reply so exquisitely inimitable that I cannot refrain from quoting a few sentences, as a specimen of his more acidulated style.

PHILIP TO MYSELF

122 Cheyne Walk
Jan. 2nd, 1921

Your letter, I regret to say, exhibits but little of the equable disposition and calm aloofness from mundane matters that might be expected from one so profoundly versed in the mysteries of metaphysics, so admirably fortified by the consolations of philosophy as Mr. Peter Gore.[1] Indeed, it is rather of Kensington Gore that I am reminded – the moral infallibility of S.W.7 expressed with a super-Ciceronian vehemence of invective – and still more of an old plantation ditty which proclaims that 'Nobody knows de trouble I've had, Nobody knows but Jesus', with such emphatic iteration that long before the last verse is reached, everyone within earshot knows all about it only too well.

And if your experience of suffering reached its maximum point in the sudden necessity of writing out in ink two very creditable articles which, I feel sure, already existed in the less durable form of pencil sketches,[2] and of correcting a few proof sheets, I can only congratulate you on having entered this vale of tears under a more fortunate disposition of starry influences than most mortals can boast of.

Personally, having no reputation to lose (except perhaps the kind of reputation which is lost on the Salvation Army's penitent stools) I have no objection to your fulminating against me, both publicly and, for that matter, privately also, amongst your

---

[1] One of the pseudonyms I had adopted in writing the contributions to the number in question.
[2] They didn't.

large circle of friends (all acquired and retained, no doubt, by persistent acts of self-sacrifice and solid worthiness) if it gives you any pleasure to do so.

. . . At this point I seem to hear renewed mutterings of the LEID-*motiv* (in the bass). 'What', you say in effect, 'what would have happened if I had simply consigned you and all your interests to the abomynable and stynkinge realm of bewgrie and let the sound of your Sackbut die away in the distance like the Felis Catus Castrensis of Carrollingian legend, until there was nothing left of it but the grin – on the lips of its enemies?'

What indeed, save that you would have had to deny yourself the extreme satisfaction you appear to derive from exhibiting yourself in the position (which in this case is hardly uncomfortable enough to be convincing) of a martyr deliberately betrayed to the torture by my beastly callousness, my detestable disregard for my fellow creatures, my loathsome and disgusting usw., etc., κτλ, – I leave the selection of more appropriate adjectives in your extremely capable hands' and so on for many pages.

It was one of his greatest faults – by no means an uncommon one – that he tried every possible interpretation before it occurred to him to consider that he might have been in the wrong. In the present instance he manifestly had no case whatever, but he persisted in adopting an attitude of injured innocence which, in the circumstances, was exceedingly diverting – so much so, indeed, that my irritation at his inconsiderate behaviour entirely melted away. There was a curiously disarming quality in even his most outrageous performances which made it impossible for anyone who knew him and loved him to harbour resentment against him for long. We met accidentally at the house of a common friend, and it was all over. One reservation I made; that never again, under any circumstances, would I enter into any kind of partnership or association with him. Even this reservation went by the board; within a short time I found myself once more collaborating with him – this time in a study of *Carlo Gesualdo, Musician and Murderer*. And again, as I ought to have known perfectly well from bitter experience, he proved as exasperating a colleague as on the former occasion, for after I had finished my share of the book it was several years before I succeeded in inducing him to finish his, and even then only by threatening to write it myself.

The *Sackbut* remained for a time in a state of suspended animation, and then, suddenly, after a few months, when everyone must have thought it was dead, the corpse suddenly sat up and gave forth the most unusual series of contributions that any musical journal in this or any other country can ever have offered to its astonished readers: including, amongst other things, a reproduction of a pen-drawing by Augustus John, a crazy article by Arthur Symons on Petronius, and a set of poems in the manner of Rimbaud by Roy Campbell. Here again, incidentally, we find another example of Philip's critical flair. Long before any of the regular literary critics, he had divined in these immature poems the remarkable talent which is to-day acclaimed as one of the foremost in modern English poetry. But what all this was doing in a musical journal is another question.

After seeing this eccentric number through the press he again abruptly vanished, like his Felis Catus Castrensis of Carrollingian legend, to reappear in North Africa, from where he wrote the following letter to Delius:

PHILIP TO DELIUS

Biskra
March 28th, 1921

I should have written to you before, but the heat and the general effect of this climate is such that one has very little energy for doing anything at all, even thinking. I suppose one benefits physically, but in other respects one feels rather dead. We have just returned from a three days' expedition in the desert, on horseback, with two camels to carry the tents and provisions. The effects of light and colour in this country are wonderful, especially in the evening about sunset; but there is a certain deadness about it that robs it – for me at any rate – of any emotional suggestiveness. And I found when riding in the Sahara that whenever I travelled in my mind to some other place, the vision seemed more intense and real than my own surroundings. The desert has a strange tendency to vanish suddenly and give place to whatever rises up in one's imagination.

The Arabs are on the whole a degenerate, depressing crew – ill-clad and evil-smelling, persistent beggars and inveterate swindlers. Most of the wares exhibited for sale here look as though they had been imported from Manchester. And as for the women, Leicester Square or the lowest pub in Limehouse has nothing so incredibly revolting to show as the 'ouled-naïls' or dancing girls who sit on the pavement in the evening and try to lure the unwary traveller into some stinking Café Maure where, as a preliminary to other things, the tedious danse du ventre is performed to the strains of a hideously strident tin-oboe and various kind of tom-tom. For glamour and poetical suggestiveness give me the barrel-organ or the automatic piano! Only a Bantock or a Holst could find them in the street of the 'old nails'.

We leave here to-morrow for Tunis and cross thence to Naples by sea. From there we make a wild rush up to Budapest where we shall be able to visit Béla Bartók. We shall arrive there about April 7th and stay five or six days . . . On the way home we shall spend a few days in Vienna and Munich, arriving back in London about April 20th – possibly a little later, but in any case before the end of the month.

Philip had always evinced a warm admiration for the music of Béla Bartók, and his visit to Budapest in order to meet him inspired an equally warm regard for the man. Writing to Delius from the Hungarian capital he says 'Bartók is quite one of the most lovable personalities I have ever met'. When Bartók visited England in the spring of the following year he stayed for a time with Philip in Wales.

After returning to England for a short time during which he brought out another – this time comparatively sane and normal – number of the *Sackbut*, he went abroad again, first to Paris and then to a little village called Camaret, near Finistère in Brittany, where he settled down for a short while. This is a letter he wrote me from there:

PHILIP TO MYSELF

Camaret
Finistère
June 21st, 1921

Curwen has taken over the *Sackbut* and is going to run it – i.e., pay all expenses and contributors, giving me an entirely free hand as editor – I made it quite clear that I would not risk a repetition of the Winthrop business – for at least a year or so. If I can get any money out of him for the 'goodwill' and other attendent phantasmagoria I shall send you some of the spoil.

I have been staying here on the Breton – and quasi-Cornish – coast for some weeks, working very hard – and, really, for a change, getting on quite well, and drinking practically nothing. In fact I haven't been anything but strictly sober since the afternoon I left Paris when, staggering towards the Gare Montparnasse with a bag in one hand and a bottle of Calvados in the other, I fell prone before a tramcar and but for timely assistance might easily have missed more than my train.

Really, there is a fortune waiting for the first man who starts a calvados trade in England. It is one of the purest and most potent drinks in existence. One can get blind in 10 minutes, unfailingly – yet it's not even imported to England – and it could be made by the gallon 'in ea parte quae dicitur West-cuntre', being but the spirit of that staple product cider.

On the cliffs facing the open sea there stands a castle with eight little towers and a portico on which is inscribed 'La beauté est l'exaltation de la vérité' – one better than Keats. It makes me think of Tristan (and more particularly of Isolde), although it seems to be overrun by white cats and I have seen a goat sitting at night, yes – on one of the window-ledges. To-morrow I am going down the coast to Quimper and thence to Carnac, the mystical centre of the Celtic world. Then I shall probably stay some time in Paris.

This letter, incidentally, raises an issue which might as well be dealt with here as elsewhere. It is a part of the legend sedulously built up by himself as much as, if not more than, by anyone else, that Peter Warlock was a drunkard. Actually he was nothing of the kind, and I do not say this out of any hypocritical desire to conceal an unpalatable truth – rather the contrary, it is with a certain sentimental regret that I am compelled by honesty to make the admission, for the destruction of legends is a form of vandalism particularly repugnant to me. I can conceive of nothing more ridiculous than the conspiracy of silence with which biographers attempt to surround this amiable and widely spread weakness in their subjects. For example, in all that has been written about a certain eminent latter-day statesman, now deceased, you will not find a word that hints at the fact, known to all – and the proof of it is that everyone who reads this knows perfectly well to whom I am referring without the necessity of mentioning his name – that he was in the habit of consuming vast quantities of alcohol, and was frequently observed in public in a state of complete intoxication. Similarly, Lytton Strachey's suggestion that General Gordon was fond of brandy raised up a storm of indignant controversy which still splutters on in the correspondence columns of our more respectable newspapers. I remember also, in this connection, reading an article by the late Arnold Bennett, in the course of which he gave utterance to the dictum that he had never known a man of genuine talent who was given to excessive indulgence in alcohol. If he really believed this I can only say that he must have been woefully mistaken in his estimate of the talents of those with whom he came into contact. My own experience, and that of most people, I should imagine, is precisely the contrary, namely, that I have seldom met anyone of pre-eminent talent who does not, on occasion at least, indulge in alcohol to what is considered an excessive extent, with the noteworthy exception of Bernard Shaw – and it is for that very reason that one is inclined to doubt the reality of his seeming greatness. As Professor William James says in his (fifty-seven?)

Varieties of Religious Experience, 'The sway of alcohol over mankind is unquestionably due to its power to stimulate the mystical faculties of human nature, usually crushed to earth by the cold facts and dry criticisms of the sober hour. Sobriety diminishes, discriminates, and says no; drunkenness expands, unites, and says yes. It is in fact the great exciter of the yes function in man. It brings its votary from the chill periphery of things to the radiant core. It makes him for the moment one with truth. Not through mere perversity do men run after it . . . The drunken consciousness is one bit of the mystic consciousness, and our total opinion of it must find its place in our opinion of that larger whole.' Is it not precisely this that is the matter with Shaw, that he is crushed to earth by the cold facts and dry criticisms of the sober hour, that he diminishes, discriminates, and says no, that he is perpetually at the chill periphery of things? And I should be the last person to deny, rather the first vociferously to proclaim, that Peter Warlock was frequently in the habit of stimulating the mystical faculties of human nature, exciting the yes function in man, and becoming one with truth, but in this he was in no way different from the overwhelming majority of men of talent, except perhaps in degree, and not even that in comparison with some of the highest genius. I need only mention the fact that one of the greatest composers of the present day is indisputably also the heaviest drinker alive. The man who never indulges in wine, like the man who cares nothing for women, or the man who is indifferent to song, is merely a pathological specimen – there is something lacking in him, he is incomplete. Philip was a devout worshipper of each member of that delectable trinity of graces; the fact that he blasphemed sometimes against one or other or all of them may be forgiven – only a true believer can blaspheme.

At the same time it would be entirely untrue to suppose that Peter Warlock was a person invariably, or even generally, under the influence of alcohol – that is quite another matter. On the contrary, I have known few people, apart from total abstainers, to be so consistently abstemious over long periods of time; often for months on end he would avoid alcohol altogether, and this not from any effort of will or as if to break himself of a habit, or anything of the kind, but merely out of indifference, disinclination, and sometimes even positive distaste. Then, after a long spell of such a mode of existence in the country he would come up to London for a short time, during which he would admittedly behave in a somewhat spectacular fashion, and after which he would retire for a further prolonged period of asceticism. The consequence was that to many casual acquaintances and people who did not know him very well he must have seemed to be in a perpetual state of intoxication, simply because he was whenever they happened to see him, which was very seldom. He certainly encouraged this belief himself, by every means in his power; nothing delighted him more than to be thought a colossal drunkard. I need hardly point out the psychological significance of this; your real drunkard is nearly always secretly ashamed of his weakness and tries to conceal it, not to flaunt it in people's faces.

The extravagance of his behaviour on festive occasions led not infrequently to conflict with the forces of law and order, and some of his more outrageous escapades ended in the police court next morning. His most disagreeable experience of this kind was in Paris, when he was found lying face downwards in the gutter of the Rue Blanche in the pouring rain, without a penny in his pocket, and removed to the Santé where he was next day stood in a row naked together with pickpockets and vagrants, and washed with a long mop dipped in cold soapy water while his clothes were baked under the assumption that they were verminous. It is only surprising that such unpleasant experiences were not more frequent than they actually were, and that they were not more often accompanied by physical injury. He once broke a leg, and once an ankle, but for the rest he seemed to bear a charmed life.

While we are on the subject it might be as well to dispose of a kindred but less innocent and harmless aspect of the Warlock legend which has grown up, namely, that he was addicted to drugs. To those who knew him the mere suggestion is utterly absurd, but unfortunately one cannot ignore the accusation as one would have preferred to do, seeing that a certain young lady who recently attained a considerable notoriety mentions, in her alleged memoirs which appeared in one of the less reputable of Sunday newspapers, the name of Peter Warlock as that of one of the many brilliant men and women she had known who 'were ruined and destroyed by their helpless slavery to drugs'. Even so one would infinitely have preferred to ignore such an obviously irresponsible statement made by a self-confessed drug-addict, were it not for the fact that the writer was the daughter of the late Lady Dean Paul, otherwise known as Poldowski – a composer of genuine if slender talent, who knew Peter Warlock fairly well. The allegation thereby gains a certain weight and substance which it would not otherwise possess, for it might well seem to be based upon personal knowledge. But even apart from Miss Dean Paul, the legend – for it is nothing else – seems to have gained a certain credence, and in consequence I feel that I have no option but to go into the matter fully, though only with the utmost reluctance; for if it is allowed to stand uncontradicted there is a danger that it might eventually be accepted as fact.

As with alcohol, the whole legend was encouraged by Peter Warlock himself in a spirit of deliberate perversity and out of a mischievous desire to shock and outrage conventional morality, but with very much less foundation in fact – indeed, practically none at all. The sole iota of truth in the allegation is that at one time, about 1920 or 1921, he experimented occasionally with the substance known as *cannabis indica*, or Indian hemp, which is capable of producing in the taker curious hallucinations and delusions, particularly with regard to the sense of time, and for that reason is especially interesting to musicians. But so far from it being a drug which one would take for pleasure, or to which one could become addicted to the extent of becoming a slave to it, the effects are for the most part so disagreeable that deliberately to invoke them on repeated occasions would demand a degree of iron resolution which Philip certainly lacked. After a short period he abandoned these experiments entirely, and never reverted to them again. It only remains to be added that in those days *cannabis indica* could be obtained at any chemist by merely signing the book; the sale of it was not illegal then, though I understand that it has since become so. As for the really dangerous drugs to which unfortunate persons do become addicted with disastrous results, such as morphine, heroin and cocaine, he had absolutely no experience of them, and no wish for it. Such was his perverse sense of humour, however, that he would often speak to people as if he had tons of the stuff in his possession, merely in order to give them the impression that he was a monster of depravity. One of Philip's minor failings, it must be frankly admitted, was an overweening impulse to *épater le bourgeois* which would never occur to anyone who was not himself, at rock bottom, a thoroughly conventional moralist. Philip, in revolt against the hypocrisy which is proverbially the national vice of the English, too often merely inverted it, and posed as being worse than he was instead of better – a more sympathetic form of the same thing, doubtless, but none the less a weakness.

It is particularly ironical, incidentally, that he of all people should be suspected of an addiction to narcotics, seeing that he had a definite aversion from even the most harmless and widespread of them all – tobacco. He is one of the few people I have known who never smoked at all. If Peter Warlock was, as has often been said, an Elizabethan born out of his time, he would certainly have been one of the leaders in the protest against the filthy new habit introduced by his eminent contemporaries, Sir Francis Drake and Sir Walter Raleigh.

To return: the *Sackbut* was eventually bought by Messrs. Curwen, but Philip was not retained as editor. He had, if I remember rightly, made up his mind to live in Paris at that time, and cherished the fantastic delusion that he could edit the paper from there. Not unnaturally, the new proprietors were of a different mind and another editor was appointed in his place. The paper still exists, and the fact that it was able to weather such formidable tempests in its early career suggests that its foundations must have been well and truly – if somewhat eccentrically – laid.

In the autumn of 1921 was published at last the novel of D. H. Lawrence already referred to, *Women in Love*, in which there appeared a malignant and scurrilous caricature of Philip. This in itself was not a surprise to him, for I had read the book in manuscript shortly after it was finished, as early as 1917, and had acquainted Philip with its contents. He can hardly have been prepared, however, for the extraordinarily venomous character of the libel, and there is no doubt that he was deeply wounded by it. It will be necessary to go into this question also more exhaustively than would otherwise be desirable on account of the indiscretions of another authoress (why must women write books?) – Mrs. Catherine Carswell – who writes as follows in her study of Lawrence entitled *The Savage Pilgrimage*: 'Secker had to inform Lawrence that Philip Heseltine, who was no longer friendly towards him, was threatening a libel action, alleging that the Halliday of the novel was a portrait of himself, which in fact it was, though Lawrence modified the character and altered the complexion for the English edition. In law, I believe Heseltine's case was very dubious; but there was already trouble enough about the book, and for peace sake Secker paid him £50 as solatium for injury to feelings and reputation.'

As a misunderstanding of facts this is hard to beat. We see clearly from the letters printed on pages 167 and 181, that Philip not only retained a warm admiration for Lawrence as an artist, but also a personal regard for the man, and nothing had happened in the years subsequent to the writing of these letters to alter his feelings. He only ceased to be friendly towards Lawrence on the publication of this offensive lampoon. Secondly, Lawrence did not modify the character and alter the complexion for the English edition until compelled to do so, as a result of the legal proceedings threatened by Philip, in consequence of which the original edition was withdrawn by the publishers, and emendations made in the text. Thirdly, if 'his case was dubious', it can only have been so on account of some legal quibble, some technical defect in the law of libel as it exists in this country, for there could on the face of it be no clearer case of defamation of character, maliciously perpetrated, than is contained in the passages in question. Lastly, the offensive innuendo contained in Mrs. Carswell's concluding sentence, to the effect that Philip was content to accept £50 as sufficient compensation for injury to feelings and reputation, is absolutely untrue, as the following extracts from letters written by Philip to his solicitors will show.

I should be glad if you would press the claim for damages in respect of the libels in copies already sold as far as ever you can without involving me in great expense or embarking upon an actual case. I can't afford to fight them, but it will be as well to give Mr. Secker and the author the impression that proceedings will certainly be taken if the matter cannot be settled out of court. I leave it to you to decide the proper sum to be claimed as damages.

. . . These (alterations) are ridiculously inadequate and make little difference to the libel. But surely the withdrawal of the book from circulation and the submitting of a proof (in Lawrence's handwriting) containing alterations in the personal descriptions, constitutes an admission of the charge of libel on the part of both author and publisher? This seems to me important and I should like to have your opinion as to how much the submitting of this proof implies, legally. If it constitutes an admission of the charge, as I suspect, then we may safely go ahead, not only in claiming damages in respect of copies already sold, but also in threatening further proceedings should the book be reissued even with the suggested alterations. If you look at these corrections you will see that they make no material difference. The circumstances and the situations remain the same.

I am inclined to accept the proposals as regards the alterations – because I fear that further demands for excisions might lead to a case in court which I could not afford – and partly because I am convinced that the second edition will be no less obscene than the first and can therefore be easily suppressed on public grounds. . . . I consider that the libels are not removed by the suggested alterations and cannot be removed except by the omission of the characters altogether. Were the character of the book other than it is, I should press the demand for their omission, since the libel is now clearly admitted by Mr. Secker. But as the second edition will without doubt provide a case for police intervention on general grounds of obscenity (there is almost enough evidence of it in the two chapters submitted in proof) I propose . . . to take such steps as may be necessary to get the book totally suppressed by the police when it next appears. . . . Another reason for not pressing the matter of excisions further is that, if it came to a case, my wife would be an essential witness and I have now finally separated from her.

. . . I purposely left in certain passages which in other circumstances I should have insisted on getting omitted, in order that there should be no dearth of evidence of certain tendencies for which to get the book suppressed by the police. Will you please communicate with Scotland Yard again immediately. Every day's delay is bound to make a difference to the circulation of the book, and I am most anxious that action should be taken in the matter at the earliest possible moment.

Apart from the chapters containing the libels, this second edition does not differ in any way from the first, and if ever a book afforded grounds for prosecution on a charge of morbid obscenity in general and the glorification of homosexuality in particular, this one does.

. . . If Scotland Yard proves dilatory, could you not address a communication to the National Council of Public Morals, urging them to take the matter up and press for police action?

Apart from the exquisitely subtle humour of the last extract (the idea of Philip of all people invoking the activities of the National Council of Public Morals is too rare for laughter – it should be reverently savoured, like the delicate bouquet of a fine old wine) it clearly appears that he was only deterred from bringing an action by lack of funds, the technical impossibility of proving special damage, and his unwillingness to bring his wife into the case. Moreover, so far from being satisfied with the £50 he did not, after receiving it, relax his efforts to have the book suppressed, not merely on personal grounds but as a matter of public interest.

Neither the police nor the National Council took any active steps in the matter; nevertheless part at least of his objective had been attained. The book had been withdrawn and considerably re-written, and his victory was celebrated in a triumphal war-chant which he sent me at the conclusion of the negotiations:

> Come, fill a vial with vintage, *vieux et sec*
> Fit for the King of Thule's golden *Becher*;
> Get half-seas-over – swamp the blooming deck.
> Swill swipes, swig swizzle, singing
> 'SUCKS TO SECKER'!

The alterations to which he had assented *faute de mieux*, however, were, as he himself rightly observed, of the most trivial and unimportant kind, consisting chiefly in slight changes of physical description, dark hair being substituted for fair, and so on, but leaving the grossness of the libel fundamentally unimpaired. The caricature, even in the revised version, remains clearly identifiable.

The whole question as to the extent to which an author is entitled to put living persons into a work of fiction is an exceedingly difficult one to decide. Admittedly one cannot expect the novelist to work entirely *in vacuo*; his work is bound to reflect to some degree his personal experience, and the characters he creates, if they are to have any semblance of reality at all, will inevitably possess traits identical with or similar to those of people with whom he has at some time or other come into contact. It is even possible that a straightforward, veracious portrait is comparatively unexceptionable; what one objects to chiefly in Lawrence's innumerable caricatures of his best friends is the spiteful way in which he combines truth and fiction, not merely exaggerating slight defects out of all proportion but also grafting others of his own invention on to the original. A curious and psychologically interesting example of this is to be found in the fact that he represents Philip, in the person of Halliday in the novel, as speaking always in a high-pitched, hysterical squeal or squeak. Actually he had rather a deep and sonorous voice; it was Lawrence himself who in real life perpetually squeaked and squealed in a ridiculous manner, like a eunuch. To ascribe thus one's own ludicrous or revolting peculiarities to one's friends is going a little too far, I think it will be admitted. Again, Lawrence does not merely confine himself to the recording and distorting of incidents which actually took place, but goes out of his way to introduce imaginary ones of inherent plausibility in order to make the conduct of the actors in them seem the more objectionable. Norman Douglas, in his admirable pamphlet *D. H. Lawrence and Maurice Magnus* complains of the way in which Lawrence has recognizably portrayed him in one of his novels and then put into his mouth uncomplimentary and spiteful remarks about his friends, also readily identifiable, which he never made. So with Philip. In Chapter xxviii of *Women in Love* an incident is recounted in which Halliday (Philip) is represented as reading aloud a private and personal letter which he has received from Birkin (Lawrence himself), to a sniggering bunch of cronies in what is obviously meant to be the Café Royal; whereupon a thinly disguised Katherine Mansfield comes up and snatches the letter from his hand in a transport of heroic indignation, and marches out of the place with it. So plausibly is it told, and so realistic and lifelike are the details, down even to the mock clerical voice in which Halliday reads out the letter – frequently adopted by Philip in satirical vein – that even knowing Lawrence and his methods it never occurred to me to doubt the substantial accuracy of the account until I came across the version of the incident given by Mr. Middleton Murry in his *Reminiscences of D. H. Lawrence*; according to which it appears that it was not a letter that was being read out, but poems from Lawrence's recently published *Amores*. This made me suspicious, because Philip at the time in question still admired Lawrence's work, and I remember well his enthusiasm over this particular volume when it was first published. I therefore wrote to Mr. Murry and asked him if he could say for certain whether Philip was one of the participants in the scene. He replied that he could not, but referred me to two eyewitnesses, one of whom, Mr. Koteliansky, was able to assure me quite definitely that Philip was not one of the party.

So here we have Lawrence deliberately ascribing to Philip an unworthy act of which he was entirely innocent – or I should say rather what he intends to be regarded as an unworthy act, for, frankly, it does not seem to me personally such a heinous offence to laugh at letters, or even poems, of Lawrence. One had to be singularly humourless, indeed, not to laugh at Lawrence on occasion. Mr. Murry, however, waxes indignant that 'his passionate poems should be jeered at by the *canaille*', and there may be others who think so. Well, all I can say is that if there is any *canaille* concerned in the matter, the term is more appropriately to be ascribed to the writer who is capable of such a cowardly and treacherous betrayal, such a stab in the back of a loyal and devoted friend, as the whole of the Halliday episode in *Women in Love*. There is not even the excuse of artistic justification, for the whole episode is dragged in in such a way as to constitute a formal blot on the work as great as that which it confers on Lawrence's reputation as a man. It is painful for me to have to say this, for I knew Lawrence well and cared for him deeply at one time; but in justice to the memory of one for whom I cared more, I have no choice.

It may be thought that all this is trivial, unimportant, unnecessary, but I think that a moment's reflection will show that it is not so. One has only to recall the case of poor Leigh Hunt, a writer of talent and in many ways an admirable man, condemned to go down to posterity in the cruel caricature of him made by Dickens in the person of Harold Skimpole; and since Mrs. Carswell has seen fit to put it on record that Halliday is a portrait of Philip Heseltine it is my obvious duty to point out that the unpleasant person he is represented to be in the pages of Lawrence is a malignant caricature, bearing only the remotest and most deceptive resemblance to actuality. I do not suggest that Lawrence is an artist of the same stature as Dickens, but it is surely none the less true that, despite the flagrant over-estimation of him at the present time which will inevitably bring an equally violent reaction in the opposite direction at no far distant date, he is destined to be regarded as one of the most important writers of his time. The danger, therefore, to which I have alluded, is by no means imaginary.

It is a remarkable fact that Philip should have served as a model for characters created by the two most talented writers of their respective generations in this country: by D. H. Lawrence in *Women in Love* and by Aldous Huxley in *Antic Hay*, which appeared two years later, in 1923. One of the chief characters in the book, indeed, the young man named Coleman with a blond fan-shaped beard and bright blue eyes, 'smiling equivocally and disquietingly as though his mind were full of some nameless and fantastic malice', who enters the Soho restaurant in Chapter IV with a peal of diabolic laughter – this is none other than Philip. More than that, it is true to say that he is the most important, as he is certainly the most vivid and arresting, character in the book, for the slender plot – if plot it can be called – is chiefly woven around the beard of which he was the possessor.

I can even recall quite clearly the occasion on which the central idea for the book presented itself to Huxley. One evening in the summer of 1922, after a Promenade Concert at which Philip and I came across Huxley in company with Eugène Goossens, we all went together to Verrey's Café in Regent Street for a drink, and there, in answer to a question asking why he had grown a beard, Philip made a witty and brilliant speech of which the essence is reproduced in the book. His inveterate propensity, moreover, for making outrageous puns and plays on words has undoubtedly suggested to Huxley many of the most entertaining witticisms in his book. 'Where the hormones, there moan I', 'I long for progeny, I live in hopes. I stope against Stopes,' and many similar others, are all in the authentic Philippic tradition.

It is very curious that the same personality should serve as a model to two such talented writers as Lawrence and Huxley for such diametrically opposed creations as Halliday and Coleman. Lawrence depicts a pitifully weak, irresolute, ridiculous, soft, effeminate nonentity; Huxley a virile, sinister, diabolic monster of vice and iniquity, and the contradiction extends down to the smallest details. The explanation, of course, is, as I have already suggested, that they were two entirely different people. Lawrence saw the one, Huxley the other. And it is curiously significant that, deeply though Philip had resented Lawrence's caricature of him, he was positively delighted with that of Huxley; the reason being that, whereas Lawrence's caricature was a caricature of his intrinsic inner self – Philip Heseltine – that of Huxley was a caricature, or rather an enhancement of the fictitious, secondary personality which he had built up for himself and as which he wished to be taken by the world – Peter Warlock. Coleman, in fact, is Peter Warlock raised to the nth power, Peter Warlock as he wished to be; Halliday is Philip Heseltine reduced to a monad of negativity.

At the same time, however, probably without being aware of it, Huxley has drawn a remarkably resembling portrait of the pre-Warlock Philip in the person of the hero or central figure of the novel, Gumbril, the Mild and Melancholy one who, inspired by the example of Coleman, buys himself a false beard, and is thereby straightway transformed into the Complete Man. 'Fan-shaped, blond, mounted on gauze and guaranteed undetectable, it arrived from the wig-maker, preciously packed in a stout cardboard box six times too large for it and accompanied by a quarter of a pint of the choicest spirit gum. In the privacy of his bedroom Gumbril uncoffined it, held it out for his own admiration, caressed its silkiness, and finally tried it on, holding it provisionally to his chin, in front of the looking-glass. The effect, he decided immediately, was stunning, was grandiose. From melancholy and all-too-mild he saw himself transformed into a sort of jovial Henry VIII, into a massive Rabelaisian man, broad and powerful and

227

exuberant with vitality and hair – great eater, deep drinker, stout fighter, prodigious lover – Cautiously and with neat, meticulous fingers he adjusted the transformation to his gummed face, pressed it firmly, held it while it stuck fast – One last look at the Complete Man, one final and definitive constatation that the Mild and Melancholy one was, for the time at least, no more; and he was ready in all confidence to set out.'

The parallel is revealingly close, for it was in precisely this way that Peter Warlock first came into existence, the only difference being that he grew his beard instead of buying it at Clarkson's. If the reader will turn back to the letter written to Colin Taylor from Ireland on p. 171 he will find a quite remarkable adumbration of the experience of Huxley's Gumbril. ('The fungus is cultivated for a purely talismanic purpose . . . it does have a certain psychological effect on me,' etc.) This is what Peter Warlock essentially was – a protection, a façade, a mask, a carapace, a defence erected against a hostile world by a gentle, sensitive nature to whom life had well nigh become unbearable without it. In one of the fragmentary and desultory diaries which he kept from time to time I find the following entry: – 'Fourth beard begun; last shave October 23rd, 1921 (nine weeks by Christmas, ten by New Year's Day'); he was never again without a beard, and from that time the definite ascendancy of Peter Warlock dates, both the man and the musician, the legend and the composer. Up till 1921 Peter Warlock had been merely a convenient pseudonym, as we have seen; the music written over that signature previous to that date was a pure self-expression of the sensitive, gentle, wistful being revealed in the letters. With the songs written in 1921 and 1922, on the other hand – *Captain Stratton's Fancy*, *Mr. Belloc's Fancy*, *Good Ale*, *Hey troly loly*, *The Bachelor*, *Piggesnie*, and so forth – we find ourselves suddenly for the first time in the presence of a wholly different personality – the lusty, roystering swashbuckling, drinking, wenching Peter Warlock of popular legend.

It need hardly be said that this spiritual 'change of life' was not as sudden and complete as it might appear to be. The separate constituent elements of this secondary personality had always been there, but hitherto they were more in the nature of the comparatively ordinary contradictions and inconsistencies of character to which everyone is subject. Neither was the change complete; the original Philip Heseltine as we shall see, continued to subsist behind the flamboyant façade of Peter Warlock up to the very end. It is true however that at about this time, 1921, the secondary Warlockian characteristics begin to group, consolidate, and organize themselves into a definite personality which tends henceforward to take the ascendancy over the former. And the psychological explanation of it is clear enough, and has indeed, already been sufficiently indicated. Philip Heseltine, from a worldly point of view, was a failure. Everything he touched went wrong, all his best-laid and most-deserving schemes invariably collapsed; but the moment he put on a mask everything succeeded, not merely in art, but in life as well. Up till the growing of the beard and the appearance of Peter Warlock, he had not been conspicuously successful with women – rather the opposite – the Hyde Park episode related on page 126 is symbolically significant in this connection; he was too timid, shy and retiring to be successful. And here again there is a quite uncanny resemblance between his experiences and those of Huxley's imaginary Gumbril. Describing a precisely similar *rencontre* Huxley writes 'The Mild and Melancholy one would have drifted to the top of the road and watched her, dumbly, disappearing for ever into the Green Park or along the blank pavements of the Bayswater Road; would have watched her for ever disappear and then, if the pubs had happened to be open, would have gone and ordered a glass of port, and sitting at the bar would have savoured, still dumbly, among the other drinkers, the muddy grapes of the Douro, and his own unique loneliness'. As it was, caparisoned in his false beard, he made a triumphant conquest. Similarly the Mild and Melancholy Philip, transformed into Peter Warlock, the Complete Man, was masterful and compelling – women could not resist him.

Philip, as opposed to Peter, exhibited the familiar romantic dichotomy in his attitude towards women; they had either to be angels of the Gretchen type, drawing him upwards into the light, or incarnate demons of the *femme fatale, Belle Dame sans Merci* order, dragging him down into the darkness – always the one or the other extreme, never anything intermediate. D. H. Lawrence showed considerable penetration when he wrote about him as followed in his *Letters* (p. 323), where the names are suppressed for good reasons: – 'His affection for M—— is a desire for the light because he is in the dark. If he were in the light he would want the dark. He wants M—— for *companionship*, not for the blood connection, the dark, sensuous relation. With P—— he has this second, dark relation, but not the first . . . Perhaps he is very split, and would always have the two things separate. For these people I really believe in two wives. I don't see why there should be monogamy for people who can't have full satisfaction in one person, because they themselves are too split, because they act in themselves separately. Monogamy is for those who are whole and clear, all in one stroke. But for those whose stroke is broken into two different directions, then there should be two fulfilments.'

In *Women in Love* he puts it more crudely and offensively, but the implications are the same, 'He (Halliday) wants a pure lily, with a baby face, on the one hand, and on the other, he must have the Pussum, just to defile himself with her. – She is the harlot, the actual harlot of adultery to him. And he's got a craving to throw himself into the filth of her. Then he gets up and calls on the name of the lily of purity, the baby-faced girl, and so enjoys himself all round. It's the old story – action and reaction, and nothing between'. And at that period, about the time I first met him, and for some years after, he would swing from the one to the other with such a pendulum-like regularity that I came to be able to calculate almost to a day the time when the inevitable reaction would occur. His intimate life was then in a kind of rondo form, in which one persistently recurring and invariable theme alternated with continually new subjects – 'A B, A C, A D', and so on. Later, with Peter Warlock, the form became plain sonata form, with two strongly contrasted subjects striving for mastery, or rather mistresshood, first one then the other being in the ascendant; later still he cultivated the contrapuntal forms with marked success and, beginning with two subjects, eventually acquired a remarkable virtuosity in combining a large number of dissimilar themes. But in these days, as I say, it was a rondo which came to an end, roughly, about the same time that Philip came to an end, and Peter began – i.e., about 1921.

It goes without saying that neither the *idée fixe* nor its alternations were the destroying vampire and the redeeming saints of his imagination, but merely innocent ciphers and symbols of purely subjective states of mind, as in calmer moments he himself well realized. As he once wrote to a friend in 1920, 'People like you and me cannot fall in love objectively. I was chiefly intrigued by this affair because for the first time in my life it seemed to me that something of the kind was happening. But it was a pure lie and has now become a perfect nightmare'.

Despite his innumerable love affairs I greatly doubt whether, like all true romantics, he was ever, ultimately, in love with any woman in his life except the incomparable lady Dulcinea del Toboso, or that Princess of Tripoli with whom the troubadour Jaufre Rudel fell in love without ever having set eyes on her, or the blue-eyed, fair-haired Jenny Colon whom Gérard de Nerval worshipped without ever having addressed a word to her – they are all the same. With Gérard, incidentally, Philip had a deep secret affinity, as we see from the following letter written to the Jenny Colon of the moment, in 1919.

PHILIP TO W.B.

Many thanks for the parcel which arrived here safely this morning, despite the extreme legibility of the wrong number on the outside.

As for 'sentimentality' I think you are in a mood to mistrust emotional utterances of all kinds, rather uncritically. For the moment you are inclined to see sentimentality everywhere, just as some people can always discover erotic symbolism in the most diverse and unlikely phenomena. If I were a Freudian I should probably say that you had a sentimental-complex! There are some things that we desire so instinctively and so profoundly that, in our perverse consciousness, we must deny them with all the force of our desire and battle against them, only to make them rush in upon us more fiercely and in the end bring fulfilment to us in the defeat of ourselves.

It matters very little by what name we call the passion — for it is nothing less – that prompts the work of men like Gérard de Nerval. It is only intensity that counts, intensity of experience; the nature or, if you like, the 'size' of the experience, counts for little beside the intensity with which it is felt.

I think there is something very beautiful about Gérard brooding long years over the image of one woman, shrouding himself in one dream till it had taken possession of his whole being and he was lost and, being lost, fulfilled in it.

Such men are burned away by the intensity of their inner fire, and that fire may be kindled by God or a woman or some apparent trivial circumstance, indifferently.

However, if one writes passionately of God, there will always be some to cry 'superstition', or if one writes passionately of a woman, 'sentimentality'; but those who cry thus can never do so with half the intensity of conviction, and more often than not they raise their voices to banish uneasy presentiments of things unknown lurking in wait for them in the darkness.

You would probably like me to think of you as a tragically disillusioned cynic, cautiously limiting your capacity for sorrow by the most utter scepticism of all possible joys – or perhaps an Elën[1]

> 'Je suis donc insensible et faite de silence,
> Et je n'ai vécu! Mes jours sont froids et vains;
> Le ciel m'a refusé les battements divins;
> On a faussé pour moi les poids de la balance', etc.

[1] The heroine of a play by Villiers de l'Isle Adam.

But I, in my simplicity (*reine Thorheit*, perhaps!) and unfashionable fairy-tale folly, shall persist in regarding you as an evilly enchanted princess who has yet to be awakened out of sleep.

The kind of love here expressed and described, the true romantic passion, feared and distrusted by all women, for they are unable to understand it, can never be realized in this world, nor in the next, nor in any other, if such there be. Gérard, madman though he was, had at least sufficient sense never to attempt to realize it; Philip, like Berlioz, continually attempted to do so, with invariably disastrous consequences.

Peter Warlock, on the other hand, treated women as they deserve, and, ultimately, as they wish to be treated, with complete cynicism, neither as angels nor devils but merely as rather inferior human beings, and was invariably as successful as Philip Heseltine was unsuccessful. The supreme irony of the situation consists in the fact that Peter frequently succeeded with the very woman by whom Philip had been contemptuously rejected. Women are like that, and the world is like that also; it had no use for the romantic idealism, the exquisite sensibility of thought and feeling, the selfless devotion to art and every form of beauty, of Philip Heseltine. To the bitter and cynical, ranting Peter Warlock it gave itself, as they did, shamelessly, at once.

In this frustration of the real self and triumph of the *alter ego* we find the clue to the whole problem of his life. In order to be accepted, in order that life should become merely tolerable even, he had to become other than he was; the only other alternative was renunciation, and to this it came in the end.

At this point it will be necessary to guard against a possible misunderstanding. I would like to make it clear that no moral issue is involved here; the duality was not of the crude and simple order exemplified in the Stevensonian fable of Jekyll and Hyde, the conflict between good and evil, darkness and light, and so on, nor even as clear-cut and sharply defined as that of Alfred de Musset, who resembled him so closely in some respects. Mme.

Allan-Despréaux, Musset's mistress, describes him thus in an interesting letter to her friend, Mme. Toussaint: 'Je n'ai jamais vu de contrastes plus frappants que les deux êtres enfermés dans ce seul individu. L'un bon, doux, tendre, enthousiaste, plein d'esprit, de bon sens, naïf, comme un enfant, bonhomme simple, sans prétention, modeste, sensible, exalté – artiste exquis en tous genres, sentant et exprimant tout ce qui est beau dans le plus beau langage, musique, peinture, littérature, théâtre. Retournez la page et prenez le contrepied: vous avez affaire à un homme possédé d'une sorte de démon, violent, orgueilleux, despotique, fou, dur, méfiant jusqu'à l'insulte, aveuglement entêté, personnel et égoiste autant que possible, blasphémant tout, et s'exaltant autant dans le mal que dans le bien. Lorsqu'une fois il a enfourché le cheval du diable il faut qu'il aille jusqu'à ce qu'il se rompe le cou. L'excès, voilà sa nature, soit en beau, soit en laid.'

I quote this interesting description at length as much on account of the differences as of the resemblances between the two cases. There is certainly a great deal in common, but that of Philip was very much more subtle and complex than that of Musset, if the long-suffering lady's account is to be taken at its face value. The difference consists in the fact that there was much in Peter Warlock that was admirable, and much in Philip Heseltine that was not so admirable. In the cruel portrait in *Women in Love* and in various passages in *The Letters* referring to Philip, Lawrence was indisputably right in detecting in him a certain invertebrate, molluscous softness, a streak of something akin to effeminacy, in comparison with which the reckless strength and virility of Peter Warlock were decidedly sympathetic.

The struggle between the Mild and Melancholy one and the Complete Man was only one part of a deadly conflict which came to be waged upon every psychological front. The critic fought against the artist in him, the Elizabethan against the modern and the medieval against both, the internationally minded pacifist with his private Cornish language against the bellicose and insular Englishman, the cultured and exquisitely refined aesthete against the beer-swilling pub-crawler, the mystic and the occultist against the cynical blasphemer; and the struggle became fiercer and more intensified as the years went on, in a gradual, inexorable crescendo. And in the same way that a nation which is rent asunder by internecine strife often makes war upon a foreign power in order to consolidate itself and divert attention from its internal chaos, so, I noticed, whenever the mental conflict threatened to become intolerable, as it frequently did, he would launch out into violent personal quarrels and public controversies in a desperate attempt to compose his inner discord. This, I think, is to a great extent the explanation of much of the agressiveness and ferocity which earned for him so many enemies, even in quarters which might otherwise have been well disposed towards him.

It is curious to observe, by the way, that the dichotomy even extended to things physiological. In the days when I first knew him his alcoholic predilection was for liqueurs and other sweet and sickly compounds; later he rarely ever drank anything but beer. At Oxford, as Mr. Nichols tells us, Philip was a vegetarian; Peter's favourite dish, inevitably therefore, was steak tartare – raw meat with a strongly flavoured sauce.

There was only one aspect of the change which seriously troubled me, personally – his attitude to children. Philip had always been fond of children, and one of his chief delights at one time was to take them to the Zoo. Peter, on the other hand, could find no words strong enough to express, not merely the irritation and impatience which every normal person feels at times and often, towards the enchanting horrors that children indubitably are, but a frenzied detestation and loathing which, I frankly confess used rather to upset me, although it certainly had its purely comic side as well. On one occasion, for example, when a well-meaning music publisher wrote to him suggesting that he might consider the composition of a set of songs suitable for children, he (the publisher) must have been somewhat taken aback on receiving in reply a vitriolic hymn of hate directed against all children past and present, and an eloquent paean in praise of the activities of Marie Stopes, expressing the pious wish that they might eventually be extended to the point at which no children would be born in future.

I see now, however, that this pose – for it was nothing more – though disagreeable in a sense, was aesthetically necessary to the complete and ideal monster that he wished to be thought. If with all his elaborate assumption of vices he did not possess, he confessed that he was fond of children, the keystone of the whole edifice would fall out; people would inevitably say that he could not be so bad as he seemed, after all, that there must be a streak of good in him somewhere, and so on – and that simply would not do at all. In this connection a little fragment scribbled on a piece of paper which was found among his things is of curious interest. 'When I see, and smell, a crowd of Battersea children swarming round the doors of Stephenson's bakery, I am minded with disgust of a swarm of obscene flies hovering over a clot of dung in the roadway. But when I turn away there sweeps over me the unspeakable poignancy of the Good Shepherd and His Lambs.' Even allowing for a certain veiled irony, the implications are clear enough; one does not write like that unless, in some way, one really believes it. I do not know of any utterance more typical of him and of the *Doppel gänger* who perpetually accompanied him.

To recapitulate: the change from Philip Heseltine to Peter Warlock was a gradual one, involving several distinct and separate phases – firstly, the adoption of a pseudonym merely as a matter of practical convenience, secondly, its use as a kind of disguise and protective armour, thirdly, when it becomes positive and takes the offensive as it were, and finally, a phase in which he takes a deliberate and perverse pleasure in turning upon and rending his former self and everything associated with him. The creation gradually assumes the upper hand over its creator, the monster over Frankenstein, and ultimately destroys him. Each man kills the thing he loves, wrote Wilde in one of his rare moments of insight, and no one ever did so more thoroughly than Peter Warlock.

Everything Philip had cared for most intensely became in the end the target of his sharpest and most envenomed darts. It was about 1921, then, that the secondary personality, hitherto in abeyance, begins to gain the mastery, both in the man and in the musician. He gradually dropped his old friends, and their place was taken by a vast horde of superficial acquaintances and boon companions. I was probably one of the few, perhaps the only one, who still remained as close a friend of Peter as of Philip, but it would be useless to try to conceal the fact that it was the latter I cared for the more. He was still there in the background and never entirely disappeared, especially when one was alone with him, but for the most part he preferred to conceal himself behind the mask of Peter Warlock. The latter was indeed a delightful companion, but there was never the same intimate comradeship with him as with Philip; and when he began writing such songs as *The Cricketers of Hambledon* and became a member of the Royal and Ancient Order of Frothblowers even I felt that he was carrying an excellent joke rather too far.

We were still to collaborate in our joint book on Carlo Gesualdo, and in the last years I contributed to the short-lived *Milo* which he edited in conjunction with Sir Thomas Beecham's Imperial League of Opera, but the old close relationship was at an end. Our paths gradually separated to a certain extent; looking back on it now, it seems to me almost as if he was trying to avoid me in a sense, not as an individual – for we remained the best of friends – but as one too strongly bound up and closely associated with the past from which he was trying to escape, and with the personality he was trying to overcome, and destroy. And the beginning of this gradual falling-off dates back to the time of the definite beginning of the ascendancy of Peter Warlock, about 1921.

PART THREE

L'art antique appliquait jadis au fronton des théâtres de la
Grèce une face d'airain, joyeuse. Cette face s'appelait la
Comédie. Ce bronze semblait rire, et était pensif. Toute la
parodie, qui aboutit à la démence, toute l'ironie, qui
aboutit à la sagesse, se condensaient et s'amalgamaient
sur cette figure; la somme des soucis, des désillusions,
des dégoûts et des chagrins se faisait sur ce front impassible,
et donnait ce total lugubre, la gaîté; un coin de la bouche
était relevé, du côté du genre humain, par la moquerie, et
l'autre coin, du côté des dieux, par le blasphème; les hommes
venaient confronter à ce modèle du sarcasme idéal l'exem-
plaire d'ironie que chacun a en soi; et la foule sans cesse
renouvelée autour de ce rire fixe, se pâmait d'aise devant l'im-
mobilité sepulcrale du ricanement. Ce sombre masque mort
de la comédie antique ajusté à un homme vivant, on pour-
rait presque dire que c'était là Gwynplaine. Cette tête in-
fernale de l'hilarité implacable, il l'avait sur le cou. Quel
fardeau pour les épaules d'un homme, le rire éternel!

Victor Hugo: *L'homme qui rit*

CHAPTER I

EYNSFORD

On his return from France in the autumn of 1921, Philip settled down to a long and steady spell of work in Wales, whence he wrote to Delius as follows:

Cefn Bryntalch
Oct. 31st, 1921

I was so disappointed that you couldn't come and spend a few days here after Bradford. The weather has been perfect and I have never seen so glorious a riot of autumnal colours as we have in our woods and on the hillsides this year.

I would love to come over and see you and it is most kind of you to offer to pay the fare – but at present I feel that I daren't stop working and leave Wales. I have been travelling about so much this year that things have got very much in arrears – and for one thing I am determined to get this book about you finally completed this year; it has been already too long hanging about halfdone.

And I am also, with great difficulty and still greater diffidence, starting composition again – an orchestral piece this time. I don't know what will come of it, but I am driven ahead, in this as in other work of a less interesting but more remunerative kind, by a fearful feeling of having to use every hour to make up for lost time. Perhaps it is good for one, in a way; but I know that if I left Wales and stopped working even for a couple of weeks, as I inevitably should if I went away, I should find it very difficult to begin again.

Jan. 27th, 1922

I feel ever so much better here than in any city and I have never been able to work so wholeheartedly before. There is great joy in turning out stuff regularly even though one knows that it is very bad! However, I am trying to cease to care about that; excessive self-criticism leads to complete sterility, which is a most horrible condition.

This is practically the last interesting letter I had from him:

Nov. 19th, 1921

Most excellent of all possible kinds of birds!

I am devastated to hear of your abstention from the cordial comforts of those compounds derived from what I believe chemists and suchlike vulgar fellows call C_2H_6O. It is a penance I myself could not by any means endure in London. The country, however, offers compensating delights to me and I am being very abstemious here, rarely attaining and never exceeding half a gallon of innocuous bitter ale *per diem*. This more than moderation is, all the same, due rather to solitude and the lack of anyone to share one's potations than to any other cause. Were you or some other genial soul to arrive I should undoubtedly revive that good old Irish custom of sitting down to dinner in a locked room, throwing the key in the fire and continuing to drink until the fire had burned out and the metal cooled (to say nothing of one's own head) sufficiently to be handled and re-inserted in the keyhole.

This is the kind of house that ought to contain rare old books and fine old wine. And it is true, there are roomfuls of books and cellars full of bottles but alas, treasures are not to be found. I am making a gradual investigation of the cellars. There are dozens of bottles which have lain there untouched and forgotten for at least sixty years but unfortunately Time, low fellow that he is, has been and —— most of them, and this operation has had its customarily degenerating effect upon their innards. Still, after I had spewed and poured down the sink several gallons of various liquids not recognizably anything between vinegar, mushroom ketchup, marking ink and bile, certain shy *virgines intactae* came forward and proffered (*a*) madeira of unspeakably lovely mellowness and (*b*) a curious concoction which I believe to be a home-brewed raisin-wine, of a rich dark amber colour and prepotent properties. The said virgins were of a most peculiar shape and size and, all things considered, there seems to be little doubt but that they have chastely contained themselves for at least a hundred years.

But Wild Wales alone holds an enchantment for me stronger

than wine or woman, and intimately associated with music. In these admirable and tranquil surroundings I can work more quietly and steadily than I have ever been able to before; and with autumn mists, wood fires, old Madeira and old Maturin,[1] who delights me even more than the Madeira, one may well be content. Congenial companionship alone is lacking – but I console myself with the reflection that if I had that also there would be more drinking and less working, and I have a great deal of lost time to make up. I have had a number of Delius piano scores to do lately, and several others to revise, make fair copies of and prepare for printing – and this has taken up most of my time, even though I work on an average six or seven hours a day. The *North Country Sketches* (piano duet) and *Hassan* (piano solo) have already reached the proof stage. Since I have been here I have arranged the *Song of the High Hills* and *In a Summer Garden* for piano solo, and both the *Dance Rhapsodies* for piano duet. . . . I have also re-translated the *Village Romeo* for a new edition. It gave me quite a pang to cross out our old friends the stage directions; however, Sali can no longer be permitted to pull the plug – he ought to think himself lucky to escape the penalty for improper use after so irregular an exploit.

My books and MSS. recently arrived from Ireland and I have re-written several compositions I had forgotten. There was much more stuff than I thought there was among the MSS.; I seem to have been quite industrious during my temporary exile. I have made, I think, quite a good thing out of that gloomy chorus by Nichols, retaining only the opening and closing bars of the original version. Apart from this I have done nothing much – two or three songs, including one good roaring one about beer, and a piece for small orchestra which is not yet scored. But as soon as the Delius book is finished and in Lane's hands, which I trust will be before Christmas, I shall begin to work seriously at composition, regardless of whether the result be good or bad. I feel sure that is the only way to set about it.

. . . Last Sunday, in response to a sudden and urgent request

---

[1] Whose 'Melmoth the Wanderer' I had presented to him.

from the Rector, I attended divine service for the first time in many years and, in the language of provincial reporting, 'presided at the grand organ', fully arrayed in cassock and surplice – to say nothing of the beard which of course has become quite profuse during my rustication. During the Communion Service in E flat by Mr. Caleb Simper(!) I discovered three pedals each of which, when depressed, shot out half a dozen stops whose names were quite unintelligible to me, with a roar, or shot them in again with a sound like an expiring bapgipe. It was almost as good fun as changing gears on a motor-car. However, the strange sounds I produced were nothing compared with the caterwauling they were supposed to accompany, and I received the congratulations of the parish on my beautiful performance. That my sobriety should be called in to assist another's incapacity seemed to me one of the best jokes of recent months. I celebrated the occasion by playing as a voluntary, while the congregation departed, that fine old Welsh tune entitled 'Ton-y-Bottel', with harmonies that must have seemed most appropriate to the villagers.

This was, indeed, probably the most prolific period of his life, from the end of 1921 to the end of 1923: his output during these years comprising the book on Delius, the *Serenade*, which was the orchestral work mentioned in his letter to the latter, *The Curlew* song-cycle, and some twenty-five or so songs, to say nothing of a large amount of arranging of works by Delius for the piano, and much transcription and editing of Elizabethan music in collaboration with Philip Wilson.

No more striking proof of the reality of his dual personality could be found than the difference that existed in this respect between Philip Heseltine and Peter Warlock. The former had always found great difficulty in expressing himself, and wrote very little and very slowly. The latter, on the other hand, seems to have found himself at once, and composed rapidly and with the utmost ease. In 1922, for example, he wrote some twenty or so songs which comprise many of the best he ever wrote such as

Sleep, the two sets of *Peterisms* and, perhaps best of all, the set of four songs entitled *Lillygay*.

Sleep, to words by John Fletcher – a poet for whom he had always a strong partiality – is perhaps the most successful example of his skill in grafting a modern harmonic idiom, and sensibility generally, on to the old Elizabethan tradition. If you look at the voice part alone you might easily imagine it to have been written by John Dowland himself, at his very best, moreover; the subtle and intricate weaving of parts, on the other hand, and the delicately tinted chromatic harmonies are of to-day, and particularly suggestive of the influence of van Dieren. At the same time the combination does not, as one would naturally expect, produce any feeling of incongruity, for the influences are so completely assimilated as to have become second nature. Furthermore, they are fused together in a curiously personal way; the separate ingredients can be analysed and defined, but not the ultimate product, which is not Dowland *plus* van Dieren, or Elizabethan *plus* modern, but simply something wholly individual and unanalysable – Peter Warlock. No one else could have written it.

In the same way that in *Sleep* and other songs he achieves this perfect synthesis of ancient and modern, and carries the Elizabethan tradition up to the present day, so in the volume entitled *Lillygay* he achieves what so many composers of the folk-song school have so persistently attempted to achieve, but without success: namely, a style based upon folk-song, yet at the same time wholly original and personal, and also belonging to its own time – even in the fine work of Vaughan Williams, who has certainly achieved a personal art based upon folk-song, one feels a certain archaism, self consciousness, and lack of inner vitality. Take, for example, the first song of the set, *The Distracted Maid*. In all the volumes of actual folk-songs that have been published you will not find a more authentic folk-song melody, or a more beautiful one, with its lovely last clause rising up to F, on which it hovers for a moment like a bird, with wings extended, and then drops gently down to ground. If the composer had been anonymous instead of pseudonymous, this melody would undoubtedly be accounted one of the finest pearls of English folk-song. But it is not only a lovely tune; it is also exquisitely wedded to the words and lends itself, moreover, to most effective contrapuntal, and particularly canonic, treatment. The accompaniment is beautifully wrought, and in the last verse, where the reality of her position breaks in momentarily upon the fantasies that the poor girl has been weaving around her lover and herself there is a stroke of sheer imaginative genius worthy of Schubert himself.

In the second of the set, *Johnnie wi' the tye*, he does the same thing for Lowland Scottish folk-song, setting to the words a melody with the characteristic Scottish 'snap', but harmonized with an almost insolent modernistic audacity. *The Shoemaker* and *Burd Ellen* are also built on melodies which one would imagine had come straight out of folk-song collections, were it not for the fact that they are almost too suspiciously good to be authentic.

All the songs in this set, incidentally, were conceived during long walks among the Welsh hills which he loved so dearly, and this circumstance is no doubt largely accountable for their characteristics. They are all of them, in fact, songs that one can sing to oneself, in the open air, without any accompaniment; at the same time the accompaniment always fits the voice part like a glove. One finds united in them, in fact, the freshness and spontaneity of folk-song and the aesthetic interest of art-song.

The method of construction employed in all of them is much the same, consisting for the most part in the resourceful exploitation of the old Elizabethan variation form, in which the theme remains unchanged throughout while every possible device of harmonic decoration and enrichment is expended on it.

In contrast to the folk-song atmospheres of the *Lillygay* songs, and the Elizabethan atmosphere of *Sleep* and most of the *Peterisms*, is the *Autumn Twilight*, set to words by Arthur Symons – a beautiful little miniature, wholly modern in its nostalgic sensibility, which in itself is enough to disprove the theory that Peter Warlock was merely an ingenious *pasticheur*. Perhaps, however, it would be more accurate to say that this song is not by Peter Warlock, but by Philip Heseltine, as, quite indubitably, is the song-cycle *The Curlew*, begun in 1920 and finished in 1922. Nothing, indeed, could be more strikingly confirmatory of the distinction that I have sought to establish between the two opposed personalities than the contrast that exists between this work and those to which I have been alluding. It is difficult – in fact impossible – to believe that they were written by the same man at the same period of his life; they have not a single feature in common. The predominating mood of the Warlock songs is robust and jovial, attaining at times to irresponsible hilarity, but never ranging further in the opposite direction than a gentle, wistful melancholy. The mood of the *Curlew* songs, on the other hand, is one of the darkest despair throughout, save only for one solitary ray of sunshine in the third number, at the words 'I know of the sleepy country'; and even this temporary, fleeting respite, a moment of escape into an imaginary world, only renders the gloom of the rest of the work all the blacker and more intense. I do not know of any music, in fact, more utterly desolating to hear than *The Curlew*, and this is not merely due to retrospective subjectivity on my part; I felt precisely the same about it when I first heard it, in 1922. To-day I cannot even bear to listen to it at all, and probably I never shall be able to again.

But it is not merely in mood that the two differ; the idiom, the technique, the very orthography, one might almost say, are at the opposite poles to each other. The writing in the Warlock songs is always neat, easy, fluent; that in *The Curlew* uneasy, hesitant, almost laboured. The former are always fundamentally diatonic in both melody and harmony, and clear-cut in rhythm; the latter is chiefly based upon a chromatic scale built up of alternating tones and semitones, and the rhythms are curiously elusive and contorted.

I can quite understand that people should prefer the Warlock to the Heseltine songs, and even that they should be considered to be very much more accomplished and better realized, but there can be no question as to which are the more ambitious and important. It is a significant fact that while he himself affected to despise, and perhaps genuinely despised, the Warlock songs, as we have seen in his letters, he always retained an affection and a respect for *The Curlew*. Writing to Gerald Cooper in June, 1922, he says, 'I am just completing *The withering of the boughs* which finishes off – to my considerable satisfaction – the Yeats song-cycle in its new guise. Though not given as a rule to flattering my own works, I think it is by far the best work I have done yet.'

I have already had occasion to draw attention to the exceptional felicity with which he was able to reproduce in his music the spirit of the words, whether in medieval poems such as *The Bailey, My gostly Fader*, in Elizabethan poems such as *Sleep*, or *Take, O, take*, and here, as in the Symons setting, he shows himself to have the same insight and understanding of modern as of ancient poetry. He has set Yeats to music as no one else has; to a greater extent than any other composer he has penetrated to the core of the poet's thought and intention. This makes it all the more sad – but also supremely comic at the same time in its irony – that the poet himself should not only have failed to realize the fact, but that he should actually have done all he could to prevent the publication of settings of his poetry by Philip. The sorry story is as follows. In 1920 several publishers had expressed a reluctance even to consider various settings he had made of poems by Yeats, on the ground that they always had trouble with the poet over the question of the copyright of the words and the necessary permission to reproduce them. In September of the same year, in Oxford, he happened to meet Yeats again, whom he had got to know in Dublin in 1918. The latter explained to him that, largely in consequence of an invitation he had once received to hear a setting of his *Lake Isle of Innisfree* – a poem which voices a solitary man's desire for even greater solitude – sung by a choir of a thousand Boy Scouts, he had set up a rigid censorship in order to prevent such things from happening, as far as possible.

Not having any ear for music himself, as he frankly confessed, the poet had appointed someone else to whom, accordingly, Philip duly submitted two settings in the following year. The songs were curtly rejected, no reason being given and no attempt being made to show in what way they were unsuitable. An acrimonious correspondence then ensued between poet and composer which was terminated by the dispatch to the former by the latter of a picture postcard representing that grotesque-looking bird with an enormous bill known as the Adjutant Stork, standing on one leg. This, by the way, was always Philip's favourite method of ending a controversy, the subtle implication being, presumably, that his antagonist had attained to such a pitch of absurdity that an adequate reply was beyond the expressive range of mere words and could only be suggested by the contemplation of the strangest freaks of Nature. Queer birds with long bills, incidentally, and the Adjutant Stork and Secretary Bird in particular, were always the object of his amazed admiration, and seem to have possessed some profound symbolical significance for him, the nature of which is exceedingly difficult to discover. In the following year, however, *The Curlew* was selected for publication under the auspices of the Carnegie United Kingdom Trust, thus making the poet look even more ridiculous than the Adjutant Stork itself, and leaving him without even its one leg to stand on, seeing that the award made any further resistance to publication morally impossible.

The whole dispute was regrettable, however, not merely because it terminated the friendly relations which had hitherto existed between them, but because one cannot help feeling a certain sympathy with the attitude of the poet, who had simply been misled by incompetent advisers. One can imagine nothing more infuriating to a poet than to have his exquisite poems mauled about by second-rate – and worse – composers, as Yeats has had; by a stroke of sheer ironic perversity, however, permission to publish was withheld from the one composer who was able to do justice to the poems, while granted in many instances to composers who have travestied them. The consequence was that

Philip never again set to music the verses of the poet with whom he had perhaps a deeper affinity than with any other, while some fine settings he had already made remain in manuscript, some are lost, and others he destroyed.

Another eminent artist with whom Philip had been on friendly terms, but with whom he had a violent quarrel about this time, was the sculptor Jacob Epstein. I cannot now remember either the cause or the course of the hostilities; I only know that they did not affect the deep admiration which Philip never ceased to express for the master's work. For the rest his feuds were mainly with musicians and generally with music critics. I do not think there was a single one of eminence who was not at some time or other the object of his aversion and the recipient of his insults and abuse, generally in writing. To one in particular he was in the habit of sending, from whatever part of the country he was in, at regular intervals, pairs of bellows, the precise significance of which must necessarily remain veiled in obscurity.

In the course of the year 1922 he finished his monograph on Delius, concerning which he wrote me as follows: 'I have just read through the MS. of my little book on Delius preparatory to sending it to be typed. It has plunged me into acute misery, it is so wretchedly bad. I am more ashamed of this dreadful production than of any little Peterisms I have ever perpetrated. But having undertaken the job I suppose I must produce something or other, and I have already waited too long in the hope of being able to turn out something better.'

All this is, of course, the wildest self-depreciation. His book on Delius is a thoroughly sound, and sometimes exceedingly brilliant piece of work, both as biography and as criticism. It is true that it is occasionally pitched in too high a key; to-day it is difficult, for example, to agree with his words on the *Mass of Life* – 'This colossal work, without a doubt the greatest musical achievement since Wagner, a Mass worthy to rank beside the great Mass of Sebastian Bach.' Certain pages also are somewhat too florally ecstatic and vacuously mystical; he himself humorously confessed to me in later years, when I asked him, that he had not the faintest notion of what he meant by the last sentence of the book: 'And as the lonely soul turns to the starry host for comfort and companionship, so may we turn to this music and hear reverberated in the tones of a lonely singer the voices of the innumerable multitudes of Eternity.' It sounds all right, but it means precisely nothing at all, and is an excellent specimen of what has been called 'blank prose'. On the other hand there are sections of the book which are among the finest things in English musical criticism, alike for soundness of aesthetic judgment and eloquence and grace of style. Particularly notable in these respects are the analysis and appreciation of *A Village Romeo and Juliet*, and the final chapter on the music of Delius viewed as a whole.

A further illustration of the mood of disillusionment and self-dissatisfaction through which he seems to have been passing at this time is to be found in another letter to me, in which he says, 'I have just revised my *Serenade* for strings which I shall send to Sir God Damfrey by way of making an excuse for a good debauch at Poole in the autumn. But it is very depressing, all this petty music-making; I am no better and no worse than I was seven years ago.' Again this is demonstrably nonsense; the *Serenade* is an admirable little work. It is frequently dismissed as imitation Delius, but this is a very superficial judgment. It was ostensibly written as a tribute to Delius on the occasion of his sixtieth birthday, and consequently reveals certain Delian characteristics, as was only fitting under the circumstances. Actually, however, Delius has never written anything remotely resembling it in essence. There is in it, for example, a sustained line drawing which Delius never attempts, for it is not in his nature. Delius's melodic writing is almost invariably broken by harmonic and colouristic considerations, whereas that of the *Serenade* is continuous and organic from beginning to end.

This phase of acute self-depreciation and dissatisfaction seems to have come to a head in 1924, when we find him writing as follows to Robert Nichols: 'Like old Father William I have long

lost any belief in myself in any capacity whatsoever, and any ambition save that of making enough money to be able to eat and
drink pleasantly has gone the same way.'

This psychological condition was, of course, in large part due
merely to the inevitable and unescapable reaction which most
artists experience after a period of creative activity. Compare,
for example, the utterances of Hugo Wolf, whose alternations of
fecundity and sterility were so alike. 'I can no longer form any
notion of what a melody or a harmony is, and I am already beginning to doubt whether the compositions bearing my name are
really mine . . . I should be glad if I could write the smallest
song – I firmly believe it is all over with me . . . In myself everything is dead, not even the smallest tone will sound, it is all silent
and desert in me, as in a snow-covered field of the dead. God
knows how and when this will end.'[1] Wolf's mood was one of a
more frantic despair, Philip's of a more bitter and cynical order,
but in their origins they were the same and invariably had the
same sequel in a renewed outburst of activity.

By the time this last letter was written he had left Wales, where
he had been living almost continuously for about three years,
from 1921 to 1924, and had settled once more in Chelsea. He did
not remain long in London, however; early in 1925, I think,
he moved to Eynsford, a pleasant little village in Kent, where he
stayed for about four years. It was during this period that the
Warlock legend, which had already begun to grow up, took
definite form and substance.

The most important members of the household at Eynsford,
both in status and number, were cats – cats masculine, feminine,
and neuter: cats young, old, and middle-aged: cats of all sizes,
breeds, and colours. Cats had always been one of the ruling
passions of his life, and it was one that grew in intensity as the
years went on until it almost became a mania with him. It was
not confined to individual specimens but extended to the entire
species. The Small Cat House in the Zoo was one of his favourite

[1] Hugo Wolf; by Ernest Newman.

haunts, and every year he attended the Cat Show at the Crystal
Palace with an almost religious fervour, exhorting others to go
and do likewise. 'You must go to the cat show at the Crystal
Palace to-morrow,' he wrote me once, 'which is the last day. I
spent an ecstatic couple of hours there to-day. Such lovely mogs
you can't imagine – including the best cat in the world, surely –
an immense short-haired grey; also the heaviest cat in England
which, though physically stoneless, weighs, by a curious chance,
two stones.'

He had a special vocabulary for defining the various grades of
feline excellence, beginning with 'pussum' and culminating in
M O G – the supreme cat, the Platonic cat, the cat in the mind
of God, the Great One of the Night of Time. His conception of
the ideal cat underwent several changes at different periods; the
authentic mog at the time when I first knew him was a gigantic
black, and as we see from this letter it was later a short-haired
grey. But in the last years the supreme object of his adoration
was that exceptional rarity known as the 'self-red', of which,
indeed, only a few specimens exist. In his consuming ambition
to possess a specimen himself he followed up clues to their existence
all over the country. I have known him to journey to the other
end of London with the sole purpose of seeing one of which he
had heard, and to leap off a bus going at full speed, into the middle
of the crowded traffic, at the sight of a reddish-hued cat which
we had passed, in order to ascertain whether it was of the authentic
variety for which he was seeking. Truly, Moby Dick, the White
Whale of Herman Melville, was not pursued with greater ardour
and tenacity by Captain Ahab than the Great Mog, the Red Cat,
was by Philip. In the end he succeeded in finding it, but, as with
Captain Ahab, it was indeed the end; the self-red survived his
master, but not for long.

On settling at Eynsford Philip threw off every vestige of the
restraint that had hitherto governed these proclivities, and both
through acquisition and the normal processes of nature the feline
population increased by leaps and bounds. On one occasion I

remember him waking up one morning to find a litter of newly born kittens on his chest – an event which he declared to be a highly auspicious omen.

It is related of Antonio Sacchini, an Italian composer of the eighteenth century, that he was unable to write music unless surrounded by cats and mistresses, and Peter Warlock must surely have possessed some secret affinity to this 'graceful, elegant and judicious composer', as Burney calls him, for in addition to the vast number of cats on the premises there was always a steady and abundant supply of the latter commodity also.

In contra-distinction to this more or less floating population of cats and women, a permanent member of the establishment was a strange character called Hal Collins, otherwise Te Akau, a New Zealander whose Maori grandmother had been a cannibal and used, within his memory, to lament the passing of the good old days when she could feast upon her kind. Besides being a graphic artist of considerable talent, particularly in woodcut, he was one of these people who, without ever having learnt a note of music or received a lesson in piano playing, have an inborn technical dexterity and a quite remarkable gift for improvisation. He used to compose systematically, also, but without being able to write it down; I remember him once playing to me a whole act of an opera he had conceived on the subject of Tristram Shandy. A song of his, incidentally, taken down in notation by Peter, called *Forget not yet*, was published by the Oxford University Press, and testifies to his genuine talent. He subsisted chiefly on stout, of which he consumed gargantuan quantities, and when elated would perform Maori war dances with quite terrifying realism. On spirits, however, he would run completely amok, in true native fashion, and on one occasion almost succeeded in massacring the entire household. Like so many members of primitive races, Te Akau had powerful intuitions and a gift of prescience which was frequently uncanny, many instances of which I witnessed myself, and many of which I have heard tell of – he certainly had some kind of gift of second sight. He was devoted to Peter as a dog to its master; the relation between them was similar to that between Mr. Jones and his secretary Ricardo in Conrad's *Victory* – save that Ricardo turned upon his master whereas Colly was faithful and devoted to the end. He died even before Peter, in 1929, of what is popularly called galloping consumption, after an illness of only a few months.

Then there was the village drunkard, who, though not a resident member of the establishment, was always coming in and out. He was met one morning with daffodils entwined in his hair, complaining bitterly that just when, in the public house, he was about to lift a glass to his lips, a kangaroo would suddenly appear from nowhere, snatch it out of his hand, swallow the contents, and then disappear as mysteriously as it had come. For the most part, however, his conversation consisted of the one solitary word 'swish', which aptly conveyed to the world the condition of unalloyed beatitude he enjoyed when not disturbed by his implacable enemy, the kangaroo.

Other familiar figures were the local police force, consisting of the sergeant, no less than seven feet in height and exceedingly lean, and the village constable, quite literally as broad as he was long. In addition there was a constant stream of visitors, some of whom stayed only for the day or for a night, others indefinitely, for months on end, and others until they had to be forcibly ejected – poets and painters, airmen and actors, musicians and maniacs of every description, including pyrophils and claustrophobes – everyone who was in any way unusual or abnormal was sure of receiving a ready welcome at Eynsford. And the central figure in this wild harlequinade, with its cats, columbines, drunken clowns, comic policemen, and eccentrics of every kind, was Harlequin himself; for Peter Warlock was indeed the very embodiment in real life of this strange symbolic personality, in all the separate phases through which it has evolved in the course of the ages – not merely the familiar posturing, acrobatic figure wearing a mask and attired in particoloured spangled tights but also the earlier form of a will o' the wisp or spirit of the air, the still earlier form of a malicious and mocking demon – a warlock in fact – and even the earliest of all, in accordance with which the *familia Herlequini* were the souls of the dead and damned. '*Haec sine dubio familia Herlequini est; a multis eam olim visam audivi, sed incredulus relationes derisi, quia certa indicia nunquam de talibus vidi. Nunc vero manes mortuorum veraciter video.*' (*Historiae Ecclesiasticae* of Ordericus Vitalis, *circa* 1100 – the first known mention in literature of Harlequin.)

Even in his comparatively innocent and modern pantomime form there is something disturbing, equivocal, and sinister about this curious figure, and so there was with Peter Warlock; behind the brightly painted drop-curtain before which the absurd masquerade was taking place, there was an ever-present sense of immanent disaster, of impending catastrophe, which centred around the leading figure in it. Nor is this impression due to mere 'wisdom after the event' on my part; many others felt precisely the same, and at the same time as I did, and no less strongly.

One evening in particular I remember vividly in this connection, when Peter gave an impromptu performance of a little-known Sea Shanty in the collection of Sir Richard Terry, entitled *Walk him along, Johnny*, which he said he wished to be performed at his funeral:

Caparisoned in his African witch-doctor's robe and a huge soft black hat, he intoned the choral lines in a hoarse whisper, hopping and capering grotesquely like a vulture, in a kind of *danse macabre*, imbuing the artless little ditty with a nameless sense of dread and horror, and seeming almost to gloat over the thought of his own immanent decease. On a certain dark and gloomy December day only a few years later, in the old cemetery at Godalming, I was to recall involuntarily this strange performance, and in my mind's eye seemed to see him leaping around his own coffin, croaking sardonically, 'Walk him along, Johnny, carry him along; carry him to the burying ground.'

Occasionally there were clear signs that Philip revolted bitterly and strenuously against this sinister stranger who so often took possession of him, body and soul, and would have given anything to be rid of him. An instance of this I remember when, in the midst of a wild and riotous gathering, he suddenly rose saying, 'One has only a short time to live, and yet one spends it like this,' and walked out, not returning until the next day.

Such moments, however, although significant, were exceptions, and recollections of days spent at Eynsford are among the happiest and most memorable of my life, and in the lives of many others besides myself. I remember particularly one Easter when we crossed over by the ferry from Gravesend to Tilbury and sat in the warm spring sunshine, drinking endless pints of beer, watching the great liners pass up and down the Thames estuary, and discoursing eloquently on every subject under the sun. The peculiar glamour and enchantment of such days, and they were many, remain indelibly associated with Philip in one's mind; it is almost as if he created this halcyon quality of perfect spring and early summer skies – as if it emanated from him, so to speak, and had no independent existence apart from him. One only knows, at any rate, that one has never experienced such days with anyone else, either before or since.

No account of Peter Warlock would be complete without reference to his harlequinesque propensity for suddenly indulging

in extravagant displays of acrobatic dancing and *pas seuls* in all
places and on all occasions, whenever he happened to be in a
state of elation – in public houses, on restaurant tables, in the
middle of Piccadilly Circus, even in the austere precincts of the
Queen's Hall itself, to the stupefaction of concert goers. But the
most vivid and characteristic recollection of the kind that I retain
was that of his departure one afternoon from Charing Cross
Station, where he had arrived just in time to catch a train back
to Eynsford, after a festive day in town. On emerging from the
booking-hall, instead of going straight to his train he suddenly
began to execute the most astonishing dance I have ever seen in
my life, worthy even of Nijinsky himself; a kind of variation on the
Russian *danse accroupie*, in which the legs, however, were shot out
sideways instead of to the front, punctuated by sudden leaps into
the air, with outspread arms, brandishing an attaché case in one
hand and a walking stick in the other. Gradually the normal
activities of the station came to a standstill; passengers hurrying
for trains, porters laden with luggage, railway officials and
policemen on duty, all gathered round to watch the strange sight.
It is a curious fact that no one laughed or jeered; on the faces of
the onlookers amusement quickly gave way to sheer astonishment, and astonishment to a kind of awestruck, spellbound admiration, as this strange, bearded, faunlike creature danced there
all by himself, seemingly quite oblivious to his surroundings.
Then, suddenly, the spell was broken. A whistle sounded, and
Peter's train began slowly to move out of the station. With one
final prodigious bound into the air he dashed to the barrier,
brushed aside the protesting ticket-collector, clambered on to the
footboard of the last carriage as it left the platform, and waved a
courtly and dignified farewell to the assembled crowd before
climbing into his compartment. The astounded spectators looked
at each other mutely for a moment, shook their heads, and resumed their normal occupations.

His returns home from London to Eynsford, incidentally, were
productive of many strange and untoward occurrences. He had

always an invincible tendency to somnolence on such occasions, and would almost invariably be taken far beyond his destination before he recovered consciousness. Many and diverse were the places at which he would find himself being turned out of the train at its terminal point in the early hours of the morning, with nowhere to go, and generally without a penny in his pocket. Eventually, in order to obviate this disagreeable contingency, he was in the habit of ringing up the station at Eynsford to tell them by which train he proposed to return, and on its arrival at the station a search party would be organized by the staff in order to discover the whereabouts of his invariably recumbent and unconscious person: which, being found, would be placed upon a luggage trolley, wheeled down the platform, and confided to the tender care of his friends. Once Peter was asleep nothing on earth could wake him; there was something almost pathological about it. On the countless occasions on which I have known him to fall asleep during concerts he succeeded in remaining unconscious throughout such things as *Ein Heldenleben*, the *Sacre du Printemps*, and *Pacific 231*, which is something of a feat; the only music that made him once stir uneasily in his seat was the *Hebridean Symphony* of Sir Granville Bantock.

Caring nothing for any form of sport, outdoor or indoor, or for any games, whether of chance or skill, his sole recreation, relaxation, solace, and distraction, apart from long country walks which were wholly compatible, was the tavern. His knowledge of inns and public houses in every part of the country was truly encyclopaedic, and I can pay no higher tribute to his eminence in that field than by quoting from an essay entitled *The Timely Inn* by Mr. Douglas Goldring, himself an acknowledged authority on the subject, in his volume *Impacts*. 'Among my colleagues in this branch of research – each of them a mine of extensive and peculiar information – it would be unjust of me not to pay a tribute in passing to', amongst others mentioned, 'Philip Heseltine. Mr. Heseltine is particularly noted for his scientific inquiry into the quality of our beer, the deterioration of which can only be regarded as a national calamity.'

He certainly went into the question with characteristic thoroughness. Among his papers I have discovered evidence of an extensive correspondence on the subject of beer conducted with such official bodies as the Ministry of Health, the Institute of Brewing, and the Brewers' Society, from which he was able to elicit, among other things, the fact that, of the materials used in brewing, in Great Britain, in the year ending September 30th, 1925, amounting to 15,520,166 hundredweights in all, and producing 26,849,703 barrels containing 36 gallons each, the quantity of pure hops used was only 362,554 hundredweights, as against 1,863,930 hundredweights of sugar, syrups, etc. Lengthy, passionate, and eloquent were the speeches in which, ever after, he was wont to inveigh against this shameful state of affairs. I have seen him rouse large audiences in public houses, and hold them spellbound with his denunciations of the treacherous conspiracy he had discovered on the part of the brewers, the publicans, and the government, all working hand in glove with each other, to poison the People by means of chemical beer, and exhorting them to rise up and overthrow their tyrannous oppressors. On one occasion, I remember, he somewhat dispelled the favourable impression he had made by winding up with an eloquent peroration on the subject of the Penge tunnel in which, he passionately asserted, the Southern Railway secretly grew vast quantities of mushrooms. Unfortunately one never learnt the explanation of these strange and subterranean activities on the part of the railway company – one only gathered that they were exceedingly reprehensible and nefarious – for in the middle of a sentence he was suddenly overcome by an irresistible desire for sleep which he proceeded instantly to gratify.

The quest of the perfect beer, as of the perfect cat, was an overmastering obsession of his later years. He firmly believed, I think, that somewhere, at sometime, he would find a beer quite unlike any that he had ever tasted before, a kind of ambrosia or nectar of the gods, but made out of pure hops and nothing else. Time and time again he fell in love with and idealized some particular brew, but always in the end it failed him and proved itself unworthy of his trust. After declaring ecstatically that So-and-So's beer was positively the most miraculous he had ever tasted he would discover to his horror that it had a larger percentage of arsenic or sulphuric acid than any other . . .

Certain critics, speaking condescendingly of Peter Warlock's 'slender output', have sought to suggest that this was due to his eccentric and disorderly mode of life, and that if he had disciplined himself more his achievement might have been very much greater. This is such a tangled thicket of nonsense that it is difficult to know where to begin to clear it. The basis of the argument is, of course, ethical, and is due to a belief in the doctrine of justification by works. In the view of those who hold it the artist ought to slave at his desk like a bank clerk, from morning to night, day after day, week after week, month after month, year after year, turning out a vast quantity of bad works rather than a few good ones. Now it is certainly true enough that fertility is the concomitant of the highest genius but it is a quality, the only quality, that it shares with mediocrity. In the same way that mental defectives, through sheer irresponsibility, are notoriously prolific in actual life, so are bad artists; those of the second highest order are almost invariably men of 'slender output'. And when one thinks of the colossal mass of bad music, bad books, bad paintings in the world, then indeed one feels about them what Peter Warlock felt about human progeny and sighs for a Marie Stopes who will find some means of suppressing the results of artistic impulses.

Actually, so far from writing too little, Peter Warlock wrote, if anything, too much; so far from being slender, his output is large, if you consider that he died at the early age of thirty-six and did not produce any of it until he was twenty-five. During these eleven years he published over a hundred songs and more than twenty various choral and instrumental works, besides a large mass of work which was not published or else was destroyed, wrote two books, collaborated in another, produced a large quantity of fine journalistic work which is being collected into a volume, edited and transcribed a vast quantity of old music, made piano arrangements of many of Delius's orchestral works, made several literary anthologies and did other editorial work – if all this, in eleven years, is a slender output, then I should like to know what a large output is. As I say, I think he wrote too much; some of the later songs of Peter Warlock are not up to the best of which he was capable. But even if his output had been slender his mode of life would not have been the cause. On the contrary, his mode of life was the result, not the cause of his mode of work. Artists mostly conform to one or other of two types; either they work slowly and deliberately, with extreme regularity, or else they are dependent on the mood of the moment and can only produce when the spirit moves them. Creators on a large scale generally conform to the former, lyricists and miniaturists to the latter, and Peter Warlock was genuinely incapable of working steadily at any creative task, over a long period of time. On the other hand, when in the vein, no one had a more phenomenal power of concentration and rapidity of execution. He would often work for twenty hours on end, and was able to keep up this rate for comparatively long periods, with the result that in the course of two or three weeks he would produce as much work as the artist of the opposite type would do in six months. The inevitable consequence of such high tension, however, was a violent reaction, and frequently he would be unable to do any work of the slightest value for months on end. While his creative faculties were in action he led a quiet and ascetic existence, going nowhere and seeing no one; but during these long periods of enforced inactivity he was inevitably driven by the law of his nature into the opposite extreme. Emphatically, he was not the type of artist who required some artificial stimulus or incentive to creation, as was, for example, Swinburne, who did his best work while practically a dipsomaniac, and, when cured by Watts-Dunton, subsided into mechanical repetition of his former achievements; on the contrary, work and dissipation of any kind were with him utterly incompatible. So long as he was able to work to good purpose he thought of nothing else.

The music he wrote during the Eynsford period shows Peter Warlock very much in the ascendant, but there are at the same time a few works in which Philip Heseltine still emerges. In such things as *Yarmouth Fair*, *The Toper's Song*, *Maltworms*, *Jillian of Berry*, *Away to Twiver*, and so on, we find the authentic Peter Warlock a popular tradition, and in *Milkmaids*, *Candlelight*, *My Own Country*, *And Wilt Thou Leave Me*, and others, the continuation of the charming folk-song vein first exploited in *Lillygay*; in the two poignant and intimate, deeply subjective and expressive settings of Arthur Symons, on the other hand – *A Prayer to Saint Anthony of Padua*, and *The Sick Heart* – and in *Hanacker Mill* and *The Night* of Hilaire Belloc, we find the old Philip Heseltine. It is interesting and significant, moreover, to observe that these latter are quite definitely the best songs of the period, few though they are in proportion to the large output of Peter Warlock who, despite his comparative fecundity, does not maintain the high standard he set up in *Lillygay* or the first book of *Peterisms*. As time goes on, in fact, one encounters a steadily increasing amount of comparatively undistinguished and even mediocre work of his, quite frankly and unashamedly written as pot-boilers and nothing else. These others, however, few though they be, are among the best things Philip Heseltine ever wrote – that is, among the best songs of modern times.

In the same vein and on a larger and more ambitious scale is the little known and never performed *Sorrow's Lullaby*, to words by Thomas Lovell Beddoes, for soprano, baritone, and string quartet. This is a highly personal and intimate utterance, strange and elusive in its mood and singularly recondite in its harmonic idiom. If it must on the whole be adjudged less successful than the foregoing songs with piano accompaniment it is because the medium is not entirely suited to the thought. There is in particular too much double-stopping for the strings, and I am inclined to think that the work could have been more satisfactorily realized in a more extended combination of chamber instruments, such as that employed in *The Curlew*.

In striking contrast, both in this and other respects, is the *Capriol* suite for strings, written in 1926, and scored two years later for full orchestra. Personally I prefer the original version, the string writing of which is particularly resourceful and effective. The work is nominally based upon tunes taken from a treatise on dancing called *Orchésographie* written by one Thoinot Arbeau in 1588, but if one compares these tunes with what the composer has made of them it will be seen that to all intents and purposes it can be regarded as an original work. Only the second number of the suite, *Pavane*, is a reconstitution of the original, while the fifth, *Pieds-en-l'air*, has not even any thematic connection whatever with Arbeau. For the rest the latter has merely provided the barest little wisps of tune, a few bars long, which have only acted as suggestions for what are in reality highly organized and individual developments. The conclusion of the last number, *Mattachins*, is a case in point, owing nothing to Arbeau or, for that matter, to anyone else. It is pure Peter Warlock, the precise musical equivalent of his dance in Charing Cross station; no one else could possibly have written it.

Pure Peter Warlock, again, are the two part-songs, *One More River* and *The Lady's Birthday*. The latter is a particularly uproarious and characteristic performance, concluding with a setting of the all-too-familiar words 'Time please gentlemen, finish your drinks, hurry up please, long past time' – a veritable Hogarth or Rowlandson in sound. And once again in striking contrast is a small group of works for the same medium set to poems of Thomas Webster – *Three Dirges* – probably the gloomiest and grisliest music that even Philip Heseltine ever wrote, which is saying a good deal. That they should have been written at precisely the same time as *The Lady's Birthday* – the climax of melancholy and desolation together with that of the most boisterous and unbridled merriment – is strikingly symbolical of his strange dichotomy. It is interesting and psychologically significant, indeed, to notice that in proportion as Peter Warlock becomes wilder and wilder as time goes on, so Philip Heseltine becomes gloomier and gloomier.

The intrinsic substance of these *Dirges* is deeply interesting and very personal, but they are so excessively difficult that I doubt whether a satisfactory performance is possible, or at least practicable without a degree of preparation and rehearsal which are seldom obtainable under present conditions. A conceivable solution of the problems of intonation which present themselves in every bar would be to have them performed as they would doubtless have been performed in Elizabethan times, either by doubling the vocal parts with instruments, or, since they are harmonic and homophonic rather than contrapuntal in texture, by singing the top line only and confiding the remaining parts to instruments alone. The experiment would be well worth the making for, abstractly considered, they are very remarkable works, especially from a harmonic point of view. They are practically unknown and never performed, but there are some good judges who admire them greatly, and even consider them to be amongst the composer's best works. I take the liberty of citing in this connection a letter written to him by Mr. Arnold Bax in which, moreover, the writer's high opinion of all his work, and particularly his harmonic gift, deserves attention as coming from such a distinguished fellow artist.

ARNOLD BAX TO PHILIP

My dear Heseltine,

I never see you, so I never have the opportunity to tell you what very great pleasure your compositions give me. I don't know a single piece of yours that I don't like, and I am prompted to write to you now since Winthrop Rogers have just sent me your latest part-songs – two of them. I think *The Shrouding of the Duchess of Malfi* is a masterly piece of tragic writing. You are one of the only modern composers in my opinion whose harmonic invention derives from an emotional and natural source.

I would rather hear pure diatonic and nothing else than the damnable brain-spun muddle and mess which is the stuff of most modern music. That is why it is exciting to find someone writing harmony that to my mind is obviously sincere and imaginative and flexible.

All good wishes from . . .

This is only one among many eloquent tributes paid to the genius of Peter Warlock by his most eminent contemporaries, and no more striking refutation could be found of the cheap sneers on the part of a small and insignificant body of critics who still refuse to acknowledge it, generally for purely personal reasons which reflect the utmost discredit upon them. Mr. Bax's remarks concerning his harmonic sense are especially acute and penetrating, for undoubtedly it is in this quality that his greatest strength, in his best works, resides. Although always essentially a development and extension of the Elizabethan tradition, his harmonic thought is at the same time often extremely daring and original. This in itself is characteristically English: for were not the Elizabethans the most daring and original harmonists of their time, as the anonymous composer of *Sumer is icumen in*, Dunstable and Purcell were of their respective times? Of all composers of his generation is it not Delius who possesses the richest and subtlest harmonic palette? It would not, I think, be going too far to say that no country has contributed so much, at so many different periods, to the enrichment and development of harmonic resource, as England has, and in this distinguished record Peter Warlock deserves an honoured place.

With regard to his work as an editor and transcriber of old, and chiefly Elizabethan, music, I am happy to be able to give here the following tribute of Sir Richard Terry – than whom there is no more eminent authority on the subject in this country – of which, moreover, the personal aspects will perhaps serve to confirm and supplement what has been written by Mr. John, Mr. Nichols and myself. His very first sentence, for example, bears out strikingly what I have written above (p. 127) concerning

266

Philip's gift for establishing at once with friends an intimate spiritual contact, even with one belonging to an older generation than his own, such as Sir Richard.

SIR RICHARD TERRY'S TRIBUTE

I cannot remember how, when, or in what circumstances I first came to meet Philip Heseltine. He was one of those rare spirits whom to know at all was equivalent to feeling that there was never a time when you had not known him, and that intimately.

I never knew which I admired the more – the sheer bigness of the man or his modesty regarding the talents which made him big.

He was a musician, but he was as different from the general practitioner as the poles are apart. Music for him was not a career to be made, but a life to be lived. Where art called, there he followed, indifferent alike to popular applause and academic censure, supremely indifferent to such success as was measured in terms of money. Not that he would foolishly deny a man's right to live by his art. He recognized the soundness of the axiom that the labourer is worthy of his hire; but he was to find, at an early stage, that something more than sound axioms is required of a composer when it comes to negotiating for the sale of his works.

He failed to reckon early enough with another factor which became responsible for his failure to attain financial success. He was ever the artist – ready with generous appreciation of the artistic achievements of others. He never varied in his reverence for the work of greater artists than himself. For him a work of art was a thing in which to take joy. Knowingly to belittle a thing which his inner consciousness told him was a work of art was something of which he was incapable. It took him some time to realize that there is a type of mind which hates everyone who produces anything superior to what it can itself achieve. He may not have been acquainted with Birrell's well-known aphorism, that every big man 'is hated on his appearance, for there is something about him which revolts the ordinary mind'. He could not have been prepared for the cold malignity with which mediocrity dogs the footsteps of every artist unless and until he becomes famous enough to be fawned upon.

Most successful artists have worn down the mediocre malignants by ignoring them (the only attitude which cows them), but Heseltine could never suffer fools gladly. Generous to a fault himself, he was revolted by pettiness in others. Meanness or discreditable conduct brought the offenders under the lash of his mordant wit, and they never forgave him. He did not realize sufficiently early the subtle freemasonry that exists between mediocrities; a freemasonry that unites them (even though strangers to each other) as one man against him who dares outstrip them. They do not come out into the open with honest criticism of an artist's work; they do not raise their voices above the proper well-bred tone; but by gossip and innuendo – judiciously distributed – they contrive to create an 'atmosphere' in 'proper quarters' hostile to the object of their attentions, who ultimately finds nearly every legitimate professional avenue closed to him. Such was the price Philip Heseltine paid for the crime of being witty at the expense of pretentious mediocrity.

To understand his career it is necessary to understand the England into which he was born.

That an original thinker should have the mediocrities and the academics arrayed against him is not a new thing. What gave it a new complexion in England was the trend of events since Edwardian days. The academics who held Elgar down till he reached his forties had fortunately no stronger weapon than a common dislike which found vent in systematic disparagement. This was sufficient to keep him in obscurity until he had worn down the opposition and caught the public ear. During his period of struggle he was able to earn at least a living wage by 'jobs' obtained after fair competition in an open market.

By Heseltine's time 'fair competition' had become a farce, and the once open market turned into a *hortus conclusus*. How did it happen?

The initial step was taken when the universities of Oxford and Cambridge imposed a three years' residence as a condition of obtaining a musical degree, on the plea that this period spent at our premier seats of learning should give the musician (poor fellow) an additional culture and so (as it was publicly announced at the time), 'raise the tone of the musical profession'. But since, in issuing these decrees, the two universities made no provision for adequate musical training and tuition, the immediate result was that their musical degrees were unobtainable by musicians, however gifted, unless they had ample private means and could afford to take from their professional life three of the most precious years to play at music in an ill-equipped university when they ought to have been working at it in a properly equipped conservatoire. This incidentally caused the flooding of the musical profession with a class of cultured amateurs of reasonable proficiency in many things and genuine distinction in none. (There were exceptions of course – organ scholars at the various colleges in those days gained their posts after open competition.)

The second step was the *rapprochement* (unofficial of course) between these universities and conservatoires. This is recent history and need not be retold. One of the immediate consequences was to increase the number of those cultured amateurs who were to 'raise the tone of the profession'. For all these 'cultured' students posts had to be found. We cannot blame the heads of institutions for looking after the interests of their *alumni*, but it has led to a disquieting state of affairs. Yet, to-day, in a manner that must appear mysterious to the uninitiated, posts formerly obtainable only in open competition are filled by nomination. And, significantly, the nominees always come from one or other of the (unofficially) allied centres. Formerly a budding composer could with reason hope to maintain himself and find time for composition by gaining on his merits, in competition with all comers, an appointment at a cathedral, or a school, or wherever teachers are needed. Nowadays he has no such chances unless he is 'inside the ring' or is prepared to pay court to the ruling mandarins. The type of student most acceptable to 'the ring' is that distinguished for docile mediocrity. Heseltine was not docile, and far from being a mediocrity, so he remained outside. But if he did not gain any 'job' he kept his soul.

There is yet another method of holding down unwelcome musicians of the calibre of a Heseltine. This is the method which one finds usually employed by cultured students who have success-fully emerged from their academic courses. Once they are safely anchored in their havens of comfortable jobs, their usefulness lies in that *ipso facto* they have become active members of the powerful Society of Log Rollers. Even then their internal dissensions and their heart-burnings persist in full comicality. Before the public, however, they always preserve a united front. They talk con-sistently about each other, and take care to talk about nobody else. They give lectures about each other (and again, nobody else). Where they gain access to the Press they use it to write about each other (and about nobody else). They magnify each other's most puny achievements and maintain complete silence about the work of every 'outsider'. The British public is apathetic and incurious; it becomes accustomed to seeing only one set of names in print; it knows of no others, and so the members of 'the ring' have succeeded in establishing themselves, in public estimation at least, as the leaders of British music.

A fourth 'holding-down' method employs the social pull. The cultured scholar who has once mixed on equal terms with 'Varsity men' becomes, by virtue of that fact alone, a Patrician. Mere musicians being Plebeians are, as such, therefore not to be encouraged. Heseltine – an old Etonian – could not very well be placed in the latter class, so 'the ring' gratuitously made him an Honorary Plebeian, on the same principle by which they had constituted themselves Honorary Gentlemen. The British public being uninquisitive, and helpless in face of organized snobbery, since they are not themselves devoid of it, the scheme was bound to succeed.

But already Time is beginning to 'bring his revenges'. The policy of holding down non-academic composers is having a sequel not contemplated by its promoters. We have at least one British institution which is not easily bluffed. I mean Fleet Street. The present attitude of Fleet Street towards British music has become one of cynical amusement. Certain time-honoured journals still maintain the time-honoured standards of musical criticism, but such criticism has disappeared in one after another of the rest where it was formerly a feature. In the journals with 'the largest circulation' British music is conspicuous by its comparative absence, or (in several cases) complete neglect. Three musical journals still occupy an impregnable position, but numerous attempts of late to start new ones have ended in failure.

This is the musical England in which Heseltine moved. The 'ring' which hunted him down will automatically destroy itself; its career will one day be ended; but that, alas, is a poor compensation for the martyred victims whose bodies it has left along its track.

I do not know how far Heseltine unburdened himself to others, but to me, if he spoke of his detractors, it was always with humorous contempt. Where lesser men might justifiably have been consumed with rage, he could console himself by the composition of scathing – and outrageously witty – limericks, gibbeting the offenders. He moved with serene assurance in the midst of the pitiful crowd of backbiters, as the true Elizabethan that he was, and his looks well matched his mentality. With his pointed beard and fine carriage he looked the part. He might have been a reincarnation of Walter Raleigh or Philip Sidney.

But if he was the Elizabethan in figure, he was even more the Elizabethan in mind. The mere scoring of Elizabethan music is well within the range of accomplishments of an intelligent plumber or gas-fitter. The artistic grasp of the score, on the other hand, demands qualities so rare as to be startling when one meets them. For Heseltine's rivals the contriving of a score of Tudor music (to say nothing of their dreary comments thereon) appeared usually to be nothing more than a matter of ink and paper. From the very first I could see that for Heseltine the score meant vastly more. And he was able to convey that meaning to others in the finished product. The music sprang to life on the page before him. Where his competitors were laboriously applying their textbook knowledge to its elucidation, his mind intuitively leaped to the music's true significance – none of the aloof academicians that imagined themselves his rivals ever reached that goal in their presumptuous absorption in technicalities and all the correlative matter which is their chief preoccupation.

There is no clearer revelation of Heseltine's marked superiority over all rivals than that shown in his handling of a comparatively small matter like *musica ficta* – that Puck-like thing, so much bewritten and so little understood; an innocent looking little *gamin* who so gloriously succeeds in tripping up the many learned pundits who would investigate its character and attributes, from the illustrious Rockstro to his egregious confrères of the present day.

When I look through the versions of Heseltine's rivals, I find them complacently peppering their scores with 'howlers' whenever they risk themselves on this slippery path. Anyone who looks for similar howlers in Heseltine's work will search in vain. Textbook lore is never a match for artistic insight.

Heseltine made no parade of learning, but he *knew*. His knowledge was equalled only by his modesty. Before he had grasped a thing thoroughly he always professed entire ignorance of it, and accepted information on the subject from whatever source with a childlike humility.

I remember how once – when he turned his attention to Tudor choral work – he asked me to instruct him about ligatures; his textbooks, it seemed, were all vague on that point. I showed him a card on which I had prepared a table of ligatures for the use of pupils. He read it through and then burst into laughter, saying: 'so that's what they make such a fuss about? I thought it must be some dark and horrible mystery'.

To Heseltine the cult of Elizabethan music was not a medium for obtaining the distinction and rewards which might come to so important a person as one who studies impressively abstruse subjects. To him it was a quest, an eagerly pursued quest, and one pursued in the same spirit of adventure as that of his Elizabethan prototypes when they scoured uncharted seas in search of new lands. His textbooks were of no more use to him than the old charts were to Drake. For such men documents are of secondary importance. To them the goal is all that matters. That is why future generations (better informed than our own) will find joy in Heseltine's transcriptions when the work of many of his more pushful competitors has been consigned to the scrap heap. For he was a scholar, but not a pedant; a consummate technician, but withal possessed of vision; a creative artist who could penetrate the minds of Elizabethan composers as no mere transcriber could ever hope to do. With his passing England lost an artist, a scholar, and, in the literal sense of a much-abused term, a gentleman.

Shortly before his death he went on a motor tour with a friend. He called at my house in Oxford, healthy, tanned, and exuberantly high-spirited.

As I was going from home for a while, we arranged for him to spend a week-end with us on my return.

I never saw him again, but I can see him now waving his farewell from the gate – virile and splendid, exultant with the joy of life. That was the Heseltine I knew. That is how one would wish to remember him, and it is a memory I shall cherish until the end.

I am glad that Sir Richard has brought out so trenchantly the peculiar conditions under which music labours in this country at the present day, for otherwise I should have been compelled to deal with the point myself – much less adequately. It is a melancholy fact that music in England is for the most part represented on the one hand by the professional musician, who practices it as a means of livelihood, and discharges his task with the same efficiency and conscientiousness that any other tradesmen, such as a carpenter or a plumber, brings to his work; and on the other hand the cultured gentleman of the public schools and the universities, for whom it is an interesting and possibly engrossing diversion. Between these two extremes of artisan and dilettante there are a few artists, the number of whom can generally be counted on the fingers (the thumb being specifically excluded) of one hand; of these Peter Warlock, whatever his stature, was one. He belonged to a different world from either of the other two – and they both knew it, and bitterly resented it.

I have only one small addition to make to Sir Richard's appreciation of Philip's genius as a scholar and editor of old works, and that is an extract from a letter which he wrote me, in 1926, dealing with that knotty problem to which Sir Richard refers, called *musica ficta*; by which is meant, briefly, the convention according to which, in old music, accidentals that were not noted in the parts were added by the performers in accordance with a definite tradition, which is now lost, and can only be supplied by aesthetic intuition.

'May I have the benefit of your advice on some very pretty problems of *musica ficta* in the near future? I have transcribed a number of songs by composers of 1560–70 from MS. sources which present great difficulties in this respect; I have also done a number of compositions from Whythorne's 1571 book, in the Tenor part of which (at Christ Church, Oxford) is a note to the effect that every accidental that is to be used is inserted in the text, and that no others should be used. The impression I get from the music is that we have all been far too free with the pepper pot in this respect' (Jan. 6th, 1926).

That he, one of the first of living specialists in the music of that period, should ask me, who knew so little about it, for the benefit of my advice on such a point, illustrates very well Sir Richard's reference to his humility and modesty, his readiness to learn from anyone, and his conviction – however ill-founded on this particular occasion – that the opinion of one whose artistic judgment he valued was of more use to him than that of any number of so-called experts.

His knowledge of the Elizabethan period was not confined to music, but covered literature also, with the remotest bypaths of which he must have been better acquainted than almost any literary critic of his time; in witness whereof one need only point to the fact that when a collection of English Madrigal Verse was issued, he drew up a list of several hundred *errata*, if I remember rightly, in the text, which was duly published by Sir (then Mr.) John Squire in *The London Mercury*. A further token of his erudition in this field of literature is afforded by his discovery, editing, and publication in the last year or so of his life of that beautiful collection of early seventeenth-century lyrics, *Giles Earle; His Booke*. This aspect of his activities I am not competent to judge, and therefore beg leave to quote the following passages from reviews by those who are. 'The collection is known in the British Museum as "Additional MS. 24665", and, besides the pleasure of handling its pages with all their scribbles, blots and smudges in faded ink, one discovers, in reading them by the side of the book Mr. Warlock has made, a very great admiration for their editor. . . . It is, says its editor, "addressed to the general body of English poetry-lovers", and it is poetry which he has illuminated with his scholarship and understanding . . . Certainly Mr. Warlock's notes on the text itself handle questions of authorship, variant readings, sources, dates, and the like with a most graceful capability . . . The book is beautifully produced, a gift to his age from a great scholar with a deep love of music and literature' (*The Observer*). Also this from *The Manchester Guardian*: 'There could have been few men better qualified to edit a collection of Elizabethan and Jacobean songs than the author of *The English Ayre*; and it was a happy thing that Peter Warlock lived to complete his edition of *Giles Earle; His Booke* . . . Warlock's editing is a characteristic piece of scholarship and insight.'

It would be a great mistake, however, to suppose that in his knowledge and love of literature he was only a period-specialist, or that his tastes were narrow and exclusive, as one might easily conclude from Mr. Nichols' memoir. Not that I question for a moment the accuracy of the impression in so far as it relates to the time with which Mr. Nichols is principally dealing – his undergraduate days at Oxford, and even for some time later. It is true that he never read much of German, Russian, Italian, or of French literature apart from that of the nineteenth century; but his knowledge of English literature was encyclopaedic, and he knew his classics well. An instructive index to the degree of his literary erudition is afforded by that entertaining compilation of his entitled 'Merry-Go-Down: a gallery of gorgeous drunkards through the ages. Collected for the use, interest, illumination, and delectation of serious topers'; including citations from, amongst many others, the Book of Genesis, Aristotle, Seneca, Plato, Athenaeus, Pliny, Lucian, Petronius, Langland, Gower, Skelton, Villon, Rabelais, Nashe, Shakespeare, Beaumont and Fletcher, Walter Raleigh, Rochester, Thomson, Boswell, Byron, Peacock, Beddoes, Poe, Borrow, Dickens, Marie Corelli(!), Norman Douglas, and James Joyce.

For the last-named writer he had a particular cult which was all the more remarkable in view of his early violent prejudice against him. Mr. Nichols says on page 66 that he greatly admired *Portrait of the Artist as a Young Man*, but this is almost certainly wrong. It may be that after getting to know *Ulysses* he found much in the earlier work, on re-reading it, that was admirable, but he had not a good word to say for it at the time of its first appearance. I remember well the months of steady persistent effort it required on my part to induce him even to look at *Ulysses*, of which I had obtained a copy on its first publication in 1922. Characteristically enough, his conversion was effected by the citation of the more lurid speeches of Private Carr in the *Walpurgis Nacht* scene. Once he was acquainted with the book, however, his admiration for it knew no bounds, and he was one of the few people I know who have equally wholeheartedly appreciated the later *Work in Progress*. But this was only natural in one who desired so greatly to have a private language of his own, and even went so far as to learn Cornish for that reason.

That Joyce should thus create a private language of his own was bound to arouse his admiration. There was more in it than that, however; the peculiar form of verbal wit of which Philip was so fond, with its plays on words, recondite associations of ideas, obscure allusions, and portmanteau combinations of words, was always strikingly akin to that of Joyce, long before he had ever become acquainted with the latter's work. A good example of it is found in the letter quoted on page 211, 'The Felis Catus Castrensis of Carrollingian legend'. The association of ideas here – the Cheshire Cat and a castrated cat, Charlemagne and Lewis Carroll – is pure Joyce of the *Work in Progress* period. Unfortunately the best of Philip's many felicitous word and phrase coinings of this type are either so arcane and esoteric in their references as only to be intelligible to a few initiates – and that, I fear, is just what is the matter with *Work in Progress* itself, astonishing *tour de force* though it is – or else simply unprintable; and this latter objection applies to his many admirable limericks. The excellence of a limerick, indeed, is in direct ratio to its unprintability, and to represent his talents in this direction by such examples as would pass the censor would be to do them a grave injustice. There is an excellent one, however, which has become deservedly famous and has already appeared elsewhere, in *The Week-end Book*, and which, through a typographical equivocation, is unexceptionable:

> Young girls who frequent picture palaces
> Don't hold with this psycho-analysis;
> And although Doctor Freud
> Is distinctly annoyed,
> They still cling to their long-standing fallacies.

For the rest they must be allowed to circulate orally only, which they will undoubtedly do for a long time, especially the superb series of fifty or so dealing with composers and music critics, by which alone many of the victims will be remembered in future – for most of them a highly appropriate form of immortality.

CHAPTER II

RECAPITULATION: CODA

THE Eynsford period lasted until the autumn of 1928, when a catastrophic financial upheaval supervened. The only surprising thing about it was that it had not occurred sooner than it did. Apart from a monthly allowance of £20 he was entirely dependent upon what he earned by his pen, and the open house he maintained at Eynsford, and his mode of life generally, must for a long time have cost him very much more than he could possibly afford. In money matters, indeed, he was, and always had been, hopelessly incorrigible – there is no distinction here between Peter and Philip – the one was as bad as the other. At the same time there is the same inexplicable contradiction, although common to both his earlier and his later personalities. From first to last he had great practical common sense, shrewdness of judgment, and organizing capacity, as his capable management of the Delius Festival under Sir Thomas Beecham in 1929 was to testify; and it is a tragedy that these valuable gifts should have been so little employed. But where his own personal monetary affairs were concerned it was a very different matter. While scrupulously honourable with regard to his own engagements and commitments he was lavish and generous to a quite quixotic degree with those of others towards him. Whenever he had occasion to borrow money from anyone, as he often did from me, it was invariably repaid, and that spontaneously, too, at the earliest possible moment and without any pressure or even solicitation on the part of the creditor – a most unusual trait, as I can vouch from an extensive and painful personal experience in these matters. On the other hand, he was repeatedly fleeced by people, and would often give away his last penny to anyone who would ask him for it. In consequence it was inevitable that he should frequently find him-

PHILIP HESELTINE (*circa* 1929)

self in difficulties; in fact he was seldom free from them, but this would probably have been the same even if he had been a millionaire. Without being extravagant, for his own tastes were frugal and his needs simple, he was utterly improvident. I remember one occasion on which he had been paid £100 by a publisher for a large amount of work, after having been for some time in exceedingly straitened circumstances. Within two days every penny of it had gone, all he had to show for it being a defective motor cycle which he had been induced to buy by a fraudulent dealer, and which a few days later he abandoned in a ditch some twenty miles outside London.

I have said elsewhere, incidentally, that he cared for no form of sport, but motor cycling may perhaps be counted an exception. Whenever he was in funds the first thing he would do would be to buy a motor cycle, but a curious fatality seemed always to pursue him in the exercise of this pastime. He must at different periods have possessed at least a dozen of them, each of which, however, came to a disastrous end after only a very short time. The last of the series, I think, was an exceptionally powerful and wicked specimen at Eynsford on which, accompanied by a friend in a sidecar, he once spectacularly charged through the doors of the saloon bar of a public house, the throttle having refused to close and the brakes to act, appropriately enough just on opening time.

In October, 1928, he returned to Wales once more, whence he wrote as follows to a correspondent:

'I have been gathering up the energy to clear out of Eynsford and have got so far as to clear myself out, never to return, though Colly, cats, and Raspberry[1] are remaining until the quite preposterous financial situation is eased a little (though nothing short of a god-from-the-machine can do it). I am still without any plans, hopes, money, or ideas. This solitary place is really beautiful, but I feel like a strayed ghost among such people. From here I seem to see the whole of the immediate past as through the wrong end of a telescope.'

[1] A composer so known on account of his complexion.

279

And again to the same correspondent:

'I feel slightly stupefied by this country-house life, which is really most pleasant when there are no tiresome visitors. One has at least a dozen empty rooms to oneself, and every one with a perfectly amazing view over long vistas of rolling hills and dense woods in all their autumnal brilliance. I seem to do nothing but eat enormously, read Dickens, and listen to German operas and symphony concerts on the wireless – being isolated on the top of a hill one hears these things exceptionally well. The prospect of being able to do any work becomes daily more and more remote; but I suppose I could stay here indefinitely, if I wanted to. . . . I feel like a vegetable.'

Here is a bitter and cynical letter written to Robert Nichols about the same time.

Cefn Bryntalch
Oct. 7th, 1928

It was kind of you to write such a long and interesting letter, and to copy out for me those remarkable extracts from Goethe. I do very much appreciate your friendly solicitude, but I am afraid you are making the same mistake about me as I have made about myself for some years, in considering me as a potential artist. I am not by nature an artist at all. I have no real desire to create anything whatsoever, and my present difficulty is entirely due to my having drifted, more or less by chance, into a *milieu* where I do not and can never really belong – in much the same way that a young man, piously brought up, might drift into the Church, only to find some years later that he had no real faith in his religion and certainly no call to expound it to others. The only honest course, a man in this position would feel, would be to resign his living and leave the Church – for the weekly sermons and services would entail unendurable hypocrisy for anyone who was sensitive on such a point; but how hard it would be to get out of such a groove after being in it for years, and to turn to other work without experience or qualifications! If I had an even moderately comfortable income, or a job that would provide me with one, I should never have anything more to do with music in any shape or form.

This reminds one inevitably of the dictum of the French composer Auber: '*J'ai aimé la musique jusqu'à trente ans, une vraie passion de jeune homme. Je l'ai aimé tant qu'elle a été ma maîtresse; mais depuis qu'elle est ma femme . . . !!*' Many musicians feel like that sometimes; at the risk of seeming to repeat myself unnecessarily, however, I must emphasize once more the fact that such statements are the expression of passing moods, and must not be taken too literally or too seriously. There is, for example, a famous letter from Wagner to Liszt which is no less self-depreciatory than anything Peter Warlock ever wrote about himself – to say nothing of Hugo Wolf. At the same time it must be admitted that this particular manifestation of depression and cynical disillusion was better founded and lasted longer than usual with him. In the first place it looked very much as if Peter Warlock had come to an end of himself as a composer; his work (as distinct from that of Philip Heseltine) had certainly undergone a certain perceptible deterioration from its first brilliant beginnings in 1921. Secondly, from a purely practical point of view, the lucrative market for songs had practically ceased to exist, largely as a result of broadcasting; formerly he had received £10 or so – sometimes more, seldom less – for a song, but now it was beginning to be difficult to dispose of them at all. Finally, his immense activities in the direction of transcribing and editing old English music had virtually ceased as a result of sheer exhaustion of the soil – very little of interest or importance in this field remained to be done. Everything, in fact, seemed to have come to an end simultaneously. As a result a very natural and understandable psychological revulsion took place. Peter Warlock, we have seen clearly enough, owed his ascendancy, his very existence, to the fact of his success. Like all tyrants he could only maintain ascendancy by means of continued success; defeat would inevitably entail deposition. The logical consequence of the defeat and failure of Peter Warlock was the resurrection and renewal of the old, fundamental personality, Philip Heseltine. This was manifested in several directions; firstly, when in the spring of 1929 Sir Thomas Beecham invited his collaboration in the organization of the Delius Festival which took place in the following autumn, and also engaged him as editor of the musical journal *Milo* which was to be run in connection with the Imperial League of Opera; secondly, in such songs as *The Frostbound Wood*, *Bethlehem Down*, and *The Fox*, in which we find the triumphant resurgence of the composer of *The Curlew*; finally, in certain letters written to the same woman to whom he had addressed the beautiful letter eleven years before, quoted on page 231, and to whom he now turned again, in reaction against the facile and superficial attachments formed by his *alter ego*, Peter Warlock.

I have already said that a violent reaction against everything that Philip Heseltine had previously cared for was one of the primary characteristics of Peter Warlock, and it is no secret that for many years past he had increasingly tended to disparage the art of Delius, exaggerating its defects and minimizing its virtues out of all proportion to actuality. But the triumphant apotheosis of the art which had meant so much to him in his youth, and for which he had worked so hard, brought about a strong reaction towards it once more. He threw himself heart and soul into the organization of the festival, the success of which must undoubtedly in large part be ascribed to his untiring efforts and enthusiasm. Similarly, the mystical sentiment and introspective melancholy of these last songs – as they were to prove to be – and the romantic idealism of the letters, were precisely those qualities against which Peter Warlock was wont to inveigh most furiously. How true it is that *on revient toujours à son premier amour*, both in art and in life; how often we find it happening! So often, indeed, that one is tempted to regard it as a natural and inevitable *coda*, a presage of the impending end.

It is only after the most anxious doubts and hesitations that I have finally decided to print here the first of the following letters, and possibly some may think that I have decided wrongly, and should have omitted it. I still feel, none the less, that it is a document of such supreme importance to an understanding of the man that I simply have not the moral right to withhold it.

PHILIP TO W. B.

3 Bramerton Street
Chelsea
June 7th, 1930

On that miraculous day, now more than two months past, when I was with you in those lovely places, I was so oppressed by the beauty of it all – and you were the key to it and all the downs and rivers and birds were you – that I was quite inarticulate, and even a little afraid of you and of all the loveliness around me. Just so, I think, one who had killed himself might feel if for an hour he might see again from afar the world from which his deed had exiled him. And I resolved to examine myself, to seek out the cause of this spiritual deadness and to try and find a new direction for my being, so that when next I spoke or wrote to you it would be with clear and purposeful words, from my open heart to yours. In the course of the last few bitter and remorseful weeks I have found in myself so many seeds of the soul's death that if I dare still hope for any regeneration, it cannot but be a slow and painful one. I think that I should rightly keep silent until I can come to you as one risen from the dead, yet in these last days I have been filled with apprehensions and forebodings, and something impels me to make certain things clear to you while there is yet time: because, since everything has fallen away from me and I am left empty in mind and spirit, the one light that is left me, burning with an ever clearer and intenser flame, is the thought of you who are, who have been and will always be my spirit's companion and my one Reality. I know now – and you have known always, I believe – that in failing you I have deliberately betrayed my own soul and all the faculties of my mind and spirit. I do not pretend to understand the source of the appalling perversity in my nature that has caused me now for years, with deliberate and callous cruelty, to torment and persecute that only precious part of myself, which is you, until I know not now whether the semblance of its death is death its very self and no semblance at all. The supreme blasphemy, the sin against the Holy Spirit, is to know the Light and, knowing it, to plunge into the darkness; and I know now by bitter experience that it is not without reason that this sin was called the soul's destruction. You came to me with the most lovely and precious gifts life has to offer – such gifts as *can* be offered only to those who know the light – and stood patiently, offering them again and again, while I betrayed you, reviled, mocked, and ill-used you with a barbarity that must surely have been implanted in me by the fiends of Hell. I do not understand and I cannot explain this devilry. But now that I have seen it face to face, examined it in detail, episode by episode, the memory of it is an incessant torment to me. I have been more vilely cruel to you, the guardian angel of my soul, than I have ever been to a dumb beast; and though you who know my heart have known that I was so encompassing my own destruction, I am writing this because I want to make full confession to you myself, kneeling at your feet, not for forgiveness but that you may know that all my cruelties have come back to revenge themselves on me, and because my one remaining joy is in the awareness of the horrors of my past actions as revealed by the anguish I am suffering at the memory of them – and I like to hope that awareness is itself a sign that I am in some small measure expiating them. I knew love only when I first saw you eleven years ago – all else that I have called love in my life has been a hideous mockery, a soul-destroying obscenity. All that is good in my work that I have ever done is you and you alone. You have believed in me with a superhuman faith, and I read and re-read in your letters words of love and faith more beautiful than any I had ever dared hope would be said to me; and I know now that if any good come of my life now, it will be through the ever-present thought of you and through the integrity of my everlasting spiritual kinship with you.

RECAPITULATION: CODA

June 15th, 1930

. . . My mind is slowly awakening from its torpor and I hope to be able to get through a considerable deal of work during the next few weeks. I have actually written some music during the last few days, but rather with the hope of selling it quickly than in the belief that it is any good at all. Still, I cling to the belief that some day, if ever I can afford a period of intensive study which will enable me to write as I would wish to, the results will be very different from any which I have achieved hitherto.

June 30th, 1930

. . . Nothing has changed for the better and there is no sign of any improvement on the horizon. I am so steeped in chronic gloom and grisliness that I am no fit correspondent for any normally cheerful person, nor fit company for any but the drunkards who live here. Everything has collapsed like a pricked balloon. I am quite literally dead broke, and utterly incapable of thought or action – my mind simply refuses to function and can produce nothing whatsoever, howsoever bad. It is like being in a cage from which the most minute inspection reveals no way out. London and the company of drunken Hampshire hogs is unbearable, but on the other hand solitude in the country at this time would simply make me suicidal. When I am so insufferably and ignominiously grisly as this, I can't bear to be seen by anyone who matters; my instinct, which I am sure is right, directs me to hide discreetly in a hole. As soon as I become bearably human again (if ever) and there is the faintest glimmer of a possibility of improving the situation in any way, I will write at once and we will meet in Ashdown Forest or where you will – but not in this detestable and increasingly loathly city . . . this abominable impotence in material things is driving me to despair.

Marriner's Farm
Bramdean, Alresford
Hants.
July 15th, 1930

The summer winds on this lonely hill-top have blown away much of my town-engendered gloom, and I feel transformed, in body and mind. Also, I have a hopeful premonition of something extremely fortunate making its way towards me. In any case I shall live no more in London unless I have some definite work to keep me there. . . . I shall sell practically everything I have except a few books, and then set out afresh, without impedimenta to tie me long in one place – and hope for the necessary god to descend from his machine.

So it continued throughout the summer, abysmal gloom alternating with renewed hopefulness and determination, and this fierce inner conflict was intensified by adverse material circumstances. After only a few numbers his new paper *Milo*, through no fault of his, had suspended publication, and his hopes of a reasonably secure future were once more dashed to the ground. Further cause for bitterness lay in the fact that one of his uncles had recently died leaving £639,366, '. . . which is a pretty adequate fortune, considering that he gave away hundreds of thousands to churches, schools, and the like during his lifetime. But never a penny came my way. . . . After this I resolved finally to abandon all further use of the family name' (Letter to Delius, Sept. 29th, 1930).

This final, decisive rejection of his original name – he never used it again – is once more deeply symbolical, for it coincides with the definitive abandonment of this last desperate attempt to realize and develop the personality associated with it. He gave up the project outlined in the last of the foregoing letters, of retiring to the country and trying to make a fresh start in both life and work. Henceforth he was again Peter Warlock, and remained to until the end.

This kind of recapitulation that we have just witnessed, this return, so to speak, to the subject-matter of the earlier years, was curiously complete. The Delius, Beecham, Sackbut, Curlew, Gérard de Nerval motives all recur; one important theme, however – in some ways the most important – was missing, seemingly: the theme of the *rondo* (p. 230). The only reason for this lay in the fact that it could not be traced, as I discovered quite by chance in, of all places, a café bar in a little village in Corsica some years later, the proprietor of which had received a letter from him inquiring as to the movements and whereabouts of a certain person who had been staying there. This completes the recapitulation.

In the following letter, written to his friend Mr. E. J. Moeran, and dated November 3rd, 1930, we find Peter Warlock very much *redivivus*, with all his scurrilous wit and gaiety.

12a Tite Street
Nov. 3rd, 1930

Ever since last Monday afternoon (starting in Ludlow where they open at four every day) I have been almost continuously drunk, with the – happily – now usual result that I have drunk myself sober and feel as fit as ever on nothing at all. From the week's haze certain events stand out with the startling quality of objects one just misses while motoring on a foggy night: an elephant in the streets of Chipping Norton who refused a pint of beer because (so the mahout assured me) he had had so much already that he was tired of it; and a very beautiful woman with one leg who attempted (without success, I may add) to induce me to share a semi- or pseudo-nuptial couch. Also the following passage from 'A plain and easy account of British Fungi' (1871) which I found in the library at Cefn Bryntalch:

'At first it (the *amanita muscaria*) generally produces cheerfulness afterwards giddiness and drunkenness, and occasionally in the entire loss of consciousness. The natural inclinations of the individual become stimulated. The dancer executes a *pas d'extravagance*, the musician indulges in a song, the chatterer divulges all his secrets, the orator delivers himself of a philippic and the mimic indulges in caricature. Erroneous impressions of size and distance are common occurrences; a straw lying in the road becomes a formidable object, to overcome which a leap is taken sufficient to clear a barrel of ale, or the prostrate trunk of a British oak. But this is not the only extraordinary circumstance connected therewith. The property is imparted to the fluid excretion of rendering it intoxicating, which property it retains for a considerable time. A man, having been intoxicated on one day, and slept himself sober by the next, will, by drinking this liquor to the extent of about a cupful, become as much intoxicated as he was before. Confirmed drunkards in Siberia preserve this as a precious liquor in case a scarcity of fungi should occur. This intoxicating property may be communicated to every person who partakes of the disgusting draught, and thus with even the third, fourth, or even fifth distillation. By this means, with a few fungi to commence with, a party may shut themselves in their room and indulge in a week's debauch.'

> He that will a fung-house keep
>   Must have three things in store:
> A chamber and a feather-bed,
>   Some fungi and a
>   hey-nonny-nonny, etc.

The return to supremacy of Peter Warlock was signalized by a more than usually violent outburst of controversial hostilities. It is not generally known, for example, that the manifesto drawn up in protest against what was thought to be an unduly offensive and denigratory attack upon Sir Edward Elgar, on the part of a Cambridge professor, was his work; and in addition to this he had many private feuds and vendettas at this time which were the occasion of solicitors' letters and threats of libel actions. I did not see much of him during these last months. It seemed to me at the time that he was inexplicably holding himself aloof from his friends, and even seeking almost to avoid them. In the light of one of the foregoing letters one can now quite understand why this was so: 'When I am so insufferably and ignominiously grisly as this, I cannot bear to be seen by anyone who matters; my instinct, which I am sure is right, directs me to hide discreetly in a hole', and there is no doubt that, despite the seeming gaiety and reckless bravado which he frequently exhibited at this time, his mood was in reality one of almost unrelieved gloom. All these quarrels and controversies, indeed, were only so many desperate efforts to seek relief from it.

The causes of this state of mind were largely to be found in material circumstances. I have already pointed out that the more lucrative sources of his income had dried up entirely, and the subsequent collapse of *Milo* and the indefinite suspension of the opera scheme had given the final blow. Many and various were the projects for earning a livelihood that he considered, some of them touchingly naive, others characteristically fantastic. Among the former should be recorded his approach to various official seats of musical learning in the hope of obtaining some post or other, seemingly quite oblivious of the fact that in such quarters he was probably more bitterly detested than any other living musician; among the latter, a plan he had evolved of buying a certain piece of ground somewhere in Kent or Sussex where there were certain caves which he proposed to furnish and let at high rents to flagellants, who could there pursue their pleasures without disturbing neighbours by screams and groans, and without arousing the undesirable attention of the authorities. He once seriously discussed this project with me at great length and with great wealth of practical detail, his eloquence being so plausible as almost to convince one of its feasibility.

On Thursday, December 11th, not having seen him for some little time, I went over to his flat in Tite Street, Chelsea, where he was then living. I found him just on the point of leaving for the Queen's Hall in order to hear a performance of his *Three Carols* for chorus and orchestra which was to be given by some amateur society or other. Knowing only too well from years of bitter experience as a music critic the kind of performance it was

T

likely to be, I tried, vainly, to dissuade him. We arranged, how-ever, to meet after the concert at a public-house near by, and I must confess that in spite of what I had told him to expect I was unprepared and even alarmed to observe the state of misery and dejection into which the performance had plunged him. After a short space of devastating silence he suddenly burst out into a furious diatribe against the infamy of compromise – how it were better to have done with everything, once and for all, rather than to tolerate the mediocre, the second-rate, the imperfect; how one should make no concessions and resolutely insist on everything or nothing. Agreeing with him wholeheartedly as I did, it was im-possible to console him, and after a short time he abruptly departed. I never saw him again, and I shall always remember these last words of his to me, so characteristic were they, and such a fitting last memory to retain of him, symbolizing and summing up his whole life and personality.

Shortly after seven o'clock on the morning of Wednesday, December 17th, a strong smell of gas was noticed to be coming from his flat, but when an attempt was made to obtain entrance there was no reply from within, and the door and windows were all shut and bolted. The police were called in and the door was broken open; he was discovered lying upon a couch, unconscious, fully clothed. On removal to St. Luke's Hospital he was found to be dead. I here append an account of the evidence given at the coroner's inquest which took place a week later.

Opening the proceedings, the coroner said that death was apparently due to coal-gas poisoning. Evidence of identification was given by his mother, Mrs. Edith Buckley Jones of Cefn Bryntalch, Abermule, Montgomeryshire. She said her son's full name was Philip Arnold Heseltine and he was thirty-six years of age; he enjoyed good health.

The Coroner. Was he sometimes depressed? – Oh yes, he got depressed at times. She last saw him in October, when he was perfectly well.

The Coroner. He was married, but had not lived with his wife for some years? – A very long time.

Has he ever threatened to take his life? – Never.

The Coroner, referring to a letter from her son dated November 15th, submitted by Mrs. Buckley Jones, observed that it was in affectionate terms, but did not throw any light on the circumstance of his death.

The Coroner read out the following part of the letter: 'I would very much rather visit you at some time other than Christmas. It is a season of the year which I dislike more and more as time goes on. The Christmas festivities throw a gloom and melancholy over me, and make me very poor company. I find it much better to remain more or less alone and devote myself to some quiet work.'

The Coroner. Had he got any real difficulties, financial or otherwise? – None.

Is there any family history of any mental trouble? – None.

Dr. R. Brontë, the pathologist who made the post-mortem examination, said that the cause of death was coal-gas poisoning. There were no signs whatever of alcohol, and no evidence in the organs to suggest that he was addicted to it, or to any drug.

The Coroner. There is no doubt at all that death was due to coal-gas poisoning? – No doubt at all.

Mr. Bernard van Dieren said that he had known Mr. Heseltine for about fifteen years. He saw him on Tuesday evening and was with him from 10.40 to 12.15. They had a drink together in the Duke of Wellington, and then went to Mr. Heseltine's flat.

The Coroner. When you left he was perfectly all right and normal? – Yes.

And sober? – Yes. He apologized to me and my wife because he had not even a bottle of beer in the house to offer us. We had a quiet talk.

You had no idea he was morbid and depressed then? – No.

If he subsequently took his own life, can you throw any light on it? – The only thing I could possibly think of is that he might in the early morning have suddenly awakened, felt miserable for some reason or other, and done something which he could not really have contemplated.

You cannot say anything definite? – No. I can say that when I left him he was in a state of mind in which that should have been the very last thing I could have expected.

You did not think that he had any suicidal intent? – No.

You were really the last person to see him alive, were you not? – Yes. I am perfectly certain that if he had expected anyone to visit him he would have told me about it.

A woman, who lived above the flat occupied by Mr. Heseltine, described how about 6.40 on Wednesday morning she heard a noise which was like the shutting of doors and windows. 'There was a lot of noise. I really wondered what was happening. I got out of bed and I looked out of the window. The place downstairs was all lit up, and I heard Mr. Heseltine speaking.'

The Coroner. Did you hear what he said? – Oh, no, I could not hear plainly what he said.

Do you mean that there were lights coming from his flat? – Yes, they were all alight. I thought a party was going on, or something of the sort, by the noise, and I was cross about it.

Did it go on long? – No.

If anyone were shutting one or two windows, that would account for it, would it not? – Yes, it would.

Witness said that when she got up about 8.20 the place was full of gas. She went over her flat looking for the gas leak, and, finding none, she told her son to ring up the gas company. 'Mrs. Warlock, as we knew her, came along, and I sent my woman down to see her. She was in the area downstairs, and said she could not get in. She said to my maid, "Send for the police." The police broke the window because it was bolted top and bottom.'

The Coroner. You looked into the yard and saw a kitten? – Yes, I did not know they had a cat. I heard the little thing crying. Apparently Mr. Warlock had put some food out. The poor little thing was terrified.

You suggested that he might have let the cat out? – Yes, he must have thought about the cat.

If Mr. Heseltine took his own life, you could not throw any light on it? – Nothing at all.

The name of Mrs. Warlock having been called, the coroner kept from the jury the name and present address of witness, and asked her how long she had been living with Mr. Heseltine. The erroneously reported answer reads 'three months', which refers only to the time they had occupied the flat.

The Coroner. When did you last see Mr. Heseltine alive? – I last saw him alive about 7.30 or 8 o'clock on Tuesday evening.

And did you go out to a dance then? – Yes.

What time did you get back? – I did not come back that night. I went to sleep at an hotel after the dance.

When did you come back to the house? – I came back in the morning at 10.45.

Did you find the door bolted? – Yes. I could not get in with the key. Later the police and a doctor were sent for.

The witness was questioned at some length regarding a gas pipe which, she said, was near a chest in the room. The pipe had a tap, but they had never used it.

The Coroner. Do you know that the gas tap turns very easily? – I came across it once when I was sweeping and turned it on. That was the first I knew of it.

Did it not strike you that it was easily turned? – I really did not notice it.

Had you known him ever to threaten to take his life? – He had threatened to, but I thought it was just talk.

You did not take it seriously? – No.

How long ago was it? – The last time was on Sunday, three days before.

Was he in trouble of any kind? – He said he felt he was a failure, and seemed worried about his work, and that he could not go on. He said he seemed not to be able to do any more.

She left him about 8 o'clock, when there were two friends with him. He knew that she would not be back until the next morning.

Was there anything in the nature of a quarrel or anything of that sort? – Oh, only tiny and unimportant.

If he took his life, can you throw any light on it? – He seemed to worry about things.

Did he have a substantial ground for taking his life? – No.

The police constable who was called to the flat said that Mr. Heseltine was lying on a sofa with his face against the wall. Gas was escaping, and he (witness) turned it off at the main. A plug was out of the end of the pipe, and this had not been found. There were a number of papers in the room, including music manuscripts, and miscellaneous letters, and on the back of one of these what seemed to be a pencil draft will, beginning, 'This is the last will of me, Peter Warlock, 12A Tite Street . . .'

The Coroner, after inspecting the documents, said that they threw no light on the tragedy.

A gas fitter, who saw the pipe after the tragedy, said that he found the tap turned on. There was no defect. There was no plug at the end of the gas pipe, neither had one been found, and he could not say whether there had been one there or whether it had been removed recently.

The local manager of the gas company said that it would be difficult for him to say whether the pipe had been plugged or not. He said that he could not understand anyone not noticing the escape of gas, since there would be a very strong hissing noise.

Mr. John Ireland, the well-known composer, offering to give evidence, said that he had known Heseltine by reputation for many years and personally for the past two or three years. He last saw him alive about a fortnight before his death.

The Coroner. Can you throw any light on this at all? – The only thing I can say is that I think he was worried about his work as a composer. I think that he felt, as, I suppose, many composers do, that he had not yet received the recognition his work deserved.

Perhaps he had not estimated his popularity in a wider circle? – I think he had not, decidedly.

Had he got any real troubles or difficulties? – None that I know of at all. I always thought he was a very bright and cheerful man.

Impulsive or temperamental? – I have only seen him impulsive when musical questions have been considered, where he had to express an opinion.

You cannot throw any actual light on his death? – None whatever. It was the greatest surprise to me.

The Coroner told the jury that they would have to decide whether the death was accidental or intentional.

The jury after consultation in private, returned a verdict that death was caused by coal-gas poisoning, but that they were unable to say whether due to accident or whether it meant suicide.

The Coroner said that no doubt the jury recognized that in this case they had no absolute proof of suicide, which was available in some cases in the form of a note left by the dead person. He would record that there was insufficient evidence on which to decide whether it was suicide or accident.

'In the untimely death of Peter Warlock', the Coroner added, 'the musical world has lost a figure prominent both in composition and literature. He will be greatly missed by a large circle, and to his family I am sure we would like to offer our sympathy in his tragic death.'

I have given a full account of the evidence because so many of the details are significant and revealing. Is there not, for example, something peculiarly poignant in the fact that Peter Warlock, the composer of *Balulalow*, *Tyrley Tyrlow*, *Bethlehem Down*, *The Sycamore Tree*, *As Dew in Aprylle*, *Chanson du jour de Noël*, and so many more carols of which the last, the *Carillon Carilla* of Hilaire Belloc, had only just been published – that the supreme carollist of modern times, possibly the greatest since the anonymous masters of the Middle Ages, should have disliked so intensely and should have died so tragically at that very season of the year which he had celebrated so often and with such incomparable felicity? Is it not touchingly and admirably characteristic that his last thought,

before committing his fatal act, should have been for his cat? –
For despite the open verdict of the jury there can be little doubt
in the mind of anyone who knew him or anyone who has read the
evidence that it was a clear case of *felo de se*, and it would be
foolish to pretend otherwise. So far as the ethical aspect of the
matter is concerned everyone must judge for himself; personally,
it troubles me not at all, and it is enough to say that those who
believe, as I do, in the right of every man to dispose of his life as
he thinks fit can point to the fact that nowhere in either Old or
New Testaments or in the sacred writings of any other established
religious system is there to be found a single word of specific condemnation of the act of self-destruction, whereas, on the other
hand, according to the moral code of pagan antiquity it was as
often as not considered not merely permissible but positively com-
mendable. Many, indeed, of their greatest heroes died by their
own hand; as Hume says, 'Cato and Brutus, Arria and Portia
acted heroically; those who now imitate their example ought to
receive the same praises from posterity', and Pliny even goes so
far as to suggest that the power to commit suicide constitutes
evidence of the superiority of men over the gods; 'Deus non sibi
potest mortem consciscere si velit, quod homini dedit optimum in
tantis vitae paenis.'

However that may be, it is at least true that severe moral condemnation of the deed, and the accounting for it on the grounds
alternatively of insanity or cowardice, is of comparatively recent
origin. So far as the first of them is concerned, there can be no
question whatsoever but that Philip was his normal self – gloomy,
despondent perhaps, but no more than that – up until midnight
on December 16th, and it is inconceivable that anyone should
suddenly become insane in such a short space of time without
giving any previous warning. Some there will be, no doubt, who
will assert that he always was mad, and that his whole life shows
it, but they could only be people who did not know him, and who
fail to realize that behind the façade of eccentricity which he
presented to the world he was as well-balanced and normal as

anyone. So far as the hackneyed reproach of cowardice is concerned, such a view might conceivably be warranted in the case of, say, a fraudulent financier fleeing from justice, or even in that of a man suffering from a painful and incurable disease, but there was no such motive here to justify that interpretation. He was in perfect health, and though no doubt he was in straitened circumstances at the time, this was such a familiar predicament with him that it could not have been a factor of importance in making his decision. In any case, it must be remembered, he was always assured of enough to exist upon, in a modest and humble style admittedly, but the sure knowledge of this can go a long way towards mitigating the discomforts of immediate deprivations – besides, as I have already said, his material needs were few and simple. Apart from that, however, he knew perfectly well that in any dire necessity there were many friends to whom he could have turned for assistance with absolute confidence. As for the 'tiny quarrel' to which allusion was made in the evidence, it can be dismissed as irrelevant; tiny quarrels, and even big ones, were of daily occurrence throughout his life. Finally, Mr. John Ireland's well-meant suggestion that the tragedy could be due to the lack of appreciation his work had encountered must be emphatically dismissed. Quite apart from the fact that there was no lack of appreciation for his work, either in musical circles or with the general public, he was the last man to care, one way or the other. It was not the approbation of others that he desired or sought, and lacked, but of his own self – the only critic, the only audience to whose opinion he attached the slightest weight or consideration. 'He said he felt he was a failure,' declared another witness, 'and seemed worried about his work. He said he seemed not to be able to do any more.' That is a very different matter, and very much nearer the truth than the suggestion that he had felt himself insufficiently recognized. It is not the whole truth, however; it is not a complete explanation. Every artist of talent feels the same at some time or other, and the more talented he is the oftener and the more intensely does he feel it; it is only the mediocrity who never experiences this sense of failure. As Señor Ortega y Gasset truly observes in his *Rebelión de las Masas*, 'He who does not feel himself lost, is lost without remission; that is to say, he never finds himself, never comes up against his own reality'; and M. Jean Cocteau, of all people, surprisingly enough, says profoundly that 'the aesthetic of failure is the only one that lasts; he who does not know failure is lost'. No one recognized the truth of this better than Philip who, on one occasion when a friend of his was suffering from an acute attack of the very same complaint, copied out and sent him as consolation that magnificent passage of George Borrow in which he says, 'how dost thou know that this dark principle is not thy best friend, that it is not that which tempers the whole mass of thy corruption? It may be, for what thou knowest, the mother of wisdom, and of great works . . . it is ever nearest the favourites of God – the fool knows little of it. Thou wouldst be joyous, wouldst thou? Then be a fool. What great work was ever the result of joy, the puny one?'

It is, of course, easy enough to be philosophic where others are concerned, and very difficult where one's own self is, and I have no wish or intention to seek to minimize unduly the significance of the fact that at the time of his death he was labouring under a more than usually violent attack of the black mood of self-distrust and sense of failure to which, as we have already seen, he was so frequently subject. It is the peculiar attribute of this state of mind, this dark night of the soul, that no matter how often it occurs to one it seems each time to be final, definitive. It is of no avail to say to oneself that one has frequently experienced it before, and that in the same way that hitherto it has always passed away so it will on this occasion as well, for it is precisely this firm conviction of finality that constitutes the essence of the malady, without which, indeed, it would possess no terrors at all; one would merely sit down and wait for it to pass, but this is the one thing one cannot do. Still, I had so often before heard him express with absolute conviction the belief that he would never write another note of music, without seeming particularly distressed at the prospect, that I cannot bring myself to believe that in itself this state of mind could be sufficient to explain his decision to put an end to his life on this particular occasion.

If it was not any single one of these causes, it may be suggested, perhaps it could have been a combination of all or of some of them: temporary financial embarrassment, the momentary conviction of having come to an end of himself as a composer, exacerbated by a trivial quarrel. Possibly, but I do not think so. The true explanation, to my mind, is to be found in the fact that there was a crucial difference, despite the superficial similarity, between this particular psychological crisis and the many others which had preceded it. It was not merely dissatisfaction with his work or any other such motive or combination of motives which finally determined his desperate act, but something much deeper and more fundamental – a conviction of having come to an end of himself, not merely as a composer, but altogether, as a personality, and in view of everything that one now knows it is difficult to resist the melancholy conclusion that he was right. The life of every man of talent, and possibly of everybody, has a certain inner logic, pattern and design which it is the task of the biographer to detect, reconstruct and interpret; it is as if he were given the separate pieces of a jig-saw puzzle which he has then to put together into a definite, coherent picture, supplying intuitively the various fragments which are missing. And after years of careful consideration, many false starts and fallacious reconstructions, I can see now clearly, in his tragic end, a certain inevitability, an inescapable fatality.

The plain truth is that he had killed his old, his real self, irrevocably. In the words of William Wilson, in the story of that name by Edgar Allan Poe, Philip Heseltine might have said to his *Doppelgänger* Peter Warlock, 'You have conquered, and I yield. Yet henceforward art thou also dead – In me didst thou exist – and in my death, see by this image, which is thine own, how utterly thou hast murdered thyself'. Always with this important reservation, however, that whereas in Poe's tale the one personality is wholly good and the other wholly evil, there was much in Peter Warlock, as I have already said, that was wholly admirable. That there was a definite strain of perversity in him is undeniable, and no one realized it more clearly than he himself. But there is assuredly something more than mere perversity in the effort made by one who was by nature weak, pliant, sentimental, self-distrustful, to become virile, hard, reckless, self-reliant; in such an effort, on the contrary, there is surely an element of moral heroism and grandeur. He despised his real self and sought to change it; the tragedy was that in thus seeking to change it he only succeeded in destroying it.

The design that his life presents when looked at as a whole is strikingly complete, a kind of musical form, consisting, like that of the sonata, in the presentation and interaction of two opposed thematic personalities, so to speak. The first subject is stated at the outset and then, after preliminary hints and anticipations, the second. A working-out section then ensues, with the second subject steadily increasing in predominance until it holds the field. Then, just before the end, there is a sudden, dramatic reversion to the first subject, reminding one strikingly of that passage in the *Don Juan* of Richard Strauss, in which the garish and riotous carnival episode is abruptly broken off, and ghost-like memories of the earlier love episodes flit past, preliminary to the final catastrophic *cours à l'abîme*. There is, indeed, a logic, an inevitability, in the formal design; the end, one feels, looking on it as a whole, had to come precisely where in fact it did, and Philip, with his impeccable feeling for style, was undoubtedly aware of this. His sense of artistic fitness was too fastidious to allow him to continue repeating himself interminably, adding on to the perfect and rounded form another working-out section, another recapitulation, and so on *ad infinitum*; his sense of human dignity was such that he preferred to leave the tavern of life at his own leisure and convenience instead of, like most of us, hanging on desperately until he heard the raucous shout of, 'Time please, gentlemen, hurry up please, long past time', or until he was forcibly ejected, indignantly protesting, into the street of eternity by that most inexorable of potmen and chuckers-out, death. Granted that nothing could be more beautiful, more admirable, more affecting, than the old age of a Goethe, a Verdi, a Titian; but nothing is more pathetic and ridiculous than the spectacle of one who was once a fine artist dragging out a meaningless, mechanical, repetitive activity long after he has said everything he had to say. The lyric talent, as opposed to the constructive, belongs to youth, and it is no mere coincidence that the possessors of it usually die young. When they do not, they usually outlive their talent, and if Peter Warlock had lived on into old or even middle age the chances are that this would have happened; his flame burned too intensely to be long-lasting.

In nothing in his life, in fact, was he more the artist than in his death. By deliberately truncating his existence at what he felt to be the right moment he made his life a coherent, perfectly shaped and rounded whole; so far from it being an act of cowardice his suicide seems to me to have been an act of the highest courage. He felt that the fitting moment had come for him to die, and he took it, unflinchingly. Most of us, I fear, outstay our welcome, and the world heaves a sigh of relief on getting quit of us; he at least died regretted. I have spoken of the tragedy of his end, but the tragedy is not his, but that of his friends, for whom life without him can never be the same. They lament, not for him, but for themselves.

The sense of finality which marks the pattern of his life at this juncture is reflected also in his art; not merely in the fact that the last songs, as we have already said, show the same momentary return to the earlier personality that we find in the letters quoted, but also in the peculiar qualities of the individual songs themselves. In the unearthliness and otherworldliness of *The Frostbound Wood*, in the obsession with the idea of death and dissolution in *The Fox*, there is a strange, morbid beauty quite different from anything else in his work, or in any other music that I know, for that matter, and only paralleled in any art by the poetry of Thomas

Lovell Beddoes. The analogy between the two extends further than this; there is, indeed, a quite uncanny resemblance between the two men – so much so as almost to induce one to believe in the doctrine of reincarnation – and it is only surprising that Warlock did not set any of Beddoes' poetry to music, with the exception of *Sorrow's Lullaby*. Beddoes has frequently been described as an Elizabethan born out of his time: 'The Last Elizabethan' Lytton Strachey calls him in his fine essay of that title devoted to him in *Books and Characters*: and so has Peter Warlock been described.

Both in character and in the material circumstances of their lives they were strikingly akin. Beddoes also was a dual personality, a poet and a man of science at the same time. He, too, was of good family, was left fatherless as a small child, went from a public school to Oxford, and spent much of his time reading in the British Museum. He, too, was something of a disreputable character, in the conventional sense of the words; he would sometimes shut himself up for weeks, drinking, and he is recorded to have attempted on one occasion to set fire to Drury Lane Theatre by means of lighted five-pound notes. Finally, and most striking of all, Beddoes also died by his own hand, in practically identical circumstances – i.e. without any discoverable material motive.

Their correspondence also presents curious parallels and evidence of close psychological affinity. For example, in a letter to his friend Kelsall, Beddoes writes: 'I will frankly confess to you that I have lost much if not all of my ambition to become poetically distinguished, and I do not think that a man may dedicate himself entirely or even in great part to the cultivation of that part of literature unless he possesses far greater powers of imagination than I do'; and again, on another occasion, 'Apollo defend us from brewing all our lives at a quintessential pot of the smallest ale Parnassian'. It might almost be Peter Warlock himself speaking. And listen to this, from Mr. F. L. Lucas's essay on Beddoes in his *Studies French and English*. After quoting a beautiful passage from Beddoes' poetry, the author says, 'Surely, if the writer of that lived withdrawn into his shell, it was precisely because he was too sensitive, and had suffered. It is as if part of him had perished young. . . . He resembles his own Wolfram, a dead thing in a living world, gentle once but hardened now. Certainly his letters show him, if no lover, at all events a good hater. He reveals a particular dislike of British Philistinism. . . . At war within, he spared neither his country, nor his contemporaries, nor himself . . . he was too hard on his own work. . . . There is often more quintessential poetry, I feel, in three lines of his than in as many pages of other poets not without repute.' Change the word poetry to music, and poets to musicians, and the above observations will apply as fitly to Warlock as to Beddoes. And just as the latter is to-day recognized by the best judges – of whom Mr. Lucas is certainly one – to be not merely an Elizabethan born out of his time but a poet of genuine originality and independence, so, I venture to predict, posterity will see in Peter Warlock a composer of rare genius in his own right and, in so far as he is indebted to an old tradition, belonging to an antique lineage stretching back far farther than even the Elizabethan masters: sharing with them, indeed, a common ancestry in the trouba- dours, *trouvères*, *jongleurs*, and minstrels of the Middle Ages. Compare, for example, such a thing as his *Balulalow* with the troubadour songs as transcribed by Beck and Aubry, and you will find yourself in identically the same world; not so much because his music sounds ancient as because theirs sounds so modern. But time does not enter into the question. Both belong to a tradition which is beyond time, which has probably existed from the beginning of the world and will probably always continue to exist – the fountain of pure, natural song springing eternally from the heart of man throughout the ages, the most ancient and in- destructible art-tradition in the world. It is because his best work belongs to this timeless tradition that it is clearly destined to outlast the more artificial, and therefore perishable, products of the majority of modern song-writers. Theirs will sink with the civilization that created them, and of which they are the expression; his will float on that wide sea of humanity which transcends and includes all temporal and transient phenomena.

Apart from the songs which constitute the major portion of his output, the other works, if comparatively few, will, I am convinced, live as long as anything in modern English music, to say the least. In the last resort, however, Philip Heseltine's greatest achievement was probably the creation of Peter Warlock. To realize such a legend, such a personality, which will assuredly endure, is in itself nothing short of genius.

COMPLETE
LIST OF PUBLISHED WORKS

COMPLETE LIST OF PUBLISHED WORKS

SONGS WITH PIANOFORTE ACCOMPANIMENT

Saudades: (i) Along the stream (Li Po, trans. L. Cranmer-Byng);
    (ii) Take, O, take those lips away (Shakespeare); (iii) Hera-
    cleitus (Callimachus, trans. W. Cory), Chester, 1916-17

To the memory of a great singer (Stevenson), Augener, 1918

As ever I saw (Anon., 16th century), Winthrop Rogers, 1918

The Bailey beareth the bell away[1] (Anon., 16th century), Win-
    throp Rogers, 1918

My gostly Fader (attributed to Charles d'Orleans), Winthrop
    Rogers, 1918

Whenas the rye (George Peele), Winthrop Rogers, 1918

Lullaby[1] (Thomas Dekker), Winthrop Rogers, 1918

Take, O, take those lips away (Shakespeare), Winthrop Rogers,
    1918

Love for love (Anon., 16th century), Winthrop Rogers, 1919

Mourn no more[1] (John Fletcher), Winthrop Rogers, 1919

Sweet Content (Thomas Dekker), Winthrop Rogers, 1919

Dedication (Sir Philip Sidney), Winthrop Rogers, 1919

There is a lady sweet and kind (Anon., 16th century), Winthrop
    Rogers, 1919

My little sweet darling (Anon., 16th century), Winthrop Rogers,
    1919

Romance (R. L. Stevenson), Curwen, 1919

Late summer (E. Shanks), Augener, 1919

The Singer (E. Shanks), Augener, 1919

Balulalow[2] (Anon., Old Scotch), Oxford University Press, 1919

Captain Stratton's Fancy (John Masefield), Augener, 1921

Mr. Belloc's Fancy (J. C. Squire), Augener, 1921

Good Ale (Anon., 16th century), Augener, 1922

Hey troly loly lo (Anon., 16th century), Augener, 1922

The Bachelor (Anon., 16th century), Augener, 1922

[1] Also in part-song arrangements.
[2] Also arranged as No. 2 of the 'Three Carols for chorus and orchestra'.

Piggesnie (Anon., 16th century), Augener, 1922

Peterisms (first set): (i) Chopcherry (George Peele); (ii) A sad song (John Fletcher); (iii) Rutterkin (John Skelton), Chester, 1922

Lillygay: (i) The Distracted Maid (Anon., Old English); (ii) Johnny wi' the tye (Anon., Old Scotch); (iii) The Shoemaker (Anon., Old Scotch); (iv) Burd Ellen and Young Tamlane (Anon., Old Scotch); (v) Rantum Tantum (V. B. Neuburg), Chester, 1922

Sleep (John Fletcher), Oxford University Press, 1922

Rest, sweet nymphs (Anon., 17th century), Oxford University Press, 1922

Tyrley Tyrlow[1] (Anon., 16th century), Oxford University Press, 1922

Adam lay ybounden (Anon., 15th century), Oxford University Press, 1922

Little Trotty Wagtail (John Clare), Oxford University Press, 1922

In an arbour green (Robert Wever), Paterson, 1922

Autumn Twilight (Arthur Symons), Oxford University Press, 1922

Peterisms (second set): (i) Roister Doister (Nicholas Udall); (ii) Spring (Thomas Nashe); (iii) Lusty Juventus (Robert Wever), Oxford University Press, 1922

Milkmaids (John Smith), Enoch, 1923

Candlelight: a cycle of twelve nursery jingles (Anon.), Augener, 1923

Peter Warlock's Fancy (Anon.), Paterson, 1923

Two short songs: (i) I held Love's head (Robert Herrick); (ii) Thou gav'st me leave to kiss (Robert Herrick), Boosey, 1924

Twelve Oxen (Anon., 16th century), Oxford University Press, 1924

Yarmouth Fair (Collins), Oxford University Press, 1924

Sweet and twenty (Shakespeare), Oxford University Press, 1925

Consider (Ford Madox Ford), Oxford University Press, 1925

I have a garden (Thomas Moore), Oxford University Press, 1925

Two songs: (i) A prayer to Saint Anthony of Padua (Arthur Symons); (ii) The sick heart (Arthur Symons), Oxford University Press, 1925

---

[1] Also arranged as No. 1 of the 'Three Carols for chorus and orchestra'.

The Countryman (John Chalkhill), Winthrop Rogers, 1925

Chanson du jour de Noël (Clément Marot), Winthrop Rogers, 1925

The Toper's Song (from an 18th century ballad sheet), Winthrop Rogers, 1925

Pretty ring-time (Shakespeare), Oxford University Press, 1925

Maltworms (in collaboration with E. J. Moeran), (John Still), Oxford University Press, 1925

The Birds (Hilaire Belloc), Williams, 1926

Robin Goodfellow (Anon., 16th century), Oxford University Press, 1926

Jillian of Berry (Beaumont and Fletcher), Oxford University Press, 1926

Fair and True (Nicholas Breton), Oxford University Press, 1926

Away to Twiver (Anon., 16th century), Oxford University Press, 1926

Ha'nacker mill (Hilaire Belloc); The Night (Hilaire Belloc); My own country (Hilaire Belloc), Oxford University Press, 1926

The Lover's Maze (Thomas Campion), Oxford University Press, 1926

Sigh no more, ladies (Shakespeare), Oxford University Press, 1926

Mockery (Shakespeare), Oxford University Press, 1926

Cradle song (John Phillip), Oxford University Press, 1926

Walking the Woods (Anon., 16th century), Winthrop Rogers, 1927

The first mercy (Bruce Blunt), Winthrop Rogers, 1927

The jolly shepherd (Anon., 17th century), Winthrop Rogers, 1927

Queen Anne (contributed to an album of children's songs), Nelson, 1927

Passing by (Anon.), Oxford University Press, 1928

And wilt thou leave me thus? (Thomas Wyatt), Oxford University Press, 1928

Youth (Robert Wever), Elkin, 1928

The Passionate Shepherd (Christopher Marlowe), Elkin, 1928

The sweet o' the year (Shakespeare), Elkin, 1928

Tom Tyler (Anon., 16th century), Augener, 1929

Elore lo (Anon., 16th century), Augener, 1929

The contented lover (James Mabbe), Augener, 1929

LIST OF WORKS

The droll lover (Anon., 17th century), Augener, 1929
The Cricketers of Hambledon (Bruce Blunt), Augener, 1929
After Two Years (Richard Aldington), Oxford University Press, 1930
The Frostbound Wood (Bruce Blunt), Oxford University Press, 1930
The Fox (Bruce Blunt), Oxford University Press, 1930
Bethlehem Down (Bruce Blunt), Winthrop Rogers, 1930

INSTRUMENTAL COMPOSITIONS
(with and without voices)

An Old Song, for small orchestra, Chester, 1917
Folk-song Preludes, for pianoforte, Augener, 1918
The Curlew: a cycle of four linked songs for tenor voice, flute, English horn, and string quartet (Yeats), Stainer and Bell, 1920-22
Serenade (to Frederick Delius on his sixtieth birthday), for string orchestra, Oxford University Press, 1923
Corpus Christi, for soprano, baritone, and string quartet, Curwen, 1923
Three Carols for chorus and orchestra: (i) Tyrley Tyrlow[1]; (ii) Balulalow[1]; (iii) The Sycamore Tree, Oxford University Press, 1925
Capriol (A) suite for string orchestra, Curwen, 1926
Capriol (B) suite for full orchestra, Curwen, 1928
Sorrow's Lullaby, for soprano, baritone, and string quartet (Thomas Lovell Beddoes), Oxford University Press, 1927

CHORAL WORKS, PART-SONGS, ETC.

Cornish Christmas Carol (H. Jenner), for mixed voices, Boosey, 1918
As Dewe in Aprylle (Anon.), for mixed voices, Boosey, 1918
Corpus Christi[2] (Anon.), for contralto, tenor and mixed chorus, Curwen, 1919

[1] Also arranged as solo songs with piano.
[2] Also in different arrangement.

The Full Heart (Robert Nichols), for mixed voices, Oxford University Press, 1921

Benedicamus Domino (Anon.), for mixed voices, Boosey, 1924

Three Dirges of Webster: (i) All the Flowers of the Spring, for mixed voices, Boosey, 1924; (ii) Call for the Robin Redbreast, for female voices, Winthrop Rogers, 1925; (iii) The Shrouding of the Duchess of Malfi, for male voices, Winthrop Rogers, 1925

The Spring of the Year (A. Cunningham), for mixed voices, Oxford University Press, 1925

The Lady's Birthday (Anon.), for male voices and piano, Winthrop Rogers, 1925

One more River (Anon.), for baritone and male voices, Winthrop Rogers, 1925

What cheer? Good cheer! (Anon.), unison with organ acc., Winthrop Rogers, 1927

Where Riches is everlastingly (Anon.), unison with organ acc., Oxford University Press, 1928

I saw a fair maiden (Anon.), for five voices, Oxford University Press, 1928

Bethlehem Down (Bruce Blunt), for mixed voices, Winthrop Rogers, 1928

The five lesser joys of Mary (D. L. Kelleker), unison with organ acc., Novello, 1929

Carillon Carilla (Belloc), for mixed voices and organ acc., Novello, 1930

TRANSCRIPTIONS AND ARRANGEMENTS

(i) Vocal Works

Englishe Ayres, Elizabethan and Jacobean, in six volumes (in collaboration with Philip Wilson), Oxford University Press

The English Lutenists (various songs by Dowland, Cooper, Ford, Rosseter, Campian, Hume, Bartlet, Cavendish, Jones), Oxford University Press

Three books of Elizabethan Songs, originally composed for one voice and four stringed instruments, Oxford University Press

Anonymous Elizabethan part-songs, for various vocal combinations, Oxford University Press

Part-songs by William Cornysshe, Edmund Turges, and Robert Fayrfax, Oxford University Press

Whythorne's Duos, or songs for two voices, Oxford University Press

Whythorne's Songs for Three, Four, and Five Voices, Oxford University Press

Ravenscroft's 'Pammelia and other Rounds and Catches', Oxford University Press

Four English Songs of the Early Seventeenth Century, Oxford University Press

Peerson's 'Private Musicke', Oxford University Press

French Ayres, from Gabriel Bataille's 'Airs de differents autheurs' (1608-18), Oxford University Press

Solo songs by Richard Edwardes, John Daniel, and John Hilton, Oxford University Press

Michael Cavendish, Eight four-part Ayres, Novello

John Danyel, 'Chromatic Tunes', Chester

Dowland, two songs from 'A pilgrim's solace', for voice, piano and violin obbligato, Chester

Miscellaneous Elizabethan and Jacobean Songs, by Edwards, Campian, Peerson, Cavendish, Greaves, Corkine, and Anon., Curwen.

Choruses for Equal Voices, by Edwards, Jones, Morley, Campian, Cavendish, Cooper, and Handford, Curwen

Part-songs for mixed voices, by Ravenscroft, Dowland, Jones, and Danyel, Curwen

(ii) Instrumental Music

Purcell: Thirteen Fantasies for strings (with A. Mangeot), Curwen

Dowland: Lute Music (for piano or harpsichord), Curwen

R. Johnson: 'A Knell of Thomson', for string quintet, Curwen

Oswald Parsley: 'Perslis Clocke', for string quintet, Curwen

R. Parsons: 'A Galliard', for string quintet, Curwen

R. Parsons: 'Te fili', for string quintet, Curwen

C. Woodcocke: 'Hackney', for string quintet, Curwen

Mathew Locke: six string quartets (with A. Mangeot), Chester

LIST OF WORKS

Mathew Locke: string trio in C, Augener.

Charles Avison: Concerto in E minor, for string orchestra, Augener

John Hilton: six pieces for string trio, Augener

Wood: Five short pieces for string trio, Augener

Transcriptions of the works of Delius

North Country Sketches (four hands), Augener

A Dance Rhapsody No. 2 (four hands), Augener

Song before Sunrise (four hands), Augener

Violin Concerto (violin and piano), Augener

Double Concerto (violin, violoncello, and piano), Augener

Violoncello Concerto (violoncello and piano), Universal

In a Summer Garden (two hands), Universal

Incidental music to 'Hassan' (Flecker) (voices and piano), Universal

Requiem (voices and piano), Universal.

LITERARY WORKS

Frederick Delius, John Lane, 1923

Songs of the Gardens, an anthology, Nonesuch Press, 1925

Arbeau's 'Orchesography' (preface by Peter Warlock), Beaumont, 1925

The English Ayre, Oxford University Press, 1926

Carlo Gesualdo, Musician and Murderer (with Cecil Gray), Kegan Paul, 1926

'The Metamorphosis of Aiax' (Sir John Harington), edited by Peter Warlock and Jack Lindsay, Fanfrolico Press, 1927

Thomas Whythorne, an unknown Elizabethan composer, Oxford University Press, 1929

Merry-Go-Down. A gallery of gorgeous drunkards through the ages. Collected for the use, interest, illumination and delectation of serious topers, by Rab Noolas and decorated by Hal Collins, Mandrake Press, 1929

English Ayres, Elizabethan and Jacobean; a Discourse, Oxford University Press, 1932

Giles Earle, His Booke; edited with preface and notes, Houghton Publishing Co., 1932

INDEX

ABBEY THEATRE, DUBLIN, 159-60, 176
Abramelin the Mage, The Book of, 163
Achill Island, 161
Adjutant Stork, The, 249
Æ (George Russell), 181
Albrechtsberger, 188, 191
Allan-Despréaux, Mme., 234
Allinson, Adrian, 117, 142
Along the Stream, 140
Andreiev, Leonid, 132
And wilt thou leave me, 263
Anhalt Studio, Battersea, 129, 131, 156
Annunzio, Gabriele D', 127
Aran Islands, 161
Arbeau, Thoinot, 264
Aristotle, 276
Arlen, Michael, 108
As Dewe in Aprylle, 25, 203, 295
As ever I saw, 159, 203
Athenaeus, 276
Auber, Daniel François, 281
Autumn Twilight, 246
Away to Twiver, 263

BACH, J. S., 23, 26, 63, 70
Bachelor, The, 228
Bailey beareth the bell away, The, 159, 204, 248
Balakirev, Mily, 71
Balulalow, 25, 204, 295, 303
Bantock, Sir Granville, 213, 259
Barker, Granville, 132
Bartók, Béla, 71, 160, 175, 184, 187, 213
Baudelaire, Charles, 22, 23
Bax, Arnold, 113, 265-6
Baylis, Donald, 135
Beaumont and Fletcher, 276
Beck and Aubry, troubadour songs, 303
Beddoes, Thomas Lovell, 263, 276, 301-3
Beecham, Sir Thomas, 39-41, 84-5, 98, 102, 131, 133, 135, 136, 137, 237, 278, 282, 287
Beethoven, Ludwig van, 22, 23, 70, 97

Beldamandis, Prosdocimus de, 150-1
Belloc, Hilaire, 263
Bennett, Arnold, 215
Beresford, J. D., 108
Berlioz, Hector, 42, 48-9, 65, 70, 77, 85, 108, 233
Berkeley, Bishop, 144
Bethlehem Down, 282, 295
Birrell, Augustine, 268
Biskra, 212
Blake, William, 105, 126-7, 144, 172, 175, 188
Boehme, Jakob, 144, 188
Bols gin, 150
Borodin, Alexander, 71
Borrow, George, 45, 69, 276, 298
Boswell, James, 276
Boughton, Rutland, 184
Brahms, Johannes, 49, 71, 97
Brett, Dorothy, 120
Bridges, Robert, 28
Brittany, 214
Browne, Sir Thomas, 191, 192
Budapest, 213
Burd Ellen, 246
Burney, Charles, 254
Busoni, Ferruccio, 70, 201
Byng, Cranmer, 140
Byrd, Thomas, 104
Byron, Lord, 26-7, 276

CAFÉ ROYAL, 11, 125, 138, 224
——— Verrey, 11, 226
Callimachus, 140
Camaret, 214
Campbell, Roy, 212
Candlelight, 263
Cannabis Indica, 218
Capriol, 264
Captain Stratton's Fancy, 228
Carillon Carilla, 295
Carnac, 162, 214
Carnegie U.K. Trust, 249
Carpenter, Edward, 67
Carroll, Lewis, 211, 277

INDEX

Carswell, Catherine, 120, 122, 169, 220-1, 225
Catullus, 23
Celtic Triad, 158
Cézanne, Paul, 59, 133
Chanson du jour de Noël, 295
Chantecler, 25
Charing Cross Station, 258, 264
Chinese Ballet, 142
Chipping Norton, 287
Chopin, Frédéric, 34, 70, 160
Coblenz, 40, 44
Cocteau, Jean, 298
Cologne, 40-9
Corelli, Marie, 276
Coleridge, S. T., 178
Collins, Hal (Te Akau), 254-5, 279
Colon, Jenny, 231
Conrad, Joseph, 69, 255
Cooper, Gerald, letter to, 248
Cornish Christmas Carol, 162, 170, 183-4
—— *Rhapsody*, 158
Cornwall, 108-16, 119, 145-57
Corpus Christi, 25, 204
Cory, William, 24, 140
Craig, Gordon, 132
Cricketers of Hambledon, The, 237
Croce, Benedetto, 187
Crystal Palace, Cat Show, 253
Curlew, The, 110-1, 244, 247-8, 264, 282, 287
Curwen, Messrs., 219

DAVIES, WALFORD, 97
Debussy, Claude, 42, 48, 70, 99, 171, 176
Dedication, 204
Delectable Ballad, A, 146-8
Delius, Frederick, 37-9, 58-60, 62-4, 69-70, 84-5, 125-6, 129, 140, 142, 158, 159, 160, 201, 251, 266, 282, 287
—— Book on, 26, 104, 155, 243, 244, 250-1
—— Letters from, 43, 45, 47, 53, 106, 110, 135, 156, 176, 202, 206
—— Letters to, 39, 40, 44, 46, 49, 54, 57, 93, 94, 99, 100, 106, 107, 109, 111, 115, 117, 131, 153, 173, 177, 179, 201, 204, 212, 241, 286
Descartes, René, 144
De Quincey, Thomas, 194
Dickens, Charles, 225, 276, 280

Dieren, Bernard van, 77, 140-1, 159, 160, 175, 187, 192, 202, 245, 291
—— Letters to, 24, 138
Dirge, 158, 264-6
Distracted Maid, The, 245
Dohnanyi, Ernest von, 71
Dolben, Digby Mackworth, 28
Dostoievski, 69
Douglas, Norman, 224, 276
Dowland, John, 25, 245
Dowson, Ernest, 50, 69, 95
Drake, Sir Francis, 219, 273
Dunstable, John, 266
Dvorak, Anton, 97

EARLE, GILES: HIS BOOKE, 275
Elgar, Sir Edward, 84, 268, 288
Ellis, Havelock, 67
Emerson, Ralph Waldo, 54
English Ayre, The, 26, 275
Epstein, Jacob, 138, 250
Eton, 34-7
Evreinov, 132
Eynsford, 253-278

FARNABY, GILES, 104
Fauré, Gabriel, 70
Finistère, 214
Flaubert, Gustave, 129, 143-4, 190
Fletcher, John, 245
Forster, E. M., 22
Fox, The, 282, 301
Fraisse, Armand, 22
Franck, César, 71, 142
Frankenstein, 236
French Symbolists, The, 186
Freud, Sigmund, 277
Frostbound Wood, The, 282, 301
Frothblowers, The Royal and Ancient Order of, 237
Fux, Johann Joseph, 188, 190, 191, 192

GALEN, 104
Gardiner, Balfour, 96, 170
Gasset, Ortega y, 298
Genesis, the book of, 276
Gesualdo, Carlo: Musician and Murderer, 26, 211, 237
Gibbons, Orlando, 104
Giles Earle: His Booke, 275
Gluck, Christoph Willibald, 77, 135
Godalming, 257
Goethe, Wolfgang von, 22, 280, 301

Goldring, Douglas, 259
Goncourt, the brothers' Journal, 207-8
Good Ale, 228
Goossens, Eugène, 104, 113, 226
Gordon, General, 215
Goss, John, 13, 14
Gounod, Charles, 97
Gower, John, 276
Gravesend, 257,
Gray, Cecil, letters to, 151, 162, 180-98, 209, 210, 214, 223, 242, 250, 253, 274
Grez-sur-Loing, 37, 50, 54
Grieg, Edvard, 62, 70, 184

Hanaker Mill, 263
Handel, George Frederick, 70, 171
Hardy, Thomas, 69
Harlequin, 255-6
Haydn, Franz Joseph, 70, 97
Hegel, G. W. F., 144
Hendecasyllabics, 151
Hermes Trismegistus, 144, 186
Heseltine, Arnold, 33
—— John Postle, 33
—— Joseph, 33, 37
—— Michael, 33
—— Philip Arnold (*See* Peter Warlock)
Hey troly loly, 228
Hogarth, William, 264
Holst, Gustav, 96, 213
Homer, 26
Horoscope, 164-7
Housman, A. E., 69
Hugo, Victor, 23
Hume, David, 296
Hungarian folk-tunes, 184
Hunt, Leigh, 275
Huxley, Aldous, 89, 106, 107, 226-9
Hy-Brasil, 149

INDIAN FOLK-SONG, 160
—— hemp, 218
Inghelbrecht, D. E., 42
Inquest, coroner's, 290-5
Imperial League of Opera, 237, 282
Ireland, John, 294, 297
Irish folk music, 184-5

JAMES, WILLIAM, 215-6
Jeffreys, Richard, 67
Jillian of Berry, 263
John, Augustus, 212
Johnnie wi' the tye, 246

Johnson, Dr., 27
Joyce, James, 66, 276-7

KANGAROO, 255
Kant, Emmanuel, 144
Keats, John, 178, 214
Keller, Gottfried, 132
Kelsall, F., 302
Kingsmill, Hugh, 128
Koteliansky, S., 89, 225
Kouyoumdjian, Dikran (Michael Arlen), 108

LADMIRAULT, PAUL, 25, 70
Lady's Birthday, The, 264
Lamartine, Alphonse de, 23
Langland, William, 276
Lawrence, D. H., 68, 85-92, 98, 105, 106-22, 145, 146, 150, 167-9, 181, 185, 220-7, 230
Leibnitz, G. W., 144, 159
Levi, Eliphas, 144, 163, 168
Liadain and Curither, 168, 181
Lillygay, 245, 246, 263
Limericks, 83, 150, 277
Li Po, 140
Liszt, Franz, 34, 201, 281
London Mercury, The, 208, 275
—— University, 96-8
Lots Road, power station, 145
Lucas, F. L., 302-3
Lucian, 276
Lucretius, 23
Luhan, Mabel Dodge, 120
Lullaby, 159, 203

MACDOWELL, EDWARD, 97
Madeira wine, 243
Maeterlinck, Maurice, 132, 134
Mahler, Gustav, 23
Maltworms, 263
Manchester Guardian, The, 275
Mansfield, Katherine, 112-3, 116, 119, 121, 224-5
Maturin, The Rev. C. R., 243
Marlotte, 37
Melville, Herman, 253
Merry-Go-Down, 276
Meyerbeer, Giacomo, 47
Michelangelo, 22
Milkmaids, 263
Milo, 237, 282, 286, 289
Mr. Belloc's Fancy, 228

INDEX

Moby Dick, 253
Moeran, E. J., 13, 287
Montaigne, Michel de, 19, 85
Monteverde, Claudio, 14, 135, 171
Moussorgsky, Modeste, 160
Mozart, W. A., 70, 97, 135, 192
Murry, J. Middleton, 112-3, 116, 119, 121, 224-5
Musica ficta, 272, 274
Musset, Alfred de, 233-4
My gostly Fader, 159, 204, 248
My own Country, 263

NASHE, THOMAS, 276
National Council of Public Morals, 222
Nerval, Gérard de, 231-3, 287
Newman, Ernest, 25, 93, 207-8
Nichols, Robert, 35, 112, 119, 122, 142, 235, 243, 275-6
—— Letters to, 98, 116, 145, 152, 251, 280
Nietzsche, Friedrich, 59, 67, 81
Night, The, 263
Nijinsky, 258
Norse folk-tunes, 184

Observer, The, 275
Occultism, 163-7
Old Song, An, 158-9, 169
One more River, 264
Orchésographie, 264
Ornstein, Leo, 71
Ouled-naïls, 213
Oxford, 49, 57, 60, 61

PARACELSUS, 144
Parry, Sir Hubert, 44, 139
Paul, B. Dean, 218
Peacock, T. L., 276
Pergolesi, G. B., 135
Peterisms, 245-6, 263
Petronius, 33, 212, 276
Pilkington, Vere, 208
Plato, 59, 276
Pliny, 276
Plotinus, 182
Poe, Edgar Allan, 22, 276, 294
Poel, William, 132
Poldowski, 218
Poole, 251
Prayer to St. Anthony of Padua, 263
Princess of Tripoli, The, 231

Propertius, 23
Purcell, Henry, 25, 135, 266

RABELAIS, FRANCOIS, 69, 276
Raleigh, Sir Walter, 219, 271, 276
Raspberry, 279
Ravel, Maurice, 70, 176
Reger, Max, 71
Rimbaud, Arthur, 212
Rimsky Korsakov, 71
Rochester, Lord, 276
Rockstro, W., 272
Rodker, John, 134
Rogers, Winthrop, 202-8
Rosseter, Philip, 24-5
Royal Academy of Music, 96
—— College of Music, 96
Rowlandson, 264
Rückert, J. M. F. 23
Rudel Jaufre, 231

SACCHINI, ANTONIO, 254
Sackbut, The, 12, 99, 102-3, 200-37, 287
Saudades, 140, 143, 158, 159
Schönberg, Arnold, 49, 70, 175
Schubert, Franz, 70, 246
Scotland Yard, 222
Scott, Cyril, 193
Scottish folk-song, 246
Scriabin, Nicholas, 160
Secretary Bird, The, 249
Secker, Martin, 220-3
Seneca, 276
Serenade, 244, 259
Shakespeare, 26, 149, 276
Shaw, G. Bernard, 130, 215-6
Shoemaker, The, 246
Shrouding of the Duchess, 265
Sibelius, Jean, 49
Sick Heart, The, 263
Sidney, Sir Philip, 271
Simper, Caleb, 244
Skelton, John, 276
Sleep, 245-6, 248
Sorabji, Kaikhosru, 77
Sorrow's Lullaby, 263
Spinoza, 144
Squire, Sir John, 275
Strachey, Lytton, 215, 302
Strauss, Richard, 41-2, 48, 62, 70, 171, 300
Stevenson, R. L., 233
Stopes, Marie, 236, 261

INDEX

Sumer is icumen in, 266
Swedenborg, Emmanuel, 188
Swinburne, A. C., 262
Sycamore Tree, The, 295
Symons, Arthur, 37, 54, 59, 69, 212, 246, 248
Synge, J. M., 181

TADEMA, ALMA, 193
Taine, Hippolyte, 207-8
Take, O take, 140, 159, 203, 248
Tarot, 163, 167
Taylor, Colin, 37, 184
—— Letters to, 48, 58, 104, 158, 159, 160-2, 169-73
Terry, Sir Richard, 26, 256, 266
—— Tribute to P. W., 267-73
There is a Lady, 204
Thompson, Francis, 35
Three Dirges of Webster, 264-6
—— *Carols,* 204, 289
Tilbury, 257
Tirley, Tirlow, 295
Titian, 301
Tolstoi, 69
Tomkins, Thomas, 104
Ton-y-Bottel (Welsh folk-song), 244
Toper's Song, The, 263
Traherne, Thomas, 144, 194
Tristram Shandy, 254
Troubadours, 303

URQUHART AND MOTTEUX, 69
Ulysses (James Joyce's), 276

VERDI, GIUSEPPE, 301
Verlaine, Paul, 23
Verrey, Café, 11, 226
Victory (Joseph Conrad's), 255
Vigny, Alfred de, 68
Villiers de l'Isle Adam, 60, 232
Villon, François, 276
Vines, Raoul, 71
Vitalis, Ordericus, 256

WAGNER, RICHARD, 47, 59-60, 70, 281
Wales, 242, 246
Walker, Dr. Ernest, 70, 73
Walk him along, Johnnie, 256
Warlock, Peter (Philip Heseltine), *passim*: birth and early life, 33-4; Eton College, 34-40; meeting with Delius, 37; stay in Cologne, 40-52; at Christ Church, Oxford, 57-92; meeting with D. H. Lawrence, 106; Chelsea, 125-144; Cornwall, 145-57; Ireland, 158-99; first songs published, 203; starts paper, *The Sackbut,* 205; visits Algiers, Tunis, Hungary, 212-3; France, 213; alcoholic propensities, 215-8; experiments with *cannabis indica,* 218-9; projected libel action, 220 *et seq.*; duality of personality, 227 *et seq.*; stay in Wales, 241-4; controversy with W. B. Yeats, 248-9; stay in Eynsford, Kent, 253-79; settles in London, 283; death and coroner's inquest, 290 *et seq.*
Webster, John, 264-6
Weininger, Otto, 67
Whenas the Rye, 159
Whitman, Walt, 67, 70
Wythorne, Thomas, 274
Wilde, Oscar, 236
Williams, Dr. R. Vaughan, 78-9, 193, 245
Wilson, Philip, 244
Wolf, Hugo, 252, 281
Wonderment, 81
Wood, Sir Henry, 97
Wordsworth, William, 178

Yarmouth Fair, 263
Yeats, Jack, 182
—— W. B., 68, 69, 83, 132, 182, 186, 188

319

A LIST OF BOOKS IN

THE LIFE AND LETTERS SERIES

at 4s. 6d. net each

JONATHAN CAPE
THIRTY BEDFORD SQUARE LONDON

A NOTE ON THE ARRANGEMENT
OF THIS CATALOGUE

The main body of the list is arranged alphabetically under the names of AUTHORS. In addition, for the convenience of readers, there is an index at the end giving the titles arranged according to their numbers in the series.

The Life and Letters Series has been reviewed by Mr. Frank Swinnerton in *The Evening News* thus: 'The first volumes of this new and handsome series should meet the most modern taste. Here in beautiful light form are books which have all been previously published within the last three or four years at much higher prices.

'Of the first titles every one is the kind of work to make any keen reader say to himself, "I wish I could afford that! If it were cheaper I'd buy it!"

'With the price 4s. 6d. a volume, the appearance handsome and very agreeable, *The Life and Letters Series* CAN be afforded. The bargain will be a good one.'

ANTHONY, Katharine

CATHERINE THE GREAT. With a Frontispiece   *No. 13*
'This lively and well-written study is a judicious treatment of a temperament and a reputation, and the whole book is a contribution to the study, not only of Catherine the Great, but of a significant period in Russian history.' *Time and Tide*

BELLOC, Hilaire

A CONVERSATION WITH AN ANGEL   *No. 27*
In this volume of essays Mr. Belloc well maintains his usual high level of pungent and witty writing. His subjects are varied as they are diverting, and include pages on poverty, academic hate and epigrams, on Renan, Gibbon and Macaulay, on witchcraft, pavement artists and bridges.

HOW THE REFORMATION HAPPENED   *No. 50*
'This book is well worth reading. . . . Mr. Belloc has marshalled the events of the Reformation into significant intervals and order and charged his narrative so richly with ideas that an old and complex story has become fresh and lucid.' *Manchester Guardian*

3

BERCOVICI, Konrad

THE STORY OF THE GYPSIES. Illustrated from photographs by E. O. HOPPÉ

No. 11

'The author of this fascinating book has not only made researches into the history of this people but has also lived, travelled and been entertained by them. Though it would be extravagant to say that he had the genius of George Borrow, it is certain that he has more respect for the truth and for scholarly fact than had that great though erratic man.' *Listener*

BIRKENHEAD, The late Earl of, edited by

THE ADVENTURES OF RALPH RASHLEIGH (a penal exile in Australia 1825-1844). Illustrated from facsimile pages of the original MS.

No. 20

This book reveals, through the sufferings and vicissitudes of a single convict transported to New South Wales for burglary, a vivid picture of the conditions under which the penal code was administered less than a hundred years ago.

BLUNDEN, Edmund

THE MIND'S EYE

No. 80

'Messrs. Cape have done well to collect in a single volume, entitled *The Mind's Eye*, some of the many articles which Mr. Edmund Blunden has contributed to the periodicals of three continents and which, but for Jonathan Cape, might have been lost for ever. Mr. Blunden is a writer of traditional but splendid prose. Few passages of modern writing seem to me so alive with the slow rhythm, the balanced reserve, peculiar to our own language as those which Mr. Blunden has written about the old mill or the bridges at Yalding. For those who enjoy our language it is a real satisfaction to find a modern writer who treats his medium as something pliable, indigenous and alive.' HAROLD NICOLSON in the *Daily Telegraph*

BONE, Alexander

BOWSPRIT ASHORE

No. 69

'Mr. Alexander Bone has given us, in *Bowsprit Ashore*, the finest set of salt-water yarns one could wish to read. Get this book, for it is worthy of a place on that salt-water shelf which holds the pick of British adventure. When I add that the woodcuts are worthy of the prose, I am paying Miss Freda Bone the highest compliment I can find.' *The Daily Mail*

4

BONE, James

THE LONDON PERAMBULATOR.   Illustrated with
drawings by MUIRHEAD BONE   *No.* 23

'The quiet humour of the writer and hand of the artist go together to
present the majesty, the beauty, the variety, the oddity of London in
a book one would not soon tire of praising.' *Times Literary Supplement*

BROWNLEE, Frank

CATTLE THIEF   *No.* 32

This is the life story of a South African native. In its divination of
the native mind the book is a little masterpiece. More than this, the
exploits of Ntsukumbini, a member of a family of professional stock
thieves, his outwitting of the police, his experiences in the gold mines,
his loves and sorrows, make really good reading.

BUTLER, Samuel

ALPS AND SANCTUARIES.   Illustrated with two maps.   *No.* 25

'*Alps and Sanctuaries* is essentially a holiday book, and no one ever
enjoyed a holiday more keenly than Butler. Here we see him in his most
unbuttoned mood, giving the rein to his high spirits and letting his
fantastic humour carry him whither it would.' *From the Introduction
by* R. A. STREATFEILD

CUMMINGS, E. E.

THE ENORMOUS ROOM. With a Frontispiece portrait of
the Author, and an Introduction by ROBERT GRAVES   *No.* 2

'He reveals himself as a man of sensibility and fortitude, and he writes
always with such good taste that I do not think anyone reading his
book could feel otherwise than that it is the work of a rare, fine spirit.'
Sunday Times

DARK, Sidney

FIVE DEANS. With five illustrations   *No.* 26

'The five Deans drawn and characterised in this book are Colet,
Donne, Swift, Stanley, and Inge. . . . It is extraordinarily brilliant,
carrying the reader on with unflagging interest from beginning to
end. The writer is gifted with a sure instinctive capacity to exclude
the dull and the heavy, and to include the humanly interesting and
attractive.' *The Church Times*

5

DE KRUIF, Paul

MICROBE HUNTERS. Illustrated by four portraits *No.* 3

This book captures for the reader something of the intellectual excitement and romance associated with the works of the greater scientists.

DIMNET, Ernest

THE BRONTË SISTERS. With four illustrations *No.* 19

The Brontë Sisters is an ideal co-mingling of critical biography and literary criticism. With great tenderness, with much sympathy, but with rigid intellectual honesty, the author recreates for us the parsonage and its inhabitants, and brings especially to the mentality of Charlotte and Emily Brontë a fresh analytical talent.

DOUGHTY, Charles M.

PASSAGES FROM ARABIA DESERTA. Selected by
EDWARD GARNETT. With Frontispiece *No.* 21

'Charles Montagu Doughty was one of the great men of our day, the author of a unique prose masterpiece. For many readers it is a book so majestic, so vital, of such incomparable beauty of thought, of observation, and of diction as to occupy a place apart among their most cherished literary possessions.' *Observer*

EDINGER, George, and NEEP, E. J. C.

HORATIO NELSON. With four illustrations *No.* 44

The British Nation has set Nelson on such a high pedestal in Trafalgar Square that nobody can see what he looks like, and biographers have always held their telescopes to the blind eye. The story of Lord Nelson is the story of the greatest conspiracy of silence of the last hundred and fifty years and is among the great love tragedies of the world.

FAUSSET, Hugh I'Anson

SAMUEL TAYLOR COLERIDGE *No.* 55

'Mr. Fausset's book is a vital and informing piece of criticism.' *Times Literary Supplement*
'A good book, a really clever book which brings out many important matters which other biographers have not observed or have neglected, and one which will be read for a long time.' *New Statesman*

FAUSSET, Hugh I'Anson

A MODERN PRELUDE *No. 75*

'It is a religious autobiography, and shows how the philosopher himself emerged from the conflicts of childhood and adolescence into the serenity of a mystical faith which realizes the underlying unity of the spirit that binds the individual to a creative whole and gives him inner freedom. Mr. Fausset's account of his youth is an unusually fine and sensitive piece of biographical writing. . . . The sincerity of the book should impress even those who differ most deeply from it, and its literary charm should commend it to all its readers.' *The Times*

GRAVES, Robert

GOOD-BYE TO ALL THAT. With eight illustrations *No. 22*

'*Good-bye to all That* is a very good book, both picturesque and honest, and excellently written. Robert Graves is a fine poet—none better to-day, in my view. All poets write good prose, and he does. . . . It is the sincere and convincing expression of a distinguished individuality.' ARNOLD BENNETT

LAWRENCE AND THE ARABS *No. 71*

A full and intimate account of Lawrence's life and adventures. The author, a personal friend of Lawrence, had his permission to write this biography as a discouragement to possible misleading and inaccurate ones. He had also the advice and assistance of many of those who were with Lawrence during the Arab campaign.

'In a work of exceptional clarity and quite absorbing interest it outlines the whole marvellous business in a manner which could not have been bettered.' *Sunday Times*

HENDY, E. W.

WILD EXMOOR THROUGH THE YEAR *No. 37*

'Mr. Hendy is one of the best writers among our naturalists, with abundant and intimate knowledge of his country and its wild inhabitants. There must be many people who will find this their book; now that we have lost our old freedom of passage across country, with the rights of way curtailed or quietly filched almost everywhere, Exmoor and Dartmoor mean more than ever.' EDWARD THOMSON in *The Observer*

HINDUS, Maurice

HUMANITY UPROOTED *No. 41*

'I have just read your book. It answers a score of questions I've been asking about Russia and a score of others I should have asked had I known enough to ask them. It is as illuminating and exciting as it is convincing. I've learnt more from it than I have from any other book I've read for years.' *From a letter to the author by* MR. H. G. WELLS

HINDUS, Maurice

RED BREAD
No. 56

'Mr. Hindus has discovered a new approach to the oft-told story of
the Russian Revolution. His method is midway between that of the
straightforward reporter and of the novelist. He travels all over Russia
collecting information and impressions. Then he returns to a village
which he knows particularly well, where indeed he was born and spent
his youth, and tests this information and these impressions by living
with and talking to the villagers. . . .

'The method and style adopted by Mr. Hindus shield him from any
suspicion of partiality or prejudice. He has neither the publicist's bias
nor the partisan's axe to grind.' *The Spectator*

HORN, Alfred Aloysius

TRADER HORN (The Ivory Coast in the Earlies). Edited by ETHELREDA LEWIS. With an Introduction by JOHN GALSWORTHY. Illustrated with portraits
No. 4

'This is a gorgeous book, more full of sheer stingo than any you are
likely to come across in a day's march among the bookshops of where-
ever you may be.' *From* MR. JOHN GALSWORTHY'S *Introduction*

THE WATERS OF AFRICA. Edited by ETHELREDA LEWIS No. 28

Even more mysterious than the cannibals and shadowy rivers of
Western Africa is the East Coast of fifty years ago with its magic
island of Madagascar and its island-sown Mozambique Channel.
Here, as in his other book, the famous conversations of Horn with his
editor amplify the old man's narrative.

JACKSON, Holbrook

THE EIGHTEEN NINETIES. With twenty-six illustrations No. 17

'The curious investigator of the future will always be able to see the
period's main outlines, and to find them clearly traced in Mr. Holbrook Jackson's animated and attractive pages.' *The Daily Telegraph*

JEKYLL, Francis

GERTRUDE JEKYLL
No. 81

'This brief but most interesting memoir, written by her nephew, Mr·
Francis Jekyll, is prefaced by an affectionate foreword by Sir Edwin
Lutyens, her friend and collaborator for over forty years, and contains
a list of three hundred and fifty gardens, in the laying out of which
she either was completely responsible or assisted by her advice. In her
long, industrious and beneficent life Miss Jekyll knew and was admired
and respected by nearly everybody worth knowing in Art and Letters.
Yet she never received any official recognition. Happily it was not
required. Her name is writ large on the face of England, which, as it was
said, no one in her lifetime except the Creator did more to beautify.' *Punch*

8

KORNITZER, Margaret
THE MODERN WOMAN AND HERSELF   *No. 61*

'I should like to thank you for publishing Margaret Kornitzer's *The Modern Woman and Herself*—a book brave, honest, poignant and revealing. If it is widely read there will be much less unhappiness.' EDWARD THOMPSON

'It differs from most books of its kind, which are, for the most part, too much like arguments with cretins. It is written in a mood of placid and intelligent inquiry. Miss Kornitzer holds, and I agree with her, that women will always find their fullest happiness in marriage, the care of children, and what is called domesticity. I find her uniformly stimulating and clever in her analysis of the cause of many present discontents.' SYLVIA LYND in *Harper's Bazaar*

LA ROCHE, Sophie v.
SOPHIE IN LONDON 1786: Being the Diary of Sophie v. La Roche. Translated by CLARE WILLIAMS. With a Foreword by G. M. TREVELYAN   *No. 72*

'It is surprising that this diary has had to wait for translation until now, for it is one of the freshest and most satisfying accounts of the life of that day we have seen. Sophie possessed an almost perfect talent for seeing the right sights—that is, the sights that you and I would choose to see if we were projected back again into the days of George III. . . . The pages of Sophie's diary abound with vivid pictures, and hours of pleasure await any reader with historical sense who dips into its pages. Professor G. M. Trevelyan, in his foreword, does it no more than justice in describing it as "a valuable addition" to the library of old travellers' tales which forms so attractive a part of modern reading.' *The Listener*

LANGDON-DAVIES, John
A SHORT HISTORY OF WOMEN   *No. 42*

A most readable and reasonable book in which the author traces the ideas and theories which have been held about the position of women and the treatment which has been meted out to them during the last six thousand years.

LEYEL, Mrs. C. F.
THE MAGIC OF HERBS   *No. 34*

'Mrs. Leyel has gone deep into her subject and has brought back wonders from the earliest dawn of science and from all parts of the world . . . treasures of curious and useful information purged of their dross are presented, not too methodically and yet methodically enough.' *Manchester Guardian*

LINKLATER, Eric

BEN JONSON AND KING JAMES *No.* 79

'If Ben Jonson could have known that nearly three hundred years after his death he was to find so robust and sympathetic a biographer as Mr. Eric Linklater, the Mermaid would have rocked to his rumbustious approval.' *Punch*

'His dazzlingly written book succeeds in giving a picture of the time so vivid that you can almost touch and very nearly smell the age of velvet cloaks and open drains. I shall make bold and say that Mr. Linklater beats Mr. Strachey in his feeling for the period.' JAMES AGATE in the *Daily Express*

LUBBOCK, Percy

EARLHAM. With a Frontispiece *No.* 7

'The book seems too intimate to be reviewed. We want to be allowed to read it, and to dream over it, and keep silence about it. His judgment is perfect, his humour is true and ready; his touch light and prim; his prose is exact and clean and full of music.' *The Times*

SHADES OF ETON *No.* 30

The author was at Eton in the 'nineties of the last century. To those years belong the figures and scenes recalled in this book—in which they appear as they seemed to a boy, and in which an attempt is made to measure the effect of Eton on a boy's imagination. Warre himself, F. W. Warre-Cornish and his wife, H. E. Luxmoore and A. C. Benson were among those who counted most deeply in that impression; these and other figures familiar to Etonians of that time are sketched in detail.

LUDWIG, Emil

GENIUS AND CHARACTER. Illustrated by sixteen portraits *No.* 9

'As in his longer biographies, it is the dramatic values of motive and action he seeks, the flashes of illumination in the chiaroscuro investing a lonely figure. This is not a ponderous book; it is a series of vivacious and sometimes very moving studies.' *The Spectator*

MacCURDY, Edward

THE MIND OF LEONARDO DA VINCI *No.* 31

Mr. MacCurdy has made a special study of the manuscripts and note-books of Leonardo, a selection of which he edited. He attempts here a biographical study of Leonardo in which the subject's mind and mentality is the selective factor. The book is in three parts and deals with the period of his life at Florence, at Milan, and during the years of his wandering.

MacCURDY, Edward
LEONARDO DA VINCI: THE ARTIST   *No.* 73

'The achievements of Leonardo da Vinci were so various that he has often been regarded as a mirror of the Italian Renaissance, and Mr. Edward MacCurdy has written a remarkable guide to his life, his painting, his sculpture, and his drawings. The main value of this book, which is the fruit of long research, is to arrive at the truth of biographical fact and of genuine ascription. Fascinated as much by the student of science and of engineering as by the artist, Mr. MacCurdy has brought a scholar's knowledge to bear on the many problems of the artist's life and work. His pages are packed with information and close reasoning, but through them shines a genuine admiration which makes the book much more than a succinct work of reference. It is the kind of study that should be kept, for the probability is that the reader of other books disappointed or in doubt about some matter will find an answer here. The details in which it abounds have been fused by long study into a style that makes agreeable reading.' *John O'London's Weekly*

MacLAURIN, C., M.B., C.M., F.R.C.S.E., LL.D.
POST MORTEM   *No.* 65

Whether the 'great man' has had any real influence on the world, or whether history is merely a matter of ideas and tendencies among mankind, are still questions open to solution; but there is no doubt that great persons are still interesting; and it is the aim of this series of essays to throw such light upon them as is possible with regard to their physical condition; and to consider how far their actions were influenced by their health. There are many remarkable people in history about whom we know too little to dogmatize, though we may strongly suspect that their mental and physical conditions were abnormal when they were driven to take actions which have passed into history. *Post Mortem* contains studies, among others, of Joan of Arc, Anne Boleyn, Napoleon and Benvenuto Cellini.

MAYO, Katherine
MOTHER INDIA. Illustrated   *No.* 5

'It is certainly the most fascinating, the most devastating, and at the same time the most important and truthful book that has been written about India for a good deal more than a generation.' *New Statesman*

MEYNELL, Viola
ALICE MEYNELL. With eleven illustrations   *No.* 47

'Miss Viola Meynell's Memoir of her mother, *Alice Meynell*, is a beautiful book. It was a difficult task to do justice to that most noble woman, with her many talents—poet, critic, journalist and—no less giftedly—wife, mother and friend. But it has been worthily done. The reader will be grateful for the liberal quotations from Mrs. Meynell's poetry and literary criticism. They enrich the Memoir greatly.' *Evening Standard*

MORLEY, F. V.

LAMB BEFORE ELIA   *No. 66*

'It is a book full of sensitive appreciation of individuals, situations, and historical setting. It is rich with liberal information and with soundly reasoned judgments. It fills the reader with warm recognition of the author's talents and personality, with a deeper understanding of the character of Charles Lamb, and with a gentler tolerance of the affections of Elia.' RICHARD CHURCH in *The Christian Science Monitor*

MUIR, Edwin

JOHN KNOX. Illustrated by four portraits   *No. 12*

The study is not concerned with the truth or the falsehood of Calvinism, but rather presents the Calvinist in all his activities from the greatest to the most trifling, and shows his creed working out, here in heroic and there in ridiculous form.

MURCHIE, Guy

MEN ON THE HORIZON   *No. 62*

'This is a book of amazing adventure, so extraordinary that no one could have invented it; and it must therefore be true. Mr. Murchie has at twenty-two seen as much as most men manage to see in a long life; he has sailed the Yukon in a rowing boat, been a stowaway, lived with a Japanese family, argued—largely in sign-language—with drunken Reds in Moscow, and has been nearly killed for his pains.' E. E. KELLETT in *The News Chronicle*

MURRAY, Max

LONG WAY TO LONDON. With an Introduction by
STEPHEN GRAHAM   *No. 59*

'If you want to know how the ordinary casual visitor, with no political axe to grind and little other equipment beyond observant eyes and a sense of humour, fares in Moscow; if you want to know how hard the seats of the Trans-Siberian railway become to those who have bounced about on them for days; if you want to meet Bulgarians who have been imprisoned in Siberia; if you want to see Chinese students, and missionaries in Japanese hotels who distribute books on sex; then read this account of a strange haphazard journey by an Australian who went from London to London by way of Russia, China, Korea, Japan and Australia. Mr. Murray is so genial a traveller, so much interested in people and places, that his journey passes all too rapidly for the entertained and enlightened reader.' *Time and Tide*

MURRY, J. Middleton

SON OF WOMAN
No. 40

'A very detailed exposition of the life-work of D. H. Lawrence, and it would be impossible—I will say that—to find a better interpretation. It will be indispensable to any future historian of this prophetic period: Mr. Murry was a great friend of Lawrence, and is excellently placed to tell us exactly the significance of every fresh development in this gospel.' WYNDHAM LEWIS in *Time and Tide*

THE LIFE OF JESUS
No. 58

'A book which must take its place among the interpretation of Jesus that really count. . . . A gift to religion as well as to modern letters.' *Times Literary Supplement*

'A fine piece of work, a sort of *Ecce Homo* for our generation. It really sheds fresh light on the central figure of all history.' THE VERY REV. DEAN INGE

REMINISCENCES OF D. H. LAWRENCE
No. 74

The publication of a narrative based on a garbled version of these Reminiscences made it necessary for Mr. Middleton Murry to publish the authentic and original text, with a series of notes and appendices throwing light on some of the crucial happenings in Lawrence's life. The book contains the full documentary evidence for the nature of the relation between Lawrence and Murry, and it is intended to dispose finally of the misleading account of that relation given to the public in some other books. It also includes a prefatory essay dealing with the deeper and more enigmatic elements of that relation, and forms as a whole a document of the first importance for the understanding of one of the outstanding figures of our times.

WILLIAM BLAKE
No. 76

'This is the most comprehensive study of Blake's genius that we have yet had. Mr. Murry has already, in his studies of Keats and D. H. Lawrence, shown his aptitude for giving something like order and coherence to the incomplete utterances of genius.' *The Times Literary Supplement*

'It is certain that Mr. Middleton Murry's new book will have to be read by all who intend to study even the simplest of Blake's poems. . . . It elevates Blake to a place far higher than he has held even with many of those who have most admired him; and it can honestly be called a profound and great piece of interpretative criticism.' *The Morning Post*

NILES, Blair

CONDEMNED TO DEVIL'S ISLAND. The biography
of a French Convict. Illustrated from drawings by B. K.
MORRIS   *No.* 10

Mrs. Blair Niles is the first woman to have been allowed to visit the most
notorious Devil's Island since it became a penal colony. She describes
this penal settlement in the person of a young French burglar, and tells an
almost unbearable tale of thousands of men starved of hope and leisure.

O'FAOLÁIN, Seán

CONSTANCE MARKIEVICZ   *No.* 82

'Mr. O'Faoláin writes admirably, and his book is packed with brilliant
descriptions of the background to the Countess's activities. It will
fascinate those who prefer history to legend.' RAYMOND MORTIMER in
the *New Statesman and Nation*

'One of Ireland's most distinguished younger writers has written an
illuminating and perspicacious biography of this dynamic woman who
spent three years of her life in prisons for the cause of Irish nationalism.
Mr. O'Faoláin's statement of twentieth-century Irish politics is
brilliantly clear, and he is enlivening to read because he is not afraid to
say what he thinks.' *Birmingham Post*

PENN-SMITH, Frank

THE UNEXPECTED   *No.* 77

'This is an autobiography which, though it may be forgotten, will be
rediscovered, and continue to bring future readers who lead cautious,
monotonous lives that sense of adventure which they can only enjoy
vicariously. . . . The power of the writing lies in those pages which
describe and narrate—too long for quotation; in those which transmit
not only scenes, dangers, and endurances, but also that something
"unexpected" in the mind of the narrator himself, which makes the
book remarkable.' DESMOND MACCARTHY in the *Sunday Times*

RANSOME, Arthur

ROD AND LINE   *No.* 38

'*Rod and Line* must be placed in the front rank of contemporary
angling literature, both for its insight into the "sunset hues" through
which most of us see our sport (in reminiscence), and for its literary
excellence. It possesses, too, just that touch of whimsical humour
with which most of us (again in reminiscence) clothe the nakedness of
those distressing times which confirm us in our conviction that Job
was no fisherman.' *Field*

READ, Herbert
WORDSWORTH   *No.* 35
'This study of Wordsworth is to me a landmark in English criticism
such as we have not had since the *Biographia Literaria.* . . . If ever
I recognized great work, proclaimed by its own strength and sim-
plicity, here is such.' RICHARD CHURCH in *The Spectator*

REISCHEK, Andreas
YESTERDAYS IN MAORILAND. Translated from the
German and Edited by H. E. L. PRIDAY   *No.* 51
Herr Reischek explored the mountain areas and the bush, and became
thoroughly conversant, not only with the flora and fauna of the
islands, but also with the Maori language. When this book first appeared, *The Times Literary Supplement* said of it: 'Mr. Priday has placed
under a deep obligation all interested in New Zealand, whether they be
students of history or of nature, of the Maori in process of civilization,
or the weka and the kiwi and the kakapo in the course of extirpation.'

RIESENBERG, Felix
LOG OF THE SEA   *No.* 70
'Other seafaring writers may have had adventures as varied as Riesenberg's, but they have not his power of conveying them to readers nor his
philosophic point of view in interpreting them. Every word he writes is
of significance. . . . Riesenberg has had his share of hazards; he has met
many strange characters; he has lived vividly; and in this "log" he
re-creates his experiences with a skilled and graphic pen. This is an
absolutely first-class book of the sea, based on two score or more years
of experience on it in all sorts of climes and all sorts of ships.' *Everyman*

ROBERTS, Michael
ELIZABETHAN PROSE   *No.* 78
'It is amazing to discover how much good Elizabethan prose there is,
and how much it tells us. Jest books, letters, recipes, vituperation,
stories, literary criticism, are among Mr. Roberts's heart-warming
selection. . . . You will certainly agree with Mr. Roberts about the
delight and amusement that can be obtained from these "pugnacious
and obstreperous writings".' *John o' London's Weekly*

ROBINS, Elizabeth
THEATRE AND FRIENDSHIP   *No.* 63
'Apart from the extremely interesting subject-matter of Miss Robins'
book, the correspondence gleams with that inimitable quality which
always characterizes Henry James's letters to his friends, and makes
him a master of that almost vanished art. He ranks in this with
Walpole and Lamb, with Charlotte Brontë and Stevenson, and however
many letters we have of his, we are always thirsty for more. We only
wish this correspondence had been longer.' E. F. BENSON in *The Spectator*

RUKEYSER, Walter Arnold

WORKING FOR THE SOVIETS *No.* 67

'Out of the mass of verbiage Soviet Russia inspires there come now and again some really informative books. Generally they are the work of technical specialists, a few of whom, alone among visitors to Russia, seem content to give facts at least equal prominence with their own ideas. And such is this account of the experiences of an American mining engineer at the Soviet asbestos plant in the Urals.' *The Times Literary Supplement*

SIEBURG, Friedrich

IS GOD A FRENCHMAN? *No.* 68

'—that the peoples outside French "culture" are in fact "lesser breeds." It is this attitude which Herr Sieburg sets himself to examine with a good deal of wit and irony, with a keen perception born of an intimate acquaintance with French life, with a depth of feeling which inspires more than one beautiful passage, admirably rendered in Mr. Alan Harris's excellent translation. . . . It is a subtly difficult task extraordinarily well performed ; and the result deserves the earnest attention not of Frenchmen only.' STUART HODGSON in *The News Chronicle*

SIEGFRIED, André

AMERICA COMES OF AGE. A French Analysis. Illustrated by eight maps and diagrams. Translated from the French by H. H. HEMMING and DORIS HEMMING *No.* 1

'It is a brilliant study of the most important, and in some ways the most interesting, though certainly not the loveliest, nation on earth.' THE VERY REV. DEAN W. R. INGE

TAYLOR, G. R. Stirling

SEVEN NINETEENTH-CENTURY STATESMEN *No.* 39

'This vivid book . . . has the virtues of penetration, skilful arrangement, clear purpose, a lively style. It makes an excellent summary of the political history of England during most of the nineteenth century . . . it has not a dull page; the author has a keen eye for character, and an enviable gift for presentation.' OSBERT BURDETT in *The Observer*

OLIVER CROMWELL *No.* 57

'Mr. Stirling Taylor writes as the enemy of every form of humbug, and it must be admitted that his subject is rich in this material. The author shows penetration and discernment; his language is always trenchant and even vivid; moreover, he has equipped himself for the task by a critical study of the best authorities. The book is a notable contribution to Cromwellian studies, as well as an interesting example of the new interpretation derived by modern writers from the study of the seventeenth century.' *The Times*

WALLAS, Graham

THE ART OF THOUGHT No. 24

A book written with the practical purpose of helping the apprentice thinker to become a competent craftsman. The author examines the proposition that the human mind is 'actuated by instinct, but instrumented by reason,' and suggests its application to our own thought.

WEST, Rebecca

THE STRANGE NECESSITY: Critical Essays No. 18

Miss Rebecca West's book is a sequence of challenging studies of modern books and authors. *The Strange Necessity*—Art—which is so inclusive of opposites. Speculating on this brings Miss West to an analysis of literature, and the discovery of a double and vital function which it fulfils for man.

WILLIAMS-ELLIS, Amabel

JOHN RUSKIN No. 52

'Mrs. Williams-Ellis' most deadly weapon is a relentless sympathy which spares Ruskin nothing. The book is sincere and moving; it is a sustained effort of sympathetic insight; and it is easily the best as well as the frankest portrait of Ruskin that has yet been attempted.' EDWIN MUIR in *The Nation*

'Mrs. Williams-Ellis has written a very readable life of Ruskin; in parts there are passages of real brilliance and her work reflects a wide study of Ruskinian literature.' *The Spectator*

WILLIAMS-ELLIS, Clough & Amabel

THE PLEASURES OF ARCHITECTURE. Illustrated from drawings and photographs No. 14

This book will bring enlightenment and entertainment to those who like a well-built house or office building when they see it, but are not quite sure as to the reasons why they like it.

WILLIAMSON, Henry

THE LABOURING LIFE No. 60

'Here is a lovely book about the life of field and stream and wood and farm, a book to be savoured in little bits, put down, and savoured again. That Mr. Williamson can write is proved by one of his titles, which is in itself a poem: *Summer Afternoon by the Sea*. His writing has the quality of surprise, of making the reader suddenly see something which he must always have known and has never yet perceived.' JAMES AGATE in the *Daily Express*

WILSON, Margaret

THE CRIME OF PUNISHMENT   *No.* 64

'If crime is destiny, then obviously punishment of criminals is a crime, and this is the thesis of a book which we have read with respect and admiration—*The Crime of Punishment* by Margaret Wilson. The author is the wife of a prison official and was moved to write this book by what she has seen of prisons and criminals. The book is well written, with rare sincerity and feeling. The historical part makes terrible reading, the account of prison reforms and experiments is interesting and valuable, and the comparison with American experience illuminating.' *The Listener*

WITHERS, Hartley

EVERYBODY'S BUSINESS   *No.* 54

'This well-linked and comprehensive chain of discourses on our economic perplexities deserves the study of everybody who is in search of information rather than of controversial propaganda. For Mr. Withers, thoughtful, shrewd, and well informed, is quite exceptionally sympathetic with all serious schools of economic thought, however antagonistic they may be to one another. He puts their arguments fairly, is never reluctant to concede a point in which he finds substance, and where he dissents does it so reasonably and so genially that his book ought to be a really useful aid to the spread of that liberal spirit in which alone we shall find an escape from economic ills.' *Manchester Guardian*

WOOLLEY, C. L.

DEAD TOWNS AND LIVING MEN   *No.* 29

Dead Towns and Living Men describes the training that goes to make a fully equipped archæologist, the sort of places, usually far away from the beaten track, that he lives in, and the sort of men, usually ignorant and sometimes half-civilised, whom he must control and live with. Archæology as a satisfying human adventure has never been better described than in this book.

YORKE, Gerald

CHINA CHANGES   *No.* 83

'This is a vital and absorbing book, which will give Western readers a far better understanding of the Chinese and their difficulties than many more pretentious volumes, and that in a most readable manner. Mr. Yorke has a deep knowledge of the best of China's literature, and he has lived cheek by jowl with all sorts and conditions of her people in monasteries, camps, verminous inns, suffocating river launches, and sardine-packed omnibuses. All of which Mr. Yorke describes with breezy vigour and many vivid little sketches of the people he encountered.' *Sunday Times*

18

THE LIFE AND LETTERS SERIES

NUMERICAL INDEX TO TITLES

1. AMERICAN COMES OF AGE. André Siegfried
2. THE ENORMOUS ROOM. E. E. Cummings
3. MICROBE HUNTERS. Paul de Kruif
4. TRADER HORN. A. Aloysius Horn
5. MOTHER INDIA. Katherine Mayo
7. EARLHAM. Percy Lubbock
9. GENIUS AND CHARACTER. Emil Ludwig
10. CONDEMNED TO DEVIL'S ISLAND. Blair Niles
11. THE STORY OF THE GYPSIES. Konrad Bercovici
12. JOHN KNOX. Edwin Muir
13. CATHERINE THE GREAT. Katharine Anthony
14. THE PLEASURES OF ARCHITECTURE. C. and A. Williams-Ellis
17. THE EIGHTEEN NINETIES. Holbrook Jackson
18. THE STRANGE NECESSITY. Rebecca West
19. THE BRONTË SISTERS. Ernest Dimnet
20. THE ADVENTURES OF RALPH RASHLEIGH. The late Earl of Birkenhead
21. PASSAGES FROM ARABIA DESERTA. Selected by Edward Garnett
22. GOOD-BYE TO ALL THAT. Robert Graves
23. THE LONDON PERAMBULATOR. James Bone
24. THE ART OF THOUGHT. Graham Wallas
25. ALPS AND SANCTUARIES. Samuel Butler
26. FIVE DEANS. Sidney Dark
27. A CONVERSATION WITH AN ANGEL. Hilaire Belloc
28. THE WATERS OF AFRICA. A. Aloysius Horn
29. DEAD TOWNS AND LIVING MEN. C. L. Woolley
30. SHADES OF ETON. Percy Lubbock
31. THE MIND OF LEONARDO DA VINCI. Edward MacCurdy
32. CATTLE THIEF. Frank Brownlee
34. THE MAGIC OF HERBS. Mrs. C. F. Leyel
35. WORDSWORTH. Herbert Read
37. WILD EXMOOR THROUGH THE YEAR. E. W. Hendy
38. ROD AND LINE. Arthur Ransome
39. SEVEN NINETEENTH-CENTURY STATESMEN. G. R. Stirling Taylor
40. SON OF WOMAN. J. Middleton Murry
41. HUMANITY UPROOTED. Maurice Hindus
42. A SHORT HISTORY OF WOMEN. John Langdon-Davies
44. HORATIO NELSON. George Edinger and E. J. C. Neep
47. ALICE MEYNELL. Viola Meynell
50. HOW THE REFORMATION HAPPENED. Hilaire Belloc
51. YESTERDAYS IN MAORILAND. Andreas Reischek
52. JOHN RUSKIN. Amabel Williams-Ellis
54. EVERYBODY'S BUSINESS. Hartley Withers

55. SAMUEL TAYLOR COLERIDGE. Hugh I'Anson Fausset
56. RED BREAD. Maurice Hindus
57. OLIVER CROMWELL. G. R. Stirling Taylor
58. THE LIFE OF JESUS. J. Middleton Murry
59. LONG WAY TO LONDON. Max Murray
60. THE LABOURING LIFE. Henry Williamson
61. THE MODERN WOMAN AND HERSELF. Margaret Kornitzer
62. MEN ON THE HORIZON. Guy Murchie
63. THEATRE AND FRIENDSHIP. Elizabeth Robins
64. THE CRIME OF PUNISHMENT. Margaret Wilson
65. POST MORTEM. C. MacLaurin
66. LAMB BEFORE ELIA. F. V. Morley
67. WORKING FOR THE SOVIETS. Walter Arnold Rukeyser
68. IS GOD A FRENCHMAN? Friedrich Sieburg
69. BOWSPRIT ASHORE. Alexander Bone
70. LOG OF THE SEA. Felix Riesenberg
71. LAWRENCE AND THE ARABS. Robert Graves
72. SOPHIE IN LONDON. Sophie v. La Roche
73. LEONARDO DA VINCI: THE ARTIST. Edward MacCurdy
74. REMINISCENCES OF D. H. LAWRENCE. J. Middleton Murry
75. A MODERN PRELUDE. Hugh I'Anson Fausset
76. WILLIAM BLAKE. J. Middleton Murry
77. THE UNEXPECTED. Frank Penn-Smith
78. ELIZABETHAN PROSE. Michael Roberts
79. BEN JONSON AND KING JAMES. Eric Linklater
80. THE MIND'S EYE. Edmund Blunden
81. GERTRUDE JEKYLL. Francis Jekyll
82. CONSTANCE MARKIEVICZ. Seán O'Faoláin
83. CHINA CHANGES. Gerald Yorke

Made and printed in Gt. Britain by The Garden City Press Ltd., Letchworth and London.